The Evangelical's Daughter

Losing My Religion
— and —
Finding I AM

A MEMOIR

DEBRA ROBERTS TORRES-REYES

The Evangelical's Daughter Losing My Religion and Finding I AM
A memoir

iUniverse books may be ordered through booksellers or by contacting:

iUniverse
1663 Liberty Drive
Bloomington, IN 47403
www.iuniverse.com
844-349-9409

Because of the dynamic nature of the Internet, any web addresses or links contained in this book may have changed since publication and may no longer be valid. The views expressed in this work are solely those of the author and do not necessarily reflect the views of the publisher, and the publisher hereby disclaims any responsibility for them.

Any people depicted in stock imagery provided by Thinkstock are models, and such images are being used for illustrative purposes only. Certain stock imagery © Thinkstock.

ISBN: 978-1-5320-1229-7 (sc)
ISBN: 978-1-5320-1228-0 (e)

Library of Congress Control Number: 2016919993

Print information available on the last page.

iUniverse rev. date: 02/20/2017

This book is dedicated to the I AM race - may you
know the Truth, abide in Truth and be set free

This book is a memoir and it is drawn from my own experience.
Certain names have been changed throughout this book in order to
afford them their privacy.

This Memoir was originally published under the Title Negroes,
Flies and Wet Toilet Paper by Debra Roberts Torres-Reyes in 2011

Contents

Book I

Training a Child
1954–1966

*Train up a child in the way that he should go and
when he is old he will not depart from it.*
—Proverbs 22:6

Let the Women Be Quiet

Newark, New Jersey
Fall 1959

[I] suffer not a woman to teach, nor usurp authority
over the man, but to be in silence.
—I Timothy 2:12[1]

Gawd ain't called no womens to preach!" screamed Reverend Cook, who looked like a big, black Buddha. He seemed to have touched on every subject in the Bible and had the congregation flipping from Genesis to Revelation. There appeared to be no end to his circumlocution.

It was Children's Day at Mt. Sinai Holiness Church of God in Christ, and I felt as though I was being held prisoner in the first pew.

I was five and wearing one of my favorite dresses: pink chiffon with a white crinoline slip that peeked out from underneath. On my feet I was wearing a pair of black patent leather shoes, so shiny, I swear I could see my reflection in them. My short sandy brown hair, parted in three pigtails and secured by three large pink and blue ribbons, stood up on end like corkscrews.

We were blessed this day with guest speaker Reverend Walter J. Cook, from a Pentecostal Holiness Church of God in Christ in Brooklyn. When his sermon began three hours earlier, he'd promised to talk to us children about going to heaven and about how wonderful life would be once we got there. "You wants to go to heaven, don't cha?" he'd asked.

---

[1] All Bible verses are taken from the King James Version.

I'd nodded. Considering the alternative, I definitely wanted to go to heaven. But hell, that had been over three hours ago. By now, my head and those of my little fellow inmates were bobbing and weaving back and forth like ping-pong balls as we desperately fought to keep our eyes open.

It had been a long day.

Early that morning, Mommy had woken my sisters and me at seven A.M., with "hurry ups" and "let's get goings" as she rushed about, fussing at us and threatening to whip us if we made her late for church. We were dressed and ready to head out the door by eight o'clock to get to Sunday school on time. It did not matter to Mommy that Sunday school didn't begin until nine and that it only took us fifteen minutes to drive there. Mommy had this thing about being on time for church. Plus, because Sunday is the Lord's Day, Mommy did not allow us to eat in the mornings. Even our dog, Goldie, had to fast.

Daddy, on the other hand, was always late. We left him sleeping. We suspected that as soon as he heard us head out the door, he would get up and head to the kitchen for a bite to eat.

Our first opportunity to eat that day would not be until eleven-thirty, after Sunday school, when our church took a thirty-minute break. If we were lucky, Uncle Percy, Mommy's brother, would walk by and give us each a quarter so we could buy something at the local deli before the noon service.

At five minutes till noon, though, Uncle Percy was nowhere to be seen, when Sister Virginia, our tone-deaf choir director, beckoned us to queue up at the back of the church. Mommy, who had already taken her seat at the piano began to tickle the ivory.

Tinny sounds emanated from the out of tune piano as I stood in line waiting with the other children. The boys wore starchy white shirts with snap-on ties. The girls were in crinoline dresses of pink, green, and yellow, our nappy heads slicked back with hair grease and, length permitting, decorated in colorful ribbons and barrettes. My stomach growled and I prayed to God that Uncle Percy would get there in time for me to get something to quiet my stomach.

Too late. Mommy began to play and nodded to Sister Virginia. Mommy only knew three chords on the piano. She used these masterfully, though, as she strained to accompany the choir or any daring soloists. The church was small. It consisted of one aisle down the middle separated by pews to the left and right. In the front of the church was our makeshift pulpit and in front of the pulpit sat a round table covered by a white frilly table cloth. This was our offering table and the place where women stood to deliver messages from God and to conduct testimony service. On both sides of the offering table sat two folding chairs. This is where our choir would stand as soon as we marched up the center aisle. On cue, we snaked our way to the front and stood before the congregation—consisting of our mothers and, if we were lucky, our fathers—singing "Jesus Loves Me."

Once Sister Virginia got us to the front, she divided us into three rows facing the audience. I was terrified of all the faces staring back at me, even though they were smiling, so I hid behind one of my older sisters. But then Sister Virginia, with a horrific frown, yanked my arm and pulled me forward, making me stand out in front for everyone to see.

"Y'all chillun sing!" she snapped. "Open your mouth and sing unto the Lord."

Nervous and wiggly, we fidgeted through the song. All the while, Mommy gave me the evil eye, frowning at me because I was not singing just right. I opened my mouth wide, and although I didn't have a clue about what we were singing, I mouthed the words and pretended I did.

Shortly thereafter, Reverend Cook started preaching and there was no end in sight. The old bait-and-switch routine was a terrible habit most Pentecostal preachers had. They'd begin their sermons with "The subject of my talk today is . . ." and then just up and switch on you. Two or three hours later, they may still not have gotten to that subject. The problem was rampant among Pentecostal ministers, because they claimed to be always "led by the Spirit."

Unlike the Baptist, Presbyterian, or Catholic minister, the Pentecostal minister didn't believe in preparing an outline or talking points, because the Spirit did not want to be confined to just one subject.

Reverend Cook was being led by the Spirit today.

"Read, Sister Cook," he bellowed.

Reverend Cook was an ordained minister, but he had never attended any fancy college or "suh-diddy" (he was trying to say *sophisticated*) seminary school. He'd only finished the third grade, and he was proud of that fact because the Spirit of God had led him to preach—and that was better than any piece of paper or fancy college degree.

When he was not administering the Word of God, he worked as a janitor at an elementary school. I suspected he could not read because he often asked his wife to read the Bible for him during the sermon. He was also grossly obese.

It seemed to me that obesity and Pentecostal preaching went hand in hand. Perhaps it was because those of the Pentecostal faith had placed so many restrictions on their lives. It was a sin to go to the movies, to see baseball games, and to go to the beach (although my family often enjoyed the beach anyway - who could resist the temptation of Coney Island and the beautiful waves of the Pacific Ocean). It was a sin to watch television, to dance, and to play cards or games that used dice. It was a sin to—well, it was pretty much a sin to do anything. The list of restrictions went on and on and seemed to be updated daily. The only thing you could do that wasn't a sin was to eat, except on Wednesdays and Fridays before three P.M. These were our fast days.

Reverend Cook's wife was the complete antithesis of her husband. She was a frail little woman with kinky short hair, which she forced into an old maid's bun. Wisps of her hair stood out on the side like porcupine needles. She sat in the front row, the place of honor, in her little flowered dress, rocking back and forth, holding a white frilly handkerchief which she waved like a pompom every time her fat husband made it from one end of the pulpit to the other. Her handkerchief served double duty to flick the bobbing heads of her five dozing daughters who were seated beside her.

"Y'all chilluns better wake up and listen to yo Daddy," she said in as loud a hushed voice as she could manage. "I'm going to whoop you when you get home."

But even she had abandoned the flicking over an hour ago, because she could no longer keep an eye on her five snoozing daughters while reading for her husband. So the girls snored brazenly: their heads tilted back, their mouths agape.

Sister Cook stood, took a deep breath, and began to read in a loud, squeaky voice.

> Let your women keep silence in the churches; for it is not permitted unto them to speak; but they are commanded to be under obedience, as also saith the law. And if they will learn anything, let them ask their husbands at home: for it is a shame for women to speak in the church.1 Corinthians 14:34–35.

"Thank you, Sister Cook," the reverend said. "You may be seated."

Reverend Cook looked around the congregation as if he knew something the rest of us didn't. He pursed his lips, puffed out his cheeks like a blow fish, and stood silent. I thought that he had forgotten what he was about to say. The silence, of course, only amplified the snoring from the children's choir. I would've fallen asleep myself, except Mommy kept looking over at my sisters and me. We didn't dare doze.

"Paul saiddah . . .," Cook finally continued, emphasizing every consonant—an annoying habit he developed over his many years of on-the-job training as a born again gospel preacher. "Letta da womens, ah ha, keep quiet in da churcha. If she has a question, let her ax her husband at home!"

Beads of sweat gathered on his forehead and rolled down the sides of his fleshy face. His white shirt was sopping wet and stuck to his body.

I blinked. *Paul who? Said what?*

I found this passage of scripture odd as I glanced around the sanctuary, because, in addition to the guest speaker's wife and her five dozing, obese daughters, there were approximately thirty other women there. There were Mommy, Sister Frankie Q. Roberts, and my three sisters: Gloria, age twelve, Cynthia, age nine, and Linda, age seven. There were Sister Esther Rogers and her two daughters, Sister Davis and her two daughters, and Mother Blackman, the grandmother of our church, who always took it upon herself to tell all the other women what they could and could not do. Then there were Sister Jeanie, Sister Mary, Sister Virginia (our choir director), and Sister Lucille. There were also a handful of overweight, colorfully dressed women donning big hats and gloves, reeking of perfume and cooking oil; these women were members of Reverend Cook's church.

In comparison, only five men were present today, or on any other given day, for that matter, two of whom were under the age of ten and one of whom was preaching. Another one was drunk and passed out in the back pew (Sister Mary's husband), and the last, Pastor Johnnie Hawkeye Roberts—my Daddy—was sitting in the pulpit, grinning like a Cheshire cat, because this was his favorite sermon.

"Preach the Word!" Daddy shouted, shaking his handsome round head and slapping his knee.

He and Mommy argued all the time after she made the terrible mistake of sharing her revelation that God called her to preach. Daddy thought that was pure blasphemy.

"Frankie, why you always lyin' on de Lawd?" Daddy asked. "'De Lawd said this! And de Lawd said that!' De Lawd ain't said nothin'! Niggahs always lyin' on de Lawd!"

Two things my Daddy did not like about Niggahs: Daddy did not like "Niggah-Mess" and he did not like Niggahs putting words in the Lord's mouth. He took it personally.

"Say amen, walls," said Daddy, while smirking in Mommy's direction.

Mommy sat at the piano, pensively studying the keys, trying desperately to avoid Daddy's gaze. This was just the kind of reaction Daddy had hoped for.

"Teach us, Lord!" Daddy shouted, slapping his leg with his left hand and running the white handkerchief in his right hand over his wavy jet-black hair. Daddy was wound up about Reverend Cook's sermon to the point that beads of sweat popped up on his forehead.

Reverend Cook looked in Mommy's direction. "You can get mad if you want to, but I'm here to tell you what the Bible says." He squeezed the podium and wiped his brow. "I ain't in no popularity contest. I've got to tell it the way God wants me to tell it, whether you like it or not!"

"Amen, preacher!" the traitorous women shouted. "Just tell it like it is, preacher!" Then they broke into a round of thunderous applause.

It was no secret that Mommy thought she had a special calling. Mother Blackman had tried to counsel Mommy on what the Bible said about women preachers. But Mommy would not listen.

"The Bible says out of the mouth of two or three, let every word be established," Mother Blackman said as she stared at the ceiling, rocking in her chair. Yes, she would say, God had sent this sermon directly to Mommy. And everybody in the church knew it was the truth—including Mommy.

But did everyone also know that a literal interpretation of this scripture would mean the end of Mt. Sinai Holiness Church of God in Christ (COGIC) and all of the churches like it?

As I sat listening and watching Reverend Cook, I wondered why, if the Bible said women were to remain silent in church, the reverend would ask Sister Cook to read the scriptures and why Sister Virginia was allowed to be our choir director. It seemed to me that although women in the COGIC could not stand in the pulpit, they could—and had to—do everything else.

As with Mt. Sinai Holiness, most of the COGIC churches were at least ninety percent women. Women were required to lead the devotional services, sing the hymns, teach Sunday school, and raise sorely needed funds by selling chicken dinners and sweet-potato pies. In fact, women could even preach, as long as it was to other women during Women's Day services, although a man would usually preach another sermon during the offering or benediction.

A woman just could not be an ordained minister, because she was not allowed to speak from that sacred place of honor: the pulpit. She wasn't even supposed to stand in the pulpit. Only a man could stand in this, the most holy of holy places, and tell the masses what "thus saith the Lord."

Mommy met the preacher's gaze and they locked eyes for a moment, before she dropped hers submissively. My stomach was in knots as the fear and embarrassment I felt for her grew. I couldn't wait until Reverend Cook sat down. But he wasn't finished with her.

He labored to the other end of the pulpit, while his frail wife dutifully waved her handkerchief, and then he returned to the podium, picked up his Bible, and waved it high in the air.

"I'm just telling you what the Bible says. A woman's place is in the home, not in the pulpit."

Daddy jumped to his feet as if struck by lightening. He was tired of coming home to a dirty house, cooking his own meals, taking care of his nappy-headed daughters, and washing their dirty clothes.

"Amen! Amen! That's right. Preach the Word! Some folks always talking about what de Lawd said. De Lawd ain't said nothin'!"

God's Peculiar People

Newark
1959

[T]he Lord hath chosen thee to be a peculiar people unto himself.
—Deuteronomy 14:2

O ur church used to be owned by a Jewish man and his wife who sold everything from bagels to life insurance policies," Daddy said to the handful of folks gathered when Mt. Sinai opened its doors on October 23, 1954, six months after I was born. "But I'm selling something that money cannot buy: Jesus."

Mt. Sinai was a converted storefront. The neighborhood where it was located had seen better days. Gone were the working middle-class Poles, Jews, and Italians, strolling the sidewalks like it was some blue-collar Easter parade. In place of the white masses were segregation, isolation, poverty, and hopelessness.

It was this sense of hopelessness that caught Daddy's attention. What used to be picture-perfect traditional homes of white families was now a resting place for winos, pimps, prostitutes, transvestites, and Mt. Sinai Holiness Church of God in Christ.

Mommy's hand-painted sign—MT. SINAI HOLINESS CHURCH OF GOD IN CHRIST–Pastor: Reverend John H. Roberts—hung in the picture window in large blocked white letters.

Our church was sandwiched between a dilapidated boarding house that was rented by the hour and bar that catered to a large transvestite and lesbian crowd. On hot, balmy summer evenings, transvestites sashayed in front of the open church doors, making pitiful passes at Daddy, who stood handsomely in the pulpit, drenched in sweat as he implored them to come to Jesus.

On other nights, the pulsating beat of the tambourines and drums spilled out of our church onto the streets, drawing in winos and the most wretched sinners, who came staggering and crying to the altar. Winos who were too drunk to walk in on their own left Mt. Sinai services sober and in their right minds. Most of them didn't stay sober for long, but those who did became devoted followers of Jesus Christ, of Mt. Sinai, and of Daddy.

Sister Virginia, our choir director, was once such a wino. She'd been a young woman who'd worn every ache and pain on her dark, comely face, until one sultry August night, during Youth Revival. Virginia staggered to the front of the church, gyrating her thick hips and snapping her fingers to the beat of the music. When she reached the front, she stood in the middle of the floor, hiked her skin-tight black skirt up above her ashy legs, and proceeded to do the nastiest of all nasty black ghetto dances, the Dog.

Gasping in disbelief, we children doubled over in fits of laughter after the initial shock wore off.

"You children better hush," Mother Blackman snapped. "It's not funny. Now behave yourselves, before I take you outside and whip you." But the more we tried to suppress our laughter, the harder we laughed. Especially when Virginia tried to run her fingers through her nappy hair. It stood straight up in the air and stayed there. Virginia must have imagined herself to be one of the beautiful blonde women she might have seen in the movies, because she tossed back her head and flipped imaginary hair from her face. Then she moved her hands down her thick hips and back up to her large, pendulous, bra-less breasts, where she paused for a moment to caress them. In her better days Virginia had been a stripper. But that night, she was a pitiful sight, trying to seduce Daddy, who stood at the altar asking if she wanted to take Jesus as her personal savior.

Virginia licked her dry, cracked lips and puckered them in a vain attempt to be sexy. "I'll take *you* as my personal savior."

"Help her, Lord," was the congregation's reply. And then one by one, they got up from their seats and formed a circle around Virginia. "Jesus. Jesus. Jesus," they chanted in soft melodious unity to the rhythmic beat of the tambourines and drum.

Virginia liked being the center of attention. She got down, low and dirty. But the saints were undaunted by her. The harder she swiveled her hips, the more they chanted.

"JesusJesus*Jesus* . . ."

Mommy left the piano and entered the circle with Virginia.

"JesusJesus*Jesus* . . ."

Mommy went up to Virginia, placed her arms around her, and hugged her tight. Virginia tried to fight her off. Mommy would not give up.

"JesusJesus*Jesus* . . ."

The more Virginia fought, the tighter Mommy hugged her. Mommy began to rock her, like a mother rocks her sick child. I wished she would hug me like that when I acted up. Virginia's arms went limp, she made another weak attempt at breaking free from Mommy's hug, and then she broke. Virginia began to sob. Then her sobs turned into loud, guttural wails.

The sound reminded me of the horny male cats who came for our cat Princess when she was in heat. It was the kind of wail that came from the pit of her stomach; a low-down kind of hurt that had been stored up over years of broken promises, neglect, fear, and abandonment. I wanted to cry for her. Even at five years old, I could sense that Virginia had lived a horrid life.

Mommy did not care how badly Virginia behaved in church during the service. Nor did Mommy care how ugly Virginia looked as the snot and tears flowed freely down her face and met at the bottom of her chin.

Mommy continued to hug and rock her, whispering, "Save her, Lord" in Virginia's ear.

Then Sister Ruth Scott began to sing.

"Save me."

And the saints sang in reply, "Save me, Lawd."

"Save me."

"Save me, Lawd."

"Help me."

"Help me, Lawd."

"Help poor me."

"Help me, Lawd."

Then Sister Nancy Davis commanded, "You kids grab your Bibles. She probably has a lot of demons in her. You don't want them coming out of her and going into you, do you?"

We children scrambled about the church looking for Bibles and, when we found them, placed them over our hearts. I found Mommy's Bible and held it tightly against my heart. The thought that someone's demons, especially the ones making Virginia act like a complete idiot, could come out of her and into me was frightening, to say the least. I hadn't even started kindergarten yet. In fact, I'd learned about demons and devils before I learned how to say my ABCs and tie my shoes.

Virginia began to growl and sputter, but the saints remained undeterred. They kept praying, and Mommy kept hugging and whispering in Virginia's ear. Then they came. Dozens and dozens of them. The demons that had possessed Virginia's soul. She began upchucking, her body lurching forward as if on its own, shaking and trembling violently as demons poured from every part of her body. She puked up enough demons to fill three garbage cans. She cried buckets of tears and used up three rolls of toilet paper. Snot dripped from her nose and just hung there like icicles. It was sickening.

Then Virginia began to shake and quicken. She dropped to the floor and began to roll around like tumbleweed, first this way and then that. All the while, Mother Blackman and Sister Lucille chased her with a lap cloth, trying to cover the nakedness revealed by Virginia's skin-tight skirt snaking its way up her ashen thighs. Then Virginia began to speak in unknown tongues.

"Praise God, she is delivered," the congregation shouted. "Praise the Lawd!" and "Thank you, Jesus!" ricocheted off the walls.

Mommy got back on the piano and struck up a joyful tune, while someone grabbed the tambourine and someone took to the drum. The music was lively and hypnotic, and the place was on fire. It started off slowly, and then like making popcorn the old-fashioned way, one saint popped up, and then another and then another, until before long, all the saints were popping up and down, praising the Lord, and dancing in the Spirit.

I watched as Daddy threw his head back, crossed his arm in front of him, and took off dancing in the Spirit. This was the only place I would ever see my parents dance, because it was a sin to dance anywhere other than in church. I never saw Daddy embrace Mommy and waltz her around the floor. The closest it ever got was when the Spirit would strike Mommy, and she'd leap from the piano and start dancing alongside Daddy.

Mimicking our parents, we children began to scream and jump and dance about. Virginia was finally saved, sanctified, and filled with the Holy Ghost. Hallelujah! She was Sister Virginia now.

When not filled with alcohol, Sister Virginia was a strikingly beautiful woman. She had been blessed with shapely long legs, an ample bust, and a beautiful face. It was this outer beauty that Mother Blackman zealously took upon herself to suppress.

Mother Blackman was a licensed mother of the Church of God in Christ, with official credentials. As such, it was her duty to take Sister Virginia under her wing, counseling her on how to walk, talk, eat, and dress. And Mother Blackman took her job very seriously.

She advised Sister Virginia to hide her ample breasts by smashing them down with a bandage. She told her to wear an oversized, plain white linen shirt over her flattened breasts and to conceal her long, shapely legs with a flowing white skirt that stopped just above her ankles. Sister Virginia also took to covering her head with an old white rag, a recalcitrant braid often defiantly escaped its confines, standing straight up in the air from the middle of her forehead.

On this Sunday afternoon, Sister Virginia looked like a unicorn as she stood before the congregation, leading the testimony service. She stood in front between the offering table and one of the folding chairs.

IwannathanktheLordforbeinghere."

"Praise God!"

"IwannathanktheLordforbeingsaved."

"Praise God!"

"Iwannathankhimbecauseyouknow . . ."

"Praise God!"

"Icould'vebeendeadandinmygrave."

"Hallejuah! PraiseGod!"

"Iwannathankhimfordeliveringmefromallmysins."

"Praise God!"

"PraymystrengthintheLord."

"Praise God!"

Then she began singing, but before she could finish the first stanza, she broke into the holy dance. She danced so hard that her head rag fell off, revealing four fatter, twisted braids. But Sister Virginia didn't care, because she was dancing in the Spirit.

"Chile, when the Spirit hits you, you've gotta' move, it don't matter how you look," Sister Virginia would often say. "I used to be a fool for Satan, but now I'm a fool for Jesus. Hey, glory!"

We children looked forward to seeing Sister Virginia at church, as she was always good for a laugh or two.

Today, I fell out of my chair laughing, until I felt Mommy's penetrating glare. I froze, the laughter stuck in my throat like a lump of coal. She was sitting at the piano, pounding out her gospel dance tunes, singing a hymn, and giving me the evil eye all at the same time. Mommy was quite gifted - she was a master at multitasking. I covered my mouth and tried to suppress the snicker, which had now oozed up my throat. A giggle escaped at the very moment I saw Sister Virginia, who had by that time, danced with arms thrashing and wild frenzied, tripped over one of the folding chairs. All the eyes from the children's section followed her as she danced *limpity, loppity, limpity, loppity* to her chair and plopped down.

Mommy must have heard my giggle, because she raised a disapproving eyebrow. My sisters and I settled down, as did the other children, because it really didn't matter whose child you were—anybody and everybody could beat you if they said you were misbehaving.

Mommy nodded to my eldest sister, Gloria, who was now twelve and back from boarding school for the summer, to pick up the song Sister Virginia had abandoned. Obediently, Gloria began to lead the song while she beat the tambourine. The congregation followed her.

"I'm a soldier."

"In the army of the Lawd."

"I'm a soldier."

"In the army."

"Got my war clothes on."

"In the army of the Lawd."

"Got my war clothes on."

"In the army . . ."

The Forsaken

Newark
Summer 1959

If any man come to me and hate not his . . .
children . . . he cannot be my disciple.
—Luke 14:26–33

I f the Lord can speak out of the mouth of an *ass* . . .," Mommy said, emphasizing the final word. Mommy wasn't speaking to anyone in particular as she removed her clothes from the hanger and folded them neatly into her suitcases.

She always seized any opportunity to use profanity. It was her only vice in her pretty much sinless life. Her life was boring, and a little curse word now and again helped break up the monotony.

"If God can speak through an ass," she repeated, "he can speak through a woman."

"Mother!" cried Cynthia. "You're not supposed to say *that* word."

Mommy looked at her second-born child as if she had just hatched from an egg. But the confusion on her face disappeared as quickly as it came. She grabbed a handful of dresses from her closet and threw them in the suitcase, some still clinging to the hangers.

"Well that's what the Bible says," Mommy replied. "It says 'ass.' If the Lord can use that word, and they can print it in the Bible, then so can I."

"Mommy, where are you going?" I asked.

"To Iowa," she said, as she put on her coat.

"Can we go too?" I asked.

"Not this time," she replied.

"Why are you leaving?" I asked. "Because Daddy hit you?"

Mommy didn't respond.

Mommy and Daddy had been arguing every day for a long time. But just before that, Mommy had been sick and we thought she was dying. We stood around her bed as some women in white prayed and sang over her. They told us to tell her good-bye.

I was terrified of losing her. Daddy had tears in his eyes, and at night I saw him slip into the room and hold her hand as he prayed for her and made promises about being a good husband and told her how much he loved her. He told her she did not have to worry about any other women, because she was the only one for him.

The women in white prayed over her around the clock back then. There was always someone in the room with Mommy, praying. We waited for a long time for her to get better, and then one day Mommy woke up. And then she was sitting up and eating. And then she was smiling and talking and walking. It was a miracle. Daddy was so happy. And so was I.

Not long after that, after Mommy was all better, she was standing at the stove making breakfast for Daddy: grits, biscuits, fried ham and eggs with molasses. I sat on Daddy's lap while he sat at the kitchen table talking to Mommy about his vision for the church. Linda and Cynthia were in school, and my oldest sister, Gloria, was away at Saint's Junior College.

"Johnnie," Mommy said, setting the ham and eggs in front of him and returning to the stove. "I can't stay. I have to go to Iowa. The Lord is calling me."

I felt Daddy's body tense. I saw his eyes darken as he gritted his teeth and clinched his hand into a tight ball.

"Now, Frankie," he told her, "the Lord did not say no such thing. We have talked about this already, and, as your husband, I forbid you to go. The Bible says, "Wives, obey your husband for this is right in the Lord."

I felt anxious. I knew my Daddy loved me, and he had never even spanked me before, just the same he had a temper, and I was afraid he was going to use it on Mommy. I hugged him tighter and started to whine. Mommy's back was to us, as she stirred the grits into the boiling water. I hoped she would not speak. I hoped she would not have to have the last word this time. I hoped she would do as the Bible said and be silent. She didn't.

And so they argued and they began yelling at each other. Daddy lifted me off his lap.

Mommy told me to be quiet when I began to cry and whine for Daddy to hold me. "Debra, go to your room right now, before I give you something to cry about." She had always been jealous of the closeness between Daddy and me. But for her information, I was trying to save her. I was trying to distract Daddy, because she did not see the fury in his eyes and his fist ball up when she just couldn't be silent.

"Go on, baby," Daddy said to me sweetly. "Daddy will take you to get some ice cream later. But right now, I need to talk to Mommy." I didn't move. I stood my ground as I looked to Daddy and then Mommy.

"Go on. Everything is going to be all right," Daddy reassured me.

Mommy turned from the stove to give me the evil eye. She wouldn't whip me in front of Daddy, but as soon as he was gone, she would. So I did as I was told and went to my room. I left the door partly open. I climbed up on my bed and sat cross legged. I grabbed my pillow placing it in my lap, hugged it and listened quietly.

"That ain't none of my baby," Daddy said. "Niggahs is always lyin.'"

Mommy said she didn't care whether Sister Scott's baby was his or not. God told her to go to Iowa to preach the Word, and she had to do what the Lord told her to do, just like Daddy had to do what the Lord told him to do. The Lord had told him to go to Iowa, too. But just because he was going to be disobedient to the Lord, didn't mean she was going to follow him to hell. She almost died, she reminded him. That is when the Lord reminded her of what he wanted her to do, she said.

Then Daddy let out a big secret. One he had promised Mommy he wouldn't talk about. "You almost died because you got rid of my son. You flushed him down the toilet. I will never forgive you for that, Frankie."

My imagination was going crazy. *Mommy flushed our baby brother down the toilet!* I pictured a little boy swirling around and around in the toilet bowl like doo-doo too big to go down. Did she have to use a plunger to get the toilet to accept him? Was he still alive now, living in the sewer like the monsters on TV?

"How could you kill my son, Frankie?" Daddy's voice was filled with pain.

"Shhh, Johnnie, Debra might hear you," Mommy said.

"I want her to hear me. You almost died. Did the Lord tell you to do that too? Is that when the Lord told you to go to Iowa? De Lawd did not say that, Frankie! Niggahs always lyin' on the Lord! The Lord told you to stay here and take care of your husband and your children."

I remembered that time when Mommy and Daddy went to Iowa. They were gone for a long time. But when they came back, Daddy made fun of Iowa. He said there was nothing there except cows and white people dressed in overalls and plaids. He said that he had no intention of moving to Iowa, that he would never raise his children in a place like that, that his children needed to grow up around their own people and their family, not in some strange place like Iowa.

I was still imagining my little brother being flushed down the toilet, when all of a sudden, I heard a loud crash that sounded as if someone threw something through our window. Then I heard a cling-clanging followed by a huge scream. Goldie, our honey-hued mutt, hence her name, started barking and growling. I ran out of the room in time to see Daddy scrambling over an upside-down kitchen chair, which was lying on the floor, and rushing toward Mommy. She was swinging a pot at him, and threatening to hit him with it if he got any closer. Hot grits were flying everywhere.

Daddy didn't flinch. He dodged the grits and the pot, first this way, and then that way, and then knocked the pot out of her hand.

He grabbed Mommy around the waist and the two of them fell to the floor while she kicked and screamed. Then Goldie bit Daddy's hand.

"Ouch!" Daddy yelled, pulling his hand away and punching at Goldie. But Goldie was too fast. She ran to my bedroom and dove under the bed. I knew she was safe, so I ran back to the kitchen. Daddy and Mommy were still on the floor, but now Daddy was lunging forward to grab Mommy's feet, and once he had them, he began to drag her. Then Mommy began to scream; wait, no, that was me.

Daddy turned to me, which gave Mommy the opportunity she needed to scramble to her feet and head for the door. She almost made it out, but Daddy was too quick. They threw punches at each other. Daddy had his hand around Mommy's neck. She kneed him in his private parts, and Daddy doubled over in pain. Mommy managed to get the door open and then darted out, screaming, "Help! Help! Somebody help me!"

I was screaming too. "Leave her alone, Daddy!"

"Go back to your room, Debra," Daddy snapped at me, as he recovered and headed for the door after Mommy. We lived on the fourth floor of a large brownstone apartment building. Daddy grabbed Mommy by her legs and would not let go.

"Johnnie, don't do it," Mommy begged. "Help me, somebody!"

The doors of other apartments opened.

"Leave her alone, before I call the police!" a neighbor yelled.

"Mind your own business," Daddy screamed back.

The neighbors tried to help Mommy, but Daddy kept tugging, trying to pull Mommy down the stairs. Mommy clung to the banister and continued kicking at him. It seemed as though nothing could deter Daddy. He was like a madman.

Then somebody yelled something that brought Daddy back to his senses. "You call yourself a preacher? You call yourself a man of God?"

Daddy released Mommy's legs and scurried down the four flights of stairs like a thwarted purse snatcher. When he reached the bottom of the stairs, he yelled, "You can go, but you are not taking my children!" and then, as though it were an afterthought, he said, "Especially not Debra!" And then he was gone.

Neighbors came to help Mommy up and back into our apartment. I was crying and so was she. They sat her down at the table next to Daddy's undisturbed breakfast of fried ham, scrambled eggs with cheddar cheese, and fresh biscuits. Goldie emerged from under the bed and came into the kitchen. She licked Mommy's hand, and after determining the coast was clear, she stood up on her hind legs, snatched Daddy's ham from his plate, and returned to her hiding place.

Later that day, when my sisters returned from school, I told them what had happened. I also told them Mommy had flushed our baby brother down the toilet. They did not believe me, so I told them to go ask Mommy.

"Mommy, did you flush our baby brother down the toilet?" Linda asked.

"Yes," Mommy said sweetly.

"Why?" I asked. She did not answer me. I think she was mad at me for telling and wanted to flush me down the toilet. I inched closer to her so she would like me again and hold me like she'd held Sister Virginia when she was bad. She didn't.

"What did he look like?" Cynthia asked.

"A white frog with a ding-a-ling," Mommy said.

We laughed. But I wondered, if Mommy can flush our baby brother down the toilet and laugh about it, what wouldn't she do to me?

Later that evening, Daddy returned home. I saw them kissing and cuddling as if nothing had happened. On Sunday, Daddy returned to the pulpit to preach the Word of God, and Mommy returned to the piano to play the gospel.

But now she is leaving us and Daddy in spite of Reverend Cook's message to her.

"Why are you going to Iowa?" Linda asked again.

Mommy kissed Linda's forehead. "I've got to do what the Lord told me to do." Then she picked up her suitcases and walked out the front door.

"When are you coming back?" Linda asked.

"When the Lord says the same," she said, and then she closed the door behind her. She was gone.

Exodus

Chicago, Illinois
November 1959

Rise up, and get you forth from among my people, both
ye and the children of Israel: and go, serve the Lord.
—Exodus 12:31

I hid behind Mommy's coat, suspiciously eyeing the colored man wearing a red suit and a crooked, matted, white beard. It was obvious he was an impostor. He had some nerve pretending to be Santa Claus. Who did he think he was fooling? By the look of it, only a handful of the colored children in line were deceived.

"He isn't Santa Claus!" Cynthia said.

"There's no such thing as a colored Santa Claus. Right, Mommy?" Linda asked.

"No. I think it is Santa Claus," Mommy said.

"Uh-uh. That isn't Santa Claus! Santa Claus is not colored!" Linda was emphatic.

"Well, do you want to see him or not?" asked Mommy.

"No, because he isn't Santa Claus!" said Cynthia, eyeing the impostor.

We stood there for fifteen minutes while they had a heated debate over whether this man was really Santa Claus. All the while, I hid behind Mommy's coat and watched him interact with the other children.

A little brown girl about my age was sitting on the impostor's lap, rattling off a litany of things she wanted him to bring to her. "I

25

want a dollhouse with furniture in it, and I want a . . ." The impostor yawned and looked off at the three colored children still waiting in line, impatiently shifting from one foot to the other. Santa rolled his eyes and sighed heavily, as another colored child eagerly joined the line. Judging from Santa's reaction, he was not happy to see that.

After watching him for a few minutes, it was clear this Santa did not have the same gentle touch and voice as the real Santa back in East Orange, New Jersey. And unlike the long lines of colored and white children that used to wait to give their wish lists to the real white Santa, this line had only a handful of children. But then that was back in East Orange. This was Chicago. Perhaps the Negro kids in Chicago were just confused and did not know any better.

Mommy came back from Iowa when Daddy called her and begged her to come and get us. He couldn't take care of us and work a full-time job, plus run his church. It seemed that as soon as she was back in the door, I saw her standing over an open suitcase, packing our clothes.

"Where are we going?" I said. "Is Daddy going, too? Can Goldie go?"

"We'll see," was her reply. Then she loaded our suitcases and me in a taxicab and directed the driver to the school. When we arrived at the school she got out of the cab and disappeared behind the school's doors. Later Mommy returned with Linda and Cynthia in tow.

"Where are we going?" Linda asked, as the two girls settled into the back of the taxi with Mommy and me.

"I'll bet we're going to see Gloria," Cynthia said.

"You'll see," was the only thing Mommy said.

The taxi dropped us off at Pennsylvania Station in downtown Newark. We could not control our excitement. The prospect of taking a train ride with Mommy and missing school in the dead of winter was more than we could handle.

Four hours later, we debarked at Union Station in Washington, D.C. Mommy's best friend, Ruthie Ann, met us and took us to her apartment, where she had fried chicken, mashed potatoes and gravy, greens, hot bread, and piping hot peach cobbler fresh from the oven—all waiting for us.

Daddy did not like Mommy's friend. Ruthie Ann was a lesbian. She never tried to hide her sexual preference even back then, when it was something no one openly admitted. Daddy often accused Mommy of having a lesbian relationship with Ruthie Ann. I heard them once, when Daddy and Ruthie Ann were fighting over Mommy's affection.

"She's my wife. Not yours," Daddy had said.

"Well, why don't you do right by her, then?" Ruthie Ann replied.

"Ain't none of your business. Niggahs always gettin' in other folks' business. I'll treat my wife any way I please."

"It is my business if you don't treat her right! Why don't you get out of the way and let someone else have her?"

"Like who? You?" Daddy laughed mockingly.

We stayed with Ruthie Ann for four days in her tiny one-bedroom apartment. Ruthie Ann went to work, and Mommy prayed a lot. We girls, on the other hand, entertained ourselves by fighting and watching television. Each morning, Mommy forced us to go outside and play in the cold. We stood by the door begging and pleading with her to let us come back in. But she stuck to her guns, tuning out our plaintive wails as she sought the Lord. By day five we were ready to go back home to Daddy, but Mommy had different plans. We boarded the train and continued our trip west.

We stopped in Chicago, where we were met by a strange wrinkled old woman we had never met before. Mother Somebody (so many people came and went in our lives, it was hard to remember their names; it was either Brother or Sister So-and-So, Mother Somebody, or Pastor What's-his-name) was a short little lady, bent at the waist, who used a cane to get around her tiny apartment in the projects. Mother Somebody wore thick heavy glasses that smashed her nose and made it spread across her face.

Mommy and Mother Somebody went on a three-day fast. They did not eat nor drink any water, and they prayed and read the Bible day and night. We girls had to fast until three o'clock every day, although even after that time, we went hungry, because Mother Somebody was so poor she could barely feed herself.

"Why do we have to fast?" My older sisters and I cried.

"Because we are sinners and we want God to save us from our sins," Mommy said.

I didn't remember sinning, and so I did not see why I had to give up eating for something I did not do.

"You and your sisters have been fighting and arguing," Mother reminded us.

I did not know fighting with my sisters qualified as sinning and would send me straight to hell. Apparently I was wrong.

"You want to go to heaven when you die, don't you?" Mother Somebody asked. "You don't want to burn in the Lake of Fire forever, where there will be weeping and gnashing of teeth, do you?"

There was that question again. I did not even know what it meant to gnash teeth. But my sisters and I argued and fought all the time, so Mommy said we had to fast the arguing and fighting demons out of us. We had no choice.

We moped around the apartment, starving to save ourselves from burning in the Lake of Fire forever. But even in our weakened states, Cynthia, Linda, and I found strength to fight. Sadly, I realized, the Roberts sisters were doomed for hell.

On day five, we finally left the apartment to go to the store. And it was there we saw the impostor sitting in his big red chair, wearing that obviously fake beard and dingy red suit.

"Okay, okay. I think he is Santa Claus's helper," Mommy said, finally settling the debate.

We accepted that explanation because it made better sense. We could easily accept his role as a helper—subservient to the white man, but never his equal. Even at five years old, I had rejected the colored man's presentation. A Santa's helper made perfect sense.

I was deathly afraid of the white Santa Claus. I never even sat on his lap. There was no way I was going to sit on this black guy's. My sisters and I decided amongst ourselves that Linda would tell him that we were moving to Sioux City, Iowa. We wanted to make sure

Santa knew not to drop off our presents in New Jersey. I pictured Santa going to our house in New Jersey and searching frantically for us, wondering what to do with all the presents his elves had worked so hard to make for us.

Linda didn't want to go alone so Cynthia accompanied her and as they approached the end of the line, Cynthia jumped in line before Linda. The colored Santa's helper's eyes followed them. He sucked his teeth and let out an audible sigh. Finally, when it was Cynthia's turn, she climbed on Santa's lap, said a couple of things to him, and then left after he handed her a candy cane.

Then Linda, who Daddy had nicknamed "Tub of Lard" because she was large and overweight for her age, struggled as Santa strained and grunted to lift her to his lap. I watched Linda's wild, excited gesturing as she talked to Santa's helper. Linda's eyes, which were large and almond color, looked like that of a fawn. She had a perfect set of deep dimples to accentuate her beautiful dark skin and her perfect white teeth. Santa seemed disinterested, but shook his head in agreement. Then he reached into his burlap sack and handed Linda a broken candy cane.

As he tried to push her off his lap, Linda pointed in my direction and planted herself firmly on his bony legs. When he looked in my direction, I flinched and hid behind Mommy's coat. He seemed to hesitate and think about something for a minute, before finally reaching into his sack and pulling out a second broken candy cane. He handed the candy cane to Linda, who slid off his lap and came bouncing toward Mommy and me. Just then, Cynthia got in line again, and Santa's helper began yelling, "No! No!" and pointing his crooked bony finger at her. Cynthia stopped dead in her tracks, the eyes of the other brown children in line all upon her.

"But . . . but . . .," Cynthia stuttered.

"You've already been up here once!" the impostor yelled. "You only get one turn!"

"But I forgot to tell you . . ."

"Doesn't matter," he said, shaking his bony finger at her. "You only get one turn." Then he as an after thought, he said, "That's okay. Santa knows everything."

Cynthia shrugged her shoulders and sighed. Head hanging low, she turned on her heels and headed back towards us. We looked at her, puzzled about what else she wanted to tell him but embarrassed for her all the same. At first too humiliated to look at us, Cynthia studied the floor. But finally, she looked up and met our eyes, a smile slowly spread across her lips. We all stared at one another for a second and then broke into fits of hysterical laughter.

"I told you he wasn't the real Santa Claus!" Cynthia said.

She was right. So Cynthia and I threw our broken candy canes in the trash can (Linda had already gobbled hers down). And with that, the Roberts sisters skipped away with Mommy.

Good for Santa's Sake

Sioux City, Iowa
December 1959

G–double O–D, good
G–double O–D, good
I try to be like Jesus
G–double O–D, good

Mommy handed Linda a twenty dollar bill as she ushered the two of us out the front door. Linda and I were dressed like we were headed for the arctic instead of the Safeway store just a block away from our house. We were wearing several layers of clothing under our winter coats and a pair of woolen mittens under our woolen socks on our hands. We could barely move.

The snow crunched underneath our feet as we trudged our way to the end of the block. West Seventh Street was a large cross-street with four lanes of traffic that ran east and west. Today the traffic was light and the street looked like the parting of the Red Sea. Large banks of snow left by snow plows stood piled high on both sides and in the middle. Linda and I had to climb up and slide down these snow mountains, to get to the other side.

By the time we entered Safeway, our hands felt like icicles. We quickly found the list of things that Mommy had asked us to get and headed to the checkout counter.

"Would you like a sack?" asked the white store clerk.

Linda and I exchanged secret looks. The word *sack* was one of the many things Daddy did not like about Sioux City, Iowa. We had

31

heard him go on and on about it with Mommy, about how "country" the folks in Iowa were and how he did not want to move his family there because of that.

"Those folks are nothing but country bumpkins," Daddy had said so many times. "Would you like a *sack*? What do you mean, a sack of potatoes? It is a grocery bag, not a sack," Daddy laughed. "Would you like a *pop* with your dinner, sir? A pop?" Then he'd ball up his fist and grab Linda by the head, pretending to bop her in the head. "I'll give you a pop. Where do you want it?"

"Yes, we would like a grocery *bag*," Linda answered the clerk, emphasizing the correct word as she handed the clerk the money.

Before Linda could stop me, I reached up, grabbed the change from the clerk's hand, and stuffed it into one of my many pants pockets. We put our socks back on our hands and headed out the door. As we turned the corner of the store, a gush of wind took us by surprise at the same time a large truck came barreling down the parking lot in our direction. The combination of the wind and the truck blew my coat open and ripped Mommy's change from my pocket. I watched in horror as the dollar bills twirled up and then down into the sewer right under my feet. We took our time getting home after that; it didn't matter how cold it was.

When we walked in the house, Mommy was in the kitchen nursing a big pot of pinto beans on the stove. Cynthia was curled up in an over-sized chair in our sparsely furnished front room, watching the farm report on one of Sioux City's two television channels. In New Jersey, we had had so many channels and had grown accustomed to staying up at night watching the late show, the late late show and the late late late television shows. Especially after Mommy left us and gone to Iowa, we stayed up all night watching television all night long. The stations stayed on all night long in New York and New Jersey. In Sioux City, both stations signed off promptly at ten o'clock each night while an Indian dressed in his Tribal regalia signed off doing the Lord's Prayer in sign language.

The house we were living in was old and drafty and had five big bedrooms with rich hardwood floors. The backyard, which was huge, was now buried deep in snow.

Linda came into the kitchen as I stood in its doorway, poised to run, if necessary. Mommy glanced over at us and then took a double-take; she must have noticed the looks of concern on our faces. Mommy didn't say anything but went back to stirring the beans with her large wooden spoon and just waited.

Linda sighed heavily. "Mommy and see there was this truck and . . . ummm . . . Debra had the . . ."

"Yeah! But I told you not to give the change to me," I lied.

"Debra! No you didn't!" Linda looked at me in disbelief.

"Yes, I did!"

"No you . . ."

Mommy stopped stirring the beans and looked at us. "Where is my change?"

In the living room, Cynthia bolted from her chair and ran into the kitchen, likely anticipating that what was about to happen would be more interesting than the farm report.

Linda and I looked at Mommy and then looked down, studying our frozen feet.

"Well, you see, Debra had your change in her . . ."

"But, I told you not to give it to me," I said.

"I *said* where is my change?" Mommy held the wooden spoon up in mid-air.

"Itfellinthesewer," Linda said quickly.

"What?" Mommy's eyes darkened. "What sewer? Where?"

"The one over there," Linda said. "It fell out of Debra's pocket and went into the sewer. We tried to . . ."

"Over where? Which one? All of it?" Mommy asked, but before Linda could reply, Mommy began whacking her about the face and arms with the wooden spoon. Linda ducked in a futile attempt to get out of the way.

"I sent *you* to the store with the money!" *Whack, whack.*

"I did not give it to Debra. I gave it to you!" *Whack, whack, whack.*

Cynthia stood in the doorway, a curious smirk on her face.

"Get upstairs, *now!*" Mommy told Linda. "And I don't want to see your ugly face again tonight." And with that, Mommy gave Linda one final whack to the back of her head, taking her by surprise.

Linda, with a tear-streaked face, glared as she walked by me. "Debra, you know you didn't tell me not to give you the change."

"I don't want to hear it!" Mommy commanded. "Get upstairs! Now!"

A sigh of relief escaped my lips, but Mommy must have heard it, because she suddenly turned her attention and the wooden spoon on me. "And you!"

My eyes felt as wide as saucers as Mommy came closer with her raised spoon. She hit me several times, but not as much as she had beat Linda.

"Stop lying and get your black butt upstairs!" she screamed.

Luckily, Linda and I were still wearing several layers of pants when Mommy beat us, but we had made the mistake of removing our extra sweaters when we took off our coats. Welts were already forming on our unprotected faces and arms by the time we climbed the stairs and crawled into bed. There would be no supper of pinto beans and cornbread for us tonight.

Later that night, Mommy had to wake and dress for work an hour earlier than usual. Normally, we had to stay up till ten in order to wake her up for her eleven to seven shift at St. Vincent's Hospital.

"Mommy," we'd call, "it is time to get up." Then my sisters and I would help her dress for work.

First, Mommy would put on her full-figure bra. She was amply endowed, and would sometimes make us laugh by making her breasts jiggle and bounce around. She looked like one of those half-naked African women I'd seen in *National Geographic* magazines. But she was not so animated tonight.

Then she'd enlist our assistance as she struggled and grunted into her girdle, and then her white stockings (Daddy had always said Mommy had beautiful legs and that that was why he'd married her). Next was her white slip, her white uniform, her nurse's hat, and her white nurse's shoes. And as the time for her to leave neared, one of us always got to call a cab for her. But tonight she told us not to. Although she did not say why, Linda and I knew it was because we had lost her money and now she was broke.

"How are you going to get to work?" Linda asked.

"The Lord will provide," she said.

Before Mommy left she tucked us in bed, and Linda apologized to her for what happened to her money. But I was stone-faced. I didn't say anything about the money.

Mommy told us a story like she did every night and then she asked God to send a guardian angel to look over us as we slept. She kissed us lightly on the foreheads and reminded us not to open the door to strangers. Then she left the house and walked to the hospital, which sat at the top of a hill fifteen blocks away.

After she was gone, the old wooden house did as it had done the past four weeks we'd lived there: it came to life as if possessed by spirits. All night long, it groaned and moaned, sounding as if someone or something was trying to break in through the back door or rise up from the basement through the kitchen door. Or, perhaps it, or he, had already broken in and was standing poised at the bottom step waiting to attack my sisters and me after we fell asleep.

Every night I snuggled between my two older sisters, Linda and Cynthia, holding Linda tightly around her waist, waiting for sleep to overtake me, so I wouldn't hear the scary noises reminding me that my sisters and I were at home alone, in a new city without our Daddy. Each night, I fell asleep with the same prayer on my lips: "Jesus, please send my Daddy home."

"Good morning," Mommy hummed the next morning. "It's time to get up. Ya'll get dressed for school."

Then Mommy told us how the Lord had provided and sent an angel to give her a ride to work, as she handed Cynthia a stack of old magazines that the hospital was about to throw out. It was a ritual with Mommy. Each morning when she returned from work she'd bring a surprise for one of us. And although it was my turn to get the surprise, I suspected that she gave the surprise to Cynthia today, because she was still mad at me for losing her money.

Linda and I got up and began to dress for school. Webster Elementary was my first school experience. When I had lived in New Jersey, Mommy had not been there to enroll me in school, and the thought had never crossed Daddy's mind.

On the first day of school, I insisted on wearing one of my favorite taffeta dresses and my black patent-leather shoes in the something-below-zero Iowa temperature.

Although Mommy tried to convince me otherwise, she finally relented, bundling me and my taffeta dress under my winter coat and pulling my snow boots up over my patent-leather shoes.

At school, Linda, Mommy, and I went to the principal's office, where the principal, a large woman who looked more like a man, escorted us to Linda's class and then to mine.

The excitement and laughter that spilled out from the kindergarten classroom into the hallway came to an abrupt halt as soon as Mommy and I entered.

"Now, class," said Miss Janie, my new teacher, "I want you to say hello to a new student, Debbie Lee Roberts." Miss Janie escorted me to the front of the room and turned me to face my fellow classmates.

The faces looking back at me belonged to nothing but little white girls and little white boys, dressed in woolen sweaters and plaids. They sat on the floor with their mouths agape and their eyes wide, staring at me like I was a creature from another planet. It was obvious to me even back then that these children had never seen a brown person before.

I began to cry when Mommy walked toward the door. Mommy looked back at me and Miss Janie.

"Don't worry about her, she'll be all right," Miss Janie said, wrapping her arms around me and pulling me close to her.

Much later, after I had stopped crying (the Iowans called it *bawling*), she squeezed me in the circle between Mary Lou, a little girl with long blonde hair and blue eyes, and Cindy Ann, a little girl with long blonde hair and green eyes.

At first Mary Lou and Cindy Ann just ogled me up and down, but they finally warmed up to me. They seemed fascinated with the color of my skin and my short, nappy Buckwheat hairstyle. (Earlier that morning, I had insisted on wearing my hair down, and now, the electric static caused by the heat and the black winter cap I'd worn there and removed once I had gotten inside left my hair standing up on end.)

Over time, I would become painfully aware of my differences from them. I was the only brown child in the class, and I was the only one who did not have a Daddy living at home. I envied the little white girls with the long flowing hair. When my sisters and I played house we began to put shirts, Mommy's stockings, or anything else we could find on our heads, pretending it was long flowing blonde hair. I wanted to be just like them.

Because I was in kindergarten, I only attended school in the morning. Linda was instructed to wait for me at lunchtime and walk me home. When we got home, Mommy was usually upstairs napping after having left our lunches for us on the kitchen table. Linda and I would eat in the living room while we watched cartoons.

Today—the day after I'd lost Mommy's money—Linda and I climbed the stairs to see Mommy after we finished our lunches.

"How was school?" she asked as she reached out her arms toward us. Linda and I climbed into her bed and into her arms. Mommy was reading the paper and wasn't wearing her cat-eye glasses like normal. She looked a lot softer, prettier. Linda and I curled up with her under the blankets and just lay there, languishing in her love and affection. Later, Linda kissed Mommy good-bye and left for school, and I went to the girls' bedroom to see what Cynthia was doing. I found Cynthia sitting on the floor surrounded by paper figures she had cut out of the magazines Mommy had given her that morning. We had been told to leave our toys in Newark when we'd left and now there wasn't any money to replace them. The only real toy we had now was Gloria's old wedding doll.

When Gloria turned thirteen, she realized she was too old to play with dolls and gave the Bride to us. Her wedding regalia and her jet-black hair, which cascaded down to the middle of her back, were always neatly coiffured. Now the bride's, hair was matted and bald in spots. She stood naked and abandoned in the corner of our bedroom.

Cynthia was making paper dolls from the figures in the magazines. She must have had about one hundred of them, all white men, women, and children.

"Oooh, can I play too?" I asked as I joined her on the floor.

"No!" Cynthia snapped, forming a protective hedge around them like a mother hen.

"Please?" I begged.

"No! And don't touch them," Cynthia warned, not taking her eyes off the young blonde woman she was cutting out of the magazine.

Cynthia had a mean streak in her. Unlike Linda, being the baby of the family and crying for hours did not move her. I sat on the floor next to her watching and hoping she'd leave a few figures in the magazines for me. Later, Mommy got out of bed and called on Cynthia to do her lessons. Cynthia did not attend Webster Elementary School because when Mommy tried to enroll her in the fourth grade, the school tested her and diagnosed Cynthia as mentally retarded. Cynthia would have to attend "special classes." This revelation was a little strange because when we lived in Newark, Cynthia attended regular classes. At the same time, the diagnosis didn't come as a shock to any of us. It always took Cynthia three times as long as it took Linda or me to comprehend something if she comprehended it at all.

The problem with the special school, however, was that the nearest one was fifteen blocks away—and Mommy did not have a car. So Mommy decided she would home school Cynthia for a while, and try to get her up to par to attend regular school again.

Every afternoon, after Mommy's nap, she and Cynthia would sit at the kitchen table and go over the basics. But Mommy lacked the patience necessary to teach any of us anything except lessons about God, the Bible, and Jesus.

"Don't touch my stuff!" Cynthia cautioned me as she headed out the bedroom door to go meet Mommy. But I knew Cynthia would be down there for a while, so as soon as I heard her footsteps reach the bottom landing, I picked up a beautiful white woman with long blonde hair and the handsome dark-haired white man I had been eyeing all afternoon. As I began to play, I could hear Mommy's voice—loud, irritated, and short—down in the kitchen.

"What is two plus ten?" she asked Cynthia again and again.

"Umm . . .," Cynthia hesitated. "Is it, umm . . ."

"Twelve," I said to myself as I made the man and woman kiss.

"What is it?" Mommy asked again.

"Umm . . . nine?" Cynthia asked.

"*Nine!*" Mommy shouted. "How can two *plus* ten equal *nine*?"

"I dunno," said Cynthia. "I just don't get it."

Whack, whack, whack!

Mommy must have hit Cynthia pretty hard because I heard the impact all the way upstairs. I left the paper dolls on the floor and went down to see what was going on. Mommy heard me before I even got to the kitchen.

"Debra!" she yelled. "Come in here."

I walked in to find Cynthia sitting at the table, blubbering. Her tears were making puddles all over her white math paper. Although I felt sorry for her, it served her right for not letting me play with her paper dolls or even leaving some figures in the magazine for Linda and me to cut out.

"Yes?" I said.

"What is two plus ten?" Mommy asked.

"Twelve," I said proudly.

"See? Your sister is only five years old and *she* gets it. You are nine years old, and we have been over this time and time again!"

Cynthia, the second born, had smooth brown skin and large dark brown eyes—almost black. She was pretty. Her nose was delicate, but right now it had snot running out of it. She took the back of her hand and wiped the snot across her face. Cynthia's hair was long and thick. She and my oldest sister Gloria had the best grade of hair of all of us girls. My hair was the worst of all. It was sandy brown, short, and nappy. Cynthia hadn't bothered to comb her hair today, though. She'd been too busy playing with her paper dolls.

"I know," cried Cynthia, wiping her nose again. "But I just don't get it."

Mommy glared at Cynthia. Then forming a circle with her third finger and thumb she began thumping Cynthia's forehead.

"Do you get it now? Huh? Do you get it now? How did I ever have such dumb-bunny children?" Mommy looked my way.

I shrugged my shoulders as if to say "beats me!" and walked away. There was a lot more thumping and beating now that Daddy was not around. I would be glad when God finally sent Daddy to join us.

Days later, when Mommy did not have to go to work, she dragged us to a church called the Gospel Lighthouse. The whole week before that, Mommy had made us practice singing religious songs, just in case someone wanted to hear a selection from the Roberts girls.

Tonight, she informed us, as we crossed the Missouri River into South Sioux City, Nebraska, would be our opening debut. The Gospel Lighthouse was a white Evangelical church.

When we walked in before that evening's service, we immediately noticed that our fancy dresses with crinoline slips and patent leather shoes were sorely out of place. Some people were on their knees in prayer while others walked aimlessly, as if in a trance, crying and speaking in tongues.

Mommy seized the moment. She ushered us to the front of the church and then took her place at the piano. I stood shyly behind Linda, never taking my eyes off my black patent leather shoes, as Mommy played the introduction and then nodded at us to begin. Linda, Cynthia, and I stood, singing in soft, squeaky voices:

G–double O–D, good
G–double O–D, good
I try to be like Jesus
G–double O–D, good

The white folks clapped politely at the end of our song. Then Mommy insisted we sing another.

After the sermon, the minister had an altar call, and everybody, whether he or she wanted to or not, had to come to the altar. The minister put drops of the blessed oil on his palm and then smacked it against the forehead of the person for whom he was praying. Behind the person being prayed for stood the minister's small, frail, pale assistant.

When the minister got to me, he smacked me in the forehead, pushing my head back until I lost my balance. Meanwhile, his assistant was behind me, pulling my body down to the floor. I went down quietly when I realized what they were doing. I was slain in the Spirit. Well, sort of. Although I did not actually fall out under the anointing of the Spirit, while I lay there, I did have the sensation of floating on a cloud. Pretty soon everybody was on the floor, having also been slain in the Spirit in some form or another. I lay there for awhile. Then I opened my eyes to see what was going on around me. The church floor was covered with bodies—people crying, weeping, and speaking in tongues. Some of the children were looking around like I was. I lay back down and closed my eyes and waited until I heard the rest of the people stirring and getting up.

Back at home that night, Mommy critiqued our singing performance. She wasn't too happy with it because we didn't sing loud enough and we didn't make eye contact with the audience. And most of all, we didn't use enough hand gestures.

Mommy insisted that we act out whatever we were singing. When we were singing "Oh, Be Careful, Little Hands," she wanted us to point to our hands or our feet or the ceiling. The next time, she warned, she would whip us if our performance did not improve.

Please, God, send my Daddy home, I prayed silently. Well, "the next time" came a lot sooner than my sisters and I had hoped. It came when we started to attend the church of Elder Colbert, a large jet-black man with huge hands and large bubble eyes. He looked like a walrus. I was deathly afraid of him even though he was supposed to be saved, sanctified, and filled with the Holy Ghost. He reminded me of this story Mommy made up about a man who looked like a walrus and attacked a little girl after she disobeyed her mother and opened the door to a stranger.

Elder Colbert was the pastor of the Macedonia Church of God in Christ. Every Sunday, no matter the weather, Mommy, my sisters, and I began walking the five blocks along West Sixth Street to the church, which was across the street from the Catholic elementary school and St. Barnabas Catholic Church. Elder Colbert's church, maximum capacity, sat one thousand people. However, it only had ten adult members, all of whom were women, not counting their children or grandchildren.

On the other hand, St. Barnabas Catholic held three to four masses every Sunday morning, and it was said that they had standing room only. Elder Colbert seemed to address this difference in attendance numbers in every Sunday morning sermon.

"Just because St. Barnabas has a lot of people attending it," he'd say (*and we don't,* I'd think), "does not mean they are on their way to heaven." (*But we are?* I wondered.)

He would then open his Bible to Matthew 7:13 and read,

> Enter ye in at the strait gate: for wide is the gate, and broad is the way, that leadeth to destruction, and many there be which go in thereat: Because strait is the gate, and narrow is the way, which leadeth unto life, and few there be that find it.

I felt sorry for the Catholics who attended St. Barnabas. They were in for a strange awakening when they died and tried to enter the pearly gates of heaven. God was going to tell them, "Depart from me, you workers of iniquity."

Today, Elder Colbert sat dozing in the pulpit, while Mother Blueford, dressed in a woolen blue suit and matching blue hat, stood before the congregation at the offering table, asking the saints to give unto the Lord. Mommy sat at the piano manipulating "Amazing Grace." Linda, Cynthia, and I sat nearby so she could keep an eye

42

on us; and we were within thumping distance, should one of us get out of line.

After Mother Blueford collected the offering, she said, "Now, we'll have a selection from the Roberts girls."

The small congregation's clapping woke Elder Colbert with a start. "Thank you, Jesus," he said in a deep pious voice, hoping no one had seen him sleeping. And then pretending to be deep in prayer, he nodded his head back down and began to speak in tongues. "Ohhhshanana."

Mommy sat at the piano beaming, while Linda, Cynthia, and I sighed heavily and slumped in our pew. Mommy gave us the cue.

"Come on, girls," Mommy said, leaning over, so only we could hear. All the while, she gave us that look. "Whatever you are going to do, the Bible says, do it unto the Lord."

We pried ourselves off the front pew and dragged our feet to the front of the church. Mommy snapped her fingers, and all three of us turned to look at her as she mouthed through gritted teeth, "You better straighten up."

"Bless them, Lord," said Mother Baldwin, a little light-skinned lady wearing a pink outfit.

"Come on, children, sing unto the Lord," said Sister Bonnie, a heavyset dark-skinned woman.

We must have done well, because later that night, we took our act to the east side of town. And from then on, Mommy began parading us around, promoting our act like we were the Jackson Five.

Will Santa Claus Come to Sioux City?

Sioux City
Christmas 1959

As Christmas neared, our excitement and anxiety grew. We badgered Mommy with questions on a daily basis.

"Does Santa know we moved? How will he find us? Do you think that the colored Santa's helper gave Santa our new address?"

Mommy's only reply was, "We'll see."

Linda and I had dragged the full-sized Christmas tree that Miss Janie gave me three blocks from her home. It sat in front of the large picture window in our living room. We had decorated it with stringed popcorn and paper decorations that Linda and I had made at school.

On Christmas Eve, while Mommy dressed for work, Linda, Cynthia, and I set out cookies and a glass of milk for Santa. But as soon as we had neatly arranged his snack on the coffee table next to the large over-sized chair, Cynthia changed her mind, snatched up two of the cookies, and began to stuff both of them into her mouth at once, spraying crumbs everywhere.

"Santa's not getting these cookies," she said spraying cookie crumbs everywhere. Cynthia was still pretty upset about the ill treatment she'd received from the colored Santa's helper and was taking no chances that the impostor might get his lips on her cookies.

"Cynthia!" Linda and I screamed, as we covered the other four cookies.

"These are for Santa. You better not touch them," I warned her.

Cynthia eyed the cookies anyway, but then gave in quickly, probably realizing it wasn't worth the hassle, not to mention Mommy's wrath. Shrugging her shoulders, she plopped down on the couch in front of the TV.

"Well, he's not getting my cookies. I'd rather eat them myself. He shouldn't have talked to me that way in the first place. I just wanted to tell him that I wanted a dollhouse for Christmas."

"What difference does it make? He wasn't the real Santa Claus anyway. Just don't eat the cookies we set out for him," Linda warned as she sat down in the chair and began to watch a Christmas show on television. Our tree did not have any lights on it, but Linda, Cynthia, and I did a great job decorating it. I fell into the chair to snuggle with Linda to admire our hard work.

Later that night, as Mommy kissed me on my forehead and tucked me into bed, I asked her, "Do you think Santa knows we moved?"

"We'll see," she said again. She said a prayer over us and left for work.

That night in our bedroom, before any of us had fallen asleep, Cynthia said she heard Santa's sleigh, and Linda and I jumped out of our beds and ran to the window. But we saw nothing. And then I felt foolish after I looked over and saw Cynthia snickering.

Later, when we were supposed to be sleeping, Cynthia started talking again, telling us she was not going to let us play with the dollhouse Santa would bring her. We had a big argument and a pillow fight that Linda and I lost, but not before we all destroyed a couple of pillows and our bedroom. Cynthia readily used her long, sharp nails and large teeth to keep her younger siblings in line, and by the time Linda and I finally got to sleep, we had plenty of scratches to show for it.

Christmas morning, I awoke to Linda's brilliant brown eyes beaming above me. She was standing over me, still wearing her pajamas. Her dark brown, thickly braided hair was matted to her head and had little white feathers in it—a reminder of the pillow fight we'd gotten into the night before. At seven, Linda was three times larger than most children her age. She was also much darker than the rest of our family.

"Wake up, Debra," she said cheerfully. "It's Christmas!"

I stretched and opened my mouth wide, yielding to a large yawn.

"Ugh! Your breath stinks!" Linda recoiled like a snake about to strike. I giggled.

"Get up!" she commanded. "Let's go see what Santa Claus brought us." She grabbed the covers off me and yanked me onto the floor.

Today was Christmas, but it did not feel like it. For some reason, it made me think of photographs I'd seen in our picture album that showed what our past Christmases had been like. We'd always taken pictures of our big tree, decorated with lots of lights and ornaments, and tons of presents underneath; Santa had always been generous. There were pictures of Daddy standing at the head of our elaborately decorated table, which was outfitted with Mommy's fine china and the expensive silverware she kept in a mahogany silverware box that smelled of deep, rich wood. Gloria, Cynthia, Linda and I, sat around the table wearing deliriously happy smiles on our faces, waiting for servings of golden brown turkey. Our Christmas dinners were always a feast: a large turkey, of course, accompanied by mashed potatoes, yams, greens, stuffing, cranberry sauce, and piping hot dinner rolls.

Today, the smells were missing and so were Mommy and Daddy. Mommy had yet to return from work and Daddy was still in Newark, even though when he'd called us the week before, he promised to make it to Sioux City for Christmas.

I pulled myself up off the floor, shuffled over to the window, and looked outside. It was a sunny day and everything was covered in brilliantly white, freshly fallen snow. Cars, trees, houses, and rooftops peeked out from underneath mountains of it. I thought it strange that I did not see tracks left by Santa's sleigh. That should have been my first clue. The fact that my sisters' and my behavior our first month in Sioux City was less than "G–double O–D" should have been my second.

Cynthia was still snoring. We left her and headed down the stairs. I peered around the living room wall and could see the large over-stuffed chair. Next to the chair was the coffee table. On the coffee table sat our cookies and milk, untouched by Santa Claus. My heart began to race and my palms begin to sweat. Linda and I looked at the cookies and then at each other. *Maybe Santa was just too full to eat our cookies,* I hoped.

So I looked the other direction, toward the large picture window where our Christmas tree sat. I caught a glimpse of a our beautifully decorated tree. Linda took my hand in hers. We rounded the staircase, approaching the living room together, filled with anticipation, excitement, and dread all mixed together. And then we saw it. Except for the pine needles that had fallen off during the night, there was nothing under the tree. My hand flew to my mouth in shock, and a loud gasp escaped my lips.

Perhaps today really wasn't Christmas, I told myself. Perhaps we had gotten our dates mixed up. It felt like there was a hollow ball in the pit of my bowels which crawled slowly up my body and lodged itself in my throat.

I tried in vain to force the feeling back down, but it wouldn't budge. So I plopped myself on the cold hardwood floor and began to cry.

"Santa Claus forgot us," I wailed.

"Don't cry, Debra," Linda begged, trying to comfort me. But the sadness was contagious and, before long, she was crying too and joined me on the floor. Our crying must have awakened Cynthia, because I looked up, through my tears and snot, to find her standing there glaring at the empty Christmas tree.

"Umph! Santa didn't come!" Cynthia sucked her teeth and plopped down on the couch.

Then we heard Mommy on the front porch, so we jumped up and raced to open the door.

"Santa didn't bring us anything," I shouted before Mommy even got her key in the door.

"Oh," she said nonchalantly, when she finally got in and began removing her coat and boots.

"Come look, Mommy," Linda said.

Mommy moved into the living room slowly and looked as surprised as we did to find nothing under the tree. Our red, teary eyes looked up to her for answers. "Well, maybe you guys weren't good," she said as she shrugged her shoulders.

"Oh yes, we were good," we each murmured in our own way, trying to defend our honor.

"I don't know," she said, sighing.

"Do you think Santa left our gifts at Daddy's house?" Linda asked.

"I don't know," she said and then slowly climbed the stairs.

"Can we call Daddy and ask him?" Cynthia asked as we followed behind her.

"Not right now. I am going to take a nap first." She paused at her bedroom door.

"Can we call Daddy when you wake up?" I asked.

"We'll see," she said, disappearing behind her bedroom door. The loud click of the door latching shut in front of us echoed through the air and hung there.

We stood staring at the door for a moment, and then headed back downstairs to the empty tree. While Linda and I shared our cookies with Cynthia, we commiserated about what had happened and which one of us was to blame. After thinking about all the bad things we had done to bring this upon ourselves, I started crying again.

"Don't cry, Debra," Linda said. "I bet Santa Claus left our presents in New Jersey at our old house."

"Yeah," Cynthia chimed in. "I know whose fault it was. It was that mean old colored Santa's fault. He forgot to tell Santa that we moved to Iowa."

And at that, I stopped crying—at least for a while. Funny, although neither God nor Santa showed up that Christmas, my faith wasn't shaken in either of them. But my faith in the colored man, well, that was a different story. Right then and there, I formed the opinion that he couldn't be trusted—that somehow he would fail me every time.

The Book of Life

Sioux City
Summer 1961

*Whosoever was not found written in the book
of life was cast into the lake of fire.*
—Revelation 20:14–15

"Blink," Evangelist Missionary Blaylock commanded. About fifty pair of children's eyelids did as they were told. It was the last day of Children's Summer Revival, which Mommy had organized. Elder Tartlet had agreed to let her hold it at his storefront church on the east side of town.

I blinked my eyes several more times, as did others, enjoying the game.

"See how fast that is?" Evangelist Missionary Blaylock said. "That is how fast Jesus will return to this earth on a cloud in the sky. If you are not saved when he comes—in the twinkling of an eye—well, as you can see, you will have no time to repent."

During the first few days of children's revival Mommy and Evangelist Missionary Blaylock lured us in with Bible games, cookies and Kool-Aid, and little toys for those who could name the books of the Bible. Then on the last day—no more games, no more snacks, and no more prizes. Instead, they unveiled the "scared straight" tactic and spoke to us about the Rapture.

Evangelist Blaylock, a young woman with a caramel-colored complexion, stood in the makeshift pulpit, drenched in sweat, preaching about how the world was to end any day and about how Jesus would come on a cloud to gather his chosen few.

"If you are not saved, you are going to be left on this earth. And if your parents are saved, when Jesus returns, they will be caught up in the sky to be with him in the twinkling of an eye.

"Blink," she commanded again. "That is how fast your parents and all those whose names are written in the Lamb's Book of Life will be gone. If you are not saved, then your name is not written in the Lamb's Book of Life, but don't think for second that just because your parents are saved, you will be too. No! You have to know Jesus for yourself."

We continued blinking on our own to see just how fast our parents would be taken from us. As I blinked, I thought about what it would be like to be left on the earth with the very devil himself, and I became terrified. My heart beat wildly and I shook all over. But then that is what Evangelist Blaylock wanted—to scare us into salvation.

"There are just as many small graves as there are big graves," she reminded us. "Y'all remember that little white boy who died on Mother's Day weekend?"

I remembered him. His brother had been in my first grade-class that previous year, at the new school. I was now attending Hopkins Elementary. Unlike Webster, Hopkins was a predominately black school, but also had a good number of white children. Most Negroes who lived on the west side of Sioux City sent their children there.

At Hopkins, I was never the only brown child in the class, but most of the Negro children did not like me because I was a holy roller, of the Pentecostal non-denominational faith. Still, some of the less fortunate children, like those whose parents were on welfare or other outcasts, like I was, played with me. I was comfortable at Hopkins. I had some white friends and some Negro friends. Plus, the teachers liked me. I was special to them.

Anyway, people said that the boy, who was in Linda's third-grade class, had fallen to his death from the roof of the Sioux City Auditorium while trying to catch pigeons. His mother said he was going to catch pigeons and then sell them to get her a Mother's Day gift.

"Well, if that little white boy wasn't saved when he fell off the roof and died, he is in hell right now. Burning forever!" She paused so that would sink in.

I tried to imagine that little boy in the middle of the Lake of Fire, screaming in torment. I knew for a fact he wasn't saved, because the last time I saw him, which was after school on the Friday before he died, he was cursing like a sailor while threatening to beat up a boy twice his size.

I used to call his brother Mr. Pee-body after the cartoon character Mr. Peabody, because he'd wet the bed at night and did not wash up in the morning. He always smelled of urine.

"You don't know," she continued, "when you are going to die. You could walk out this building right now and get run over by a semi-truck. Dead! Just like that." She snapped her fingers. "Where are you going to lift your eyes? Heaven? Or, hell?"

There it was. That question again. Where did I want to spend eternity? I was only seven years old and I did not want to die. But if I did die, of course, I wanted to go to heaven.

Who in her right mind would want to go to the other place, a place where there was weeping and gnashing of teeth? A place so dark, so pitch dark, I couldn't see my own hands right in front of me? And did I fail to mention that *Satan* would be there? Hell, yes, I wanted to be saved!

By the time Missionary Blaylock made her altar call, we children couldn't get there fast enough. However, because we were of the Pentecostal faith, we couldn't simply accept God's gift of eternal life. Rather, we had to get on our knees and beg God for that "gift." Pentecostals call this "tarrying before the Lord."

Not only that, but Pentecostals must think there is something wrong with God's hearing because we had to call on him by shouting and screaming at him until he "inclined his ear unto us." Or maybe it was just because Missionary Blaylock and the other praying women were from the old-school church, so they applied a literal interpretation to the verse "Whosoever will call on the name of the Lord shall be saved."

We stayed on our knees for the next hour while a mixture of tears and snot poured down our little faces as we yelled and begged God to give us the gift of eternal life.

The children ranged from ages four to eighteen. Some of them were kids from the local neighborhood who either had nothing better to do or had parents who just wanted them out of their hair. Others were already converted children who had been forced to attend. I was a member of the forced group.

Paula and Cookie were a part of the "lookie lou" group—the group of kids who'd been forbidden to associate with my sisters and me because of our church. Cookie had a brother in Cynthia's special education class. When we first started to attend Hopkins, Paula, and Cookie and their friends would challenge Cynthia to a fight. Cynthia was a skilled fighter and she had weapons of destruction on her at all times: her big, oversized teeth and her long sharp nails. Plus she acted crazy when she fought, screaming and cursing, with her arms flailing like windmills. After Cynthia beat up Cookie and Paula; they continued their quest to find someone Cynthia could not beat up. Sometimes Cookie and Paula would jump on Cynthia while she was focusing on her opponent. When they did that, I would jump right in kicking and biting, while Linda stood watching from the sidelines pleading the "blood of Jesus," turning the other cheek and praying for her enemy.

Today the message must have struck a chord because Cookie and Paula were kneeling next to me at the altar begging for God's gift of eternal life. I wasn't too surprised by that, since besides fighting, they had done some pretty bad stuff.

There were others on their knees who were part of the group of Negro children that, by the beginning of our first summer in Iowa, would chase my sisters and me home, threatening to beat us up if they could catch us, all the while shouting at us, calling us holy rollers.

In the beginning, Mommy reassured us we were persecuted for Jesus' sake and our faith. "When they come after you, do not fight back. Turn the other check and pray for them. Plead the blood of Jesus," Mommy said. But when our 'blood of Jesus' mantra didn't work, Cynthia and I threw punches while Linda stood by praying.

Cookie and Paula, when they were alone, would play with us, but if any of their friends were around, they would turn on us and try to beat us up.

Paula, a pretty, light-skinned brown girl, with long straightened hair, lived with her grandmother, who forbade her from associating with us or attending Mommy's church. A well-developed twelve-year-old, Paula would allow me an introduction to the world of sex. It all happened one warm spring day, when Linda and Cynthia and I were playing at Webster's playground when we used to live on the east side of town.

Paula yelled at us from across the playground. "Hey, you guys!"

"We are not guys," Cynthia yelled back, indignant. "We are girls!" This was yet another indication for us of how uncultured Iowa was; they called everybody "guys."

Paula was a temperamental friend—sometimes friendly, sometimes downright mean. Today, she was alone and seemed to be in one of her better moods. She crossed the playground to join us on the jungle gym. She was wearing a flowered dress and her long hair appeared to have been freshly washed and pressed. She was beautiful, and I envied her.

The four of us were sitting and talking when a group of boys showed up—three brothers. They were very mean, very black, and very, very ugly. Today, though, they acted differently. They didn't shout at my sisters and me and call us holy rollers; they didn't threaten to beat us up if we did not leave the playground. Instead, the oldest one, who must have been fourteen, called to her.

She looked worried as she tried to ignore him, but he kept calling her to go over. Finally, she told my sisters and me to wait for her, that she'd be right back.

We watched her go, and when she got over to them, we saw the two younger brothers use their bodies to form a shield between us and Paula, who stood next to the oldest brother. We strained to see what they were doing. I could hear Paula telling him, "No, don't! I don't want to." Then I saw him lift up her dress and pull down her panties. My sisters and I gasped.

Then, while his brothers stood guard, the boy "did it" to Paula right there on the playground. When he was finished, he traded places with one of his brothers. When they were all finished with Paula, they left and she came skipping back over. We just sat with puzzled looks on our faces.

I did not know anything about sex yet, so I asked, "What were they doing to you, Paula?"

"Nothing," Paula said, looking down at her shoes. "He just wanted to talk to me."

"Were you doing the nasty, Paula?" Cynthia asked. She was always direct.

Paula hung her head. She didn't need to answer.

"Do you like it?" Cynthia asked.

"It's okay—I guess."

We sat there, staring at her. Nobody said anything for a while. And then we got up and went to play on the swings.

I hadn't done anything as bad as Cookie or Paula. I for sure hadn't done the nasty. But it didn't matter to God. If you lied to your parents or fought with your brother or sisters, you were going to hell. I definitely qualified. I lied to Mommy and fought with my sisters all the time. I remembered this as I knelt at the altar next to Paula, thinking I, too, should call out to be saved.

The praying, moaning woman yelled in our ears, "Call him! Ask him to save you!"

Ma Harris, a woman with a mysterious past and a severe case of halitosis, stood over me, clapping her hands and yelling in my ears like a Marine drill instructor, "SavemeJesus! SavemeJesus! SavemeJesus!"

Later, after the women were satisfied with how much we were crying and how loudly we were yelling, they asked us whether we thought God had heard our prayers for salvation. I really did not know. But I thought so.

Well, if we thought he did, they said, the next step was to thank God for the gift of eternal life and ask him to fill us with his Holy Spirit, which would keep us from sinning. And so for the next hour, we stayed on our knees and prayed some more, this time for the Holy Spirit to manifest itself in us through the speaking of tongues.

Over and over I yelled, "ThankyouJesus! ThankyouJesus! ThankyouJesus! ThankyouJesus!" The words sprayed through my mouth like a machine gun. I had to say the mantra faster and faster until my words began to slur.

"Let him have your tongue!" Ma Harris shouted in my ear.

I did not know how to do that, so I just opened my mouth, stuck out my tongue, and tried to say "ThankyouJesus" as fast as I could with my tongue sticking out. What came out was something like "thay-oo-zee-us." After a while, however, I began to speak in an unknown tongue. It seemed a bit forced and contrived. Much later when playing church with my school friends, we would pick a word, any word and let it ricochet through our mouth and we came up with same affect. As a child I believed I was baptized with the Holy Spirit but I did not know what I was saying because there was no one there to interpret what I was saying. Besides, the tongues were supposed to keep me from sinning. That never happened. Missionary Blaylock, also a skilled pianist, began to play the piano while Elder Tartlet picked up his guitar. My sister Gloria, who had joined us in Sioux City in the summer of 1960—because there was no money left to keep her in private school and because Mommy needed someone to watch us while she started her church—got up and began to beat the tambourine. My childhood friends and I euphorically danced before the Lord while we spoke in tongues. Then the music stopped.

Then Mommy called for testimony service, in which each of us must stand and say something on behalf of the Lord. Most of us were afraid of our own shadows. We were painfully shy, even though we saw each other every day. But we had no choice but to speak out because, as Mommy reminded us, "If you are ashamed to speak up for Jesus here on earth, he will be ashamed of you when you try to enter heaven. He will say to his father, God, he is ashamed of you."

Mommy gave us that dark evil eye, because even after her little speech, nobody budged.

Then finally, Linda, always the Mommy-pleaser, stood. "I want to thank the Lord for being here. I want to thank the Lord for being saved, sanctified, and filled with the Holy Ghost. I want to thank the Lord for my mother and father. Pray my strength in the Lord."

"Praise the Lord and thank you, Jesus!" echoed through the storefront as Linda took her seat.

Mommy looked pleased and then looked in my direction. I stood and spoke the best I could, and then so did Cynthia. And then the rest of the children, one by one, stood up and mimicked us, with very little variance in their litany.

But it was okay then just to copy the person who testified before you. We were baby saints in training, we were told. Only when we became seasoned saints would the Lord give us the words to say.

Unfortunately, we were also told that, unlike the certainty of death, salvation brought no guarantees. We were told that this kind of salvation, our salvation, could be easily lost.

I often imagined God holding a small pencil that had a giant eraser. One minute, he'd write my name in the Lamb's Book of Life, and the next minute, in a twinkling of an eye, he'd erase it because I told a lie or got mad at my sister or my mother or something—anything.

All I had to do was make him mad and he would snatch back his gift of eternal life so fast, it'd make my little halo spin. And the worst part about that was, no one really knew what might piss God off. In fact, it was probable that I wouldn't even know my name had been removed from the Book of Life, until after I died and was standing before God. I often imagined that scene. I am standing there, and he is searching for my name in the book of Life, when finally, he shakes his head and looks up at me, saying, "Nope! It's not in here!"

"What?" I'd say, feigning surprise. I knew very well my name couldn't last on the "Welcome to Heaven" list. "Let me see that book. Are you sure my name is not in there?"

And God would give me that look which said "Come on, now! You didn't really think *your* name would be in the Book of Life, did you?" Then he'd say, "Sorry. Depart from me, you worker of iniquity."

I did not have any peace or comfort in that type of salvation because it was contingent on only me and my behavior—and I was one of those hardheaded Negro children who got into everything. I did not have a guilty conscience like my sister Linda. My mottos were "Avoid getting beat at any cost" and "Lie, when the truth would do just as good." So I knew that any salvation contingent on my behavior was not a good thing. What if, in the twinkling of an eye when Jesus returned, I was telling a lie or getting mad at my sister? No matter how good I'd been up until then, no matter how hard I'd tried, I was still doomed in that moment. There were no guarantees.

School would start in two weeks, I thought. That would be the perfect testing ground for the salvation I'd renewed at the children's revival. If they tried to beat me up again, I would just "plead the blood of Jesus." But, then, if that didn't work, I wouldn't hesitate to pick up a brick and throw it at them. After all, I was doomed to fail anyway. The next Sunday, our church met at Crystal Lake at five in the morning for a baptismal service. After the service, we would stay for a church picnic and swimming.

The uniform of the day, as it always was for baptismal services, was white in some form or another. Since it was a sin for women to wear pants, we wore skirts or dresses, which we then pinned between our legs like a big diaper, so that it wouldn't float up and reveal anything while we were being submerged in the lake for our baptism. Unlike the Catholics, there was none of that sprinkling stuff. In fact, that was another reason Catholics wouldn't go to heaven—they hadn't been baptized right.

The ministers, one of whom was Mommy, stood waist high in the water, waiting for ushers to lead us out to them, one by one. The rest of the saints stood on the bank of Crystal Lake, praying and praising the Lord in song, as Ma Harris led them in a round of "Take me to the water/Take me to the water/Take me to the water to be baptized."

Ma Harris dominated every song she led. She sang over everyone else, and as soon as the rest of us neared the end of the verse, she'd race to the beginning of the next. We could never catch up with her, because when we did, she'd jump ahead.

One by one, the new saints, the old saints, adults and children, whites, Negroes, and Indians, were led into the water. When it was my turn, the usher led me in Mommy's direction. She was standing waist deep in the water, dressed in white, and was smiling at me as I walked toward her. She was not wearing her glasses and she looked soft, young, and pretty. When I finally got up next to her, she stretched one hand toward heaven and put the other in the small of my back.

"In the name of the Father, the Son, and the Holy Ghost, I baptize you, Debra Lee Roberts." Then she placed her free hand over my mouth and nose. "Hold your breath," she said gingerly, and as I did, she squeezed my nose tight. Then she and her assistant submerged my body in the cold, dirty waters of Crystal Lake.

When she brought me back up, she told me that my rising from the water symbolized my resurrection with Jesus.

"Behold, you are now a new creature in Christ," she said.

"Praise God, I am saved," I said. "I am sanctified and filled with the Holy Ghost."

And with that, my name was written in the Lamb's Book of Life. Well, at least for the time being.

Entertaining Angels

Sioux City
Summer 1962

Be not forgetful to entertain strangers; for thereby
some have entertained angels unawares.
—Hebrews 13:2

Mommy worked as a registered nurse at night and a minister by day. She and Daddy were buying a large duplex on top of a hill on Fourteenth Street. Daddy usually came to visit us twice a year and we would return to Newark with him. Later that summer, Mother would drive to Newark to visit and to return us to Sioux City.

Sometimes Mother would quit her nursing job because she said the Lord told her not to work. During these times, we lived off the tithes and offerings of the church. During these times, times were rough.

Sometimes our gas and electricity would get shut off and stay that way the whole summer. We'd burn candles at night while Mommy played catch-up with the enormous gas bill from the previous winter. Fortunately, Iowa's Electric and Gas Company dared not turn off the power during the winter, for fear the pipes would freeze.

Other times, it would be our water that got shut off, and we'd have to borrow water from our next-door neighbor. And food was always scarce, but the little we had, we shared with others. Mommy never turned any stranger away.

"Be not forgetful to entertain strangers; for thereby some have entertained angels unawares," Mommy would quote from the Bible when my sisters and I complained about another overnight house-guest. Though I learned right away that those people were far from angels, because on those rare occasions when the Lord blessed us with enough money to buy "real" food—those times when we would drool with anticipation at the thought of eating something besides pinto beans and rice, or ox tails and rice, or black-eyed peas and rice—inevitably, the Lord would send someone to eat up the groceries with which he had just blessed us.

It was on just such a rare occasion when the Armstrongs, a white family from the South, arrived. We had just put the last package of Oreo cookies in the cupboard when their pea-green Chevy hugged the curb outside and lurched to a stop.

"Praise the Lord," Reverend Armstrong said, squeezing out from behind the steering wheel. This I had to see. Because as grossly obese a man as Reverend Armstrong was, he was dwarfed by his two large sons and daughter, who had to weigh in at about two hundred pounds a piece.

Sister Armstrong, the wife, was too fat to move. She waved at us from the front seat of the car and smiled, revealing two missing front teeth, which apparently caused her to have a speech impediment, because she said, "Pwaise de Wowd, Sistah Wobetts."

"Well, come on in. Praise the Lord," Mommy said. "Cynthia, Linda, and Debra, the Lord sent us some company. You girls go change your bed sheets and straighten up your room."

What Mommy meant was that we had to turn our bedroom over to the three fat Armstrong children. And Gloria, who had finally just gotten a room to herself, had to turn hers over to Reverend and Sister Armstrong—and for several weeks, as it turned out.

During that time, we learned that Reverend Armstrong did not like the television. He called it a "one-eyed monster," preaching that it was a sin to watch television and go to movies. But every day, my sisters and I had to fight him and his family for a seat in front of the television. The Armstrong's were fascinated by the one-eyed monster.

Armstrong's sermons specialized monsters, witches, and demons, not to mention in the devil and the rapture, as well as in "crossing the deadline." No one had ever preached about "crossing the deadline" before. Apparently, he believed, there was this thing that we, the children of God, could do that would make God so angry, he would never forgive us for it—a line we could cross. No one knew what this one thing was, but whatever it was, I did not want to find myself in that position. And apparently neither did Cynthia.

Many nights after Armstrong's first sermon on crossing the deadline, Cynthia woke up, crying and tormented. She was convinced she had committed the unpardonable sin, the one God would never forgive. That was surprising to me, even then. Though she was no angel, Cynthia's only real transgression, I thought, was that of being a teenager. Then twelve, she often talked back to Mommy and fought with Linda and me. Still, she was constantly under the impression God was so angry with her that he would never forgive her and take her back into the fold.

But that didn't stop Reverend Armstrong, especially when it came to the subject of the rapture. Reverend Armstrong liked to preach about what the earth was going to be like after the saints of God were gone.

"If you think it is hard to live a saved, sanctified life on earth now, wait until all the saints of God have been gathered up and the very *devil* himself is running things. You won't be able to buy anything to eat or drink if you don't take the mark of the beast. But if you take the mark of the beast, you will be forever doomed.

"Ohhhh, saints," he would cry. Reverend Armstrong loved to cry in the Spirit. "Ohhhh, saints," he would say with tears streaming down his round face, "the moon is going to drip to blood. The sun is going to turn black. All the water is going to turn to blood."

"Ohhhh," he would moan, "what a terrible place the world is going to be. Aren't you glad to know that you have a chance to make it right with Jesus right now? Don't delay—this may be your last time."

I wasn't saved during the second week of Reverend Armstrong's revival. God was having a hard time keeping up with the number of transgressions I had committed that week. So I had to get back down on my knees and beg God to forgive and save me all over again. If I had died during that second week of the revival, I surely would have burned in hell for all eternity, right alongside the little white boy who'd died trying to catch pigeons.

One night, Barbara Jean, Reverend Armstrong's only daughter, and I walked to the park. We'd spent a lot of time together during their stay at our house and had come to enjoy each others company.

I was swinging, while Barbara Jean introduced me to the Beatles by serenading me with their songs. Her father had forbidden her to listen to the Beatles. Little did he know, Barbara Jean knew the lyrics to all of the Beatles' songs—and to all of Elvis Presley's songs too.

She also knew how to dance, for a white girl. I did not know how to dance for either a black or white girl, because it was a sin to dance.

"I'm not saved," Barbara Jean secretly confided in me. "And when I turn eighteen, I'm moving to California to join a rock 'n' roll band."

Barbara Jean also had a terrible mouth and cursed like a sailor. But we had so much fun together.

It was summer so it did not get dark that night until late. The two of us sat in the park just cursing and singing and dancing and talking, until finally I asked, "What time is it?"

"Oh, shit!" Barbara Jean shouted, though she didn't have a watch.

We raced out of the park and down the street to our little storefront church in the alley off of Sioux Street. The parking lot was filled with cars.

As soon as we walked in, Mother Goodlow gave me the evil eye, because I was wearing pants and saints don't wear pants. (Although Mommy allowed me to wear blue jeans that day, I couldn't wear them to church. She had thrown out the "no pants" restriction for children, because she said she was tired of looking up our dresses and seeing our dirty underwear.) But not only was I was wearing blue jeans; I was wearing dirty blue jeans. And to top it all off, as usual, my hair was uncombed and stood straight up on my head.

On the other hand, Barbara Jean, who was twelve, hadn't been swinging, and she did not look as though she'd been playing in a dirt box. Her long, straight, dirty-blonde hair fell neatly around her large round head down to her ample waist. And that night, she was wearing a dress that was in her favor.

We found a seat in the back, and Mommy, from her seated position in the pulpit, caught my eye and mouthed, "I'm going to get you when you get home." I dropped my gaze submissively.

All the while, Barbara Jean's father was in the pulpit crying and pleading with people to come to Jesus before it was too late.

"Ohhhh, people! What a terrible day it will be. The mountains are going to get up and move out of the way. Then the heavens will part and every eye shall see him. Jesus is trying to get you ready for that great day. Don't you want to be able to stand before God? Don't you want to be able to stand?"

I tried to imagine the face of an angry God, but when I closed my eyes, all I saw was Mommy's dark face glaring at me from behind her cat-rimmed glasses. It was getting so I couldn't distinguish between the two of them—Mommy and God. I was terrified of both.

An hour later, after he had finished preaching, Reverend Armstrong made an altar call. Other than a few new people who responded, it was mostly the same old saints kneeling at the altar. Those who had sinned or done something they didn't even know about that had caused their name to be erased from the Book of Life. I would have gone up myself, but I was dirty and wearing pants.

Instead of a two-week revival, it turned into four. The Armstrong's stayed at our house for a month. By the time they left at the end of the summer, they'd broken two of our new dining room chairs and eaten everything in sight.

Loving a Child

Sioux City
Fall 1962

*He that spareth his rod hateth his son; but he
that loveth him chasteneth him betimes.*
—Proverbs 13:24

Evangelicals weren't always the only ones waiting for the end of the world. During the cold war and the Cuban missile crisis, fallout shelters were being built all over the United States in preparation for destruction.

I was eight years old and in the third grade and John F. Kennedy was the president. The end of the world was near and everybody, including my third-grade teacher, was afraid. Bomb drills had replaced our school's fire drills, which were frightening enough, but then one day in October, they sent us home early. Our teacher told us that missiles were up and aimed at Cuba, and she shooed us out of her classroom and told us to run home.

When I got home, Mommy's car was parked outside, but I couldn't find her. I was sure the rapture had taken place and that I had been left behind. I went to the sink and turned on the faucet to see if the water had turned to blood. Good. It was still clear. Then I went to the bathroom to check the water in the toilet. That, too, looked normal. Finally, Linda and Cynthia made it home and I felt better; if I had to be left behind, at least I wouldn't be alone. But I was most relieved to see Mommy walk in the door.

After that day, Brother Armstrong's messages the previous summer about the rapture, combined with the threat of nuclear war, plagued me and kept me up at night. In the wee hours of the morning, I would often wake up and race to the bathroom to see if the water had turned to blood. And on nights when the harvest moon was surrounded by an orange glow, I would stare at it, waiting for the blood to start dripping.

And it wasn't just at night that my fear haunted me. When I returned from school, I would always look for Mommy immediately. If I could not find her, I was convinced that the rapture had taken place and that I'd been left on the earth without her, destined to fend for myself.

During school, too, I found it hard to concentrate. I was consumed with wondering, "What if Jesus returned and I was left behind? Would I be able to stand? Or would I take the mark of the beast? Would I be like Judas and deny Jesus Christ?"

And worse than the questions were their answers. Because try as I might to be good, I knew that I'd just never be able to do it. I wouldn't be able to stand. I wouldn't be able to be perfect, the way the Bible commanded us to be. Although I didn't believe, like Cynthia, that I had crossed the deadline, I knew I would be left behind, and that I'd probably take the mark of the beast.

Another, more tangible thing that kept me up at nights was my fear of Mommy sneaking into our room and beating us. Lately, she'd gotten into this habit of stockpiling our transgressions like she was the USSR, and then *bam*—surprise attack.

She prided herself on the fact she would never beat us in anger but would take a cooling-off period first. Problem was, this period could last for days, weeks, or even months. And you just never knew when it was over.

My sisters and I would be sitting around the living room watching television or playing a board game, when she would come in out of nowhere, and start beating us with an extension cord for something we'd done over two weeks ago.

"Didn't I tell you I was going to whip you?" she'd ask as the extension cord would lash into my meaty brown flesh. My sisters and I would scramble for cover, sending board-game pieces flying.

It always seemed that just when I thought she had forgotten a beating she'd promised, she'd remember. For example, one night, not long after the month long revival, I fell asleep, as usual, with nuclear holocaust and the rapture on my mind.

I had a dream about Jesus. He was standing across the street from me with a group of children behind him. He was taking them to heaven. I wanted to go with them. Jesus beckoned to me to come. "But I don't know how to fly," I replied. "I'm afraid."

"Come on," Jesus said. "You can do it. Just have faith in me."

"I can't," I replied.

Jesus tried in vain to coax me again and again. His words were gentle, but still, I was afraid.

He wasn't upset by my lack of faith. He just said, "You must develop your faith in me. But that's okay. I'll be back to get you when you are ready."

Then he left the earth, the children in tow. And as I stood watching them ascend into heaven, pain ripped through my body. I opened my eyes to see that an extension cord had lashed into my skin.

Whamp! Whamp!

Still struggling to fully awaken, I scrambled to get out of the cord's way.

Mommy was yelling, "Didn't I tell you!"

Whamp!

To be honest, I couldn't remember at four o'clock in the morning whether she had told me anything. I just wanted to run for cover. I had to get away from the crazy woman.

Whamp!

I reached for the cover on my bed. The extension cord caught me on my hand, and I jerked my hand back in pain, cowering in the corner, praying that she would stop. But she didn't. So I cried and hollered.

"Shut up!" she said as she continued to beat me. Linda and Cynthia were awake by then, wondering what was happening, hoping she wouldn't spank them, too, for something they'd done a long time ago.

Distracted by their stirring, Mommy stopped beating me and turned to them. "I want you guys to get up and clean up this room, before I give you some, too!"

Linda and Cynthia scrambled out of bed, while I continued to cower in the corner, crying.

Mommy looked at me, the extension cord dangling from her hand. "Shut up, before I give you some more to cry about with your Johnnie-Roberts-looking-self!" Then she left the room.

I prayed, "God, please send my Daddy home. And save me so that I can be good."

As usual, both prayers went unanswered.

The Boogeyman

Sioux City
Winter 1963

I will return to my house from which I came. . . . [H]e goes and takes with him seven other spirits more wicked than himself.
—Luke 11:24–26

The room was pitch black. She was sure she had left the light on in the bathroom, Cynthia told me later. Perhaps Mommy had accidentally turned it off. Our bedroom was so dark, it felt as though she could touch the darkness. And although she could not see her hands in front of her face, she saw him when he entered the room, Cynthia said.

My sister Cynthia was born with a veil over her eyes or "the gift of having spiritual eyes," as the old folks called it. Some gift. Her gift came as a package deal to compliment her learning disability. Children teased her unmercifully. They didn't call her gifted; they called her a retard.

Anyway, Cynthia said she felt his cold, black dampness as he moved about the room. Where was he exactly? There, over in the corner, grinning. Cynthia said she could tell he was grinning, because she could smell his foul, mildewy breath.

Now, it's not abnormal for children to be afraid in the dark. But normal children have normal nightmares and fears, usually about boogeymen hiding under their beds or in their closets. They, of course, had normal parents who reassured them with words like, "It's okay, honey. See, there's nothing in your closet except clothes," or "See, sweetie, there's nothing under your bed except shoes and a little dirt."

Cynthia, however, was not a normal child, and we did not come from a normal family. Our parents were Pentecostal holy rollers. Pentecostals believed in the boogeyman, too; they just called him the devil.

So whenever Cynthia woke us up in the middle of the night, screaming in terror, our Mother said things like, "You're right, there is a demon in your room. You and your sisters invited him in with all of your fighting and arguing."

And that's how Cynthia learned it did no good to scream. So this night, as she lay in the darkness, seeing the black shriveled gargoyle watching her from the corner, she tried hard to remember if we had been fighting or arguing, or if she had had any evil thoughts that day. (Thinking evil things also brought the devil to our house.) Chances are, we probably had argued that day, since we always did.

Then, he giggled, this time from a different spot in the dark room. He moved just that fast. Where was he now? Cynthia reached under her pillow for her Bible, but it wasn't there. Terror struck her heart. Where had she left it? Church? In the car? She couldn't remember.

We Roberts girls always tried to remember to sleep with our Bibles under our pillows. Mother had warned us long ago that the Bible would help ward off evil spirits and protect us. But in the movies, people used crucifixes to keep the evil spirits at bay. The Pentecostals mocked the stupidity of the movie industry's use of crucifixes, as it just reflected the beliefs of those genuflecting Catholic worshipers; and after all, the sign of the cross was the sign of the devil—at least according to a traveling Evangelical who'd explained it to us by quoting Job 1:6.

"Now there was a day when sons of God came to present themselves before the Lord," she read. "And Satan came also among them. And the Lord said unto Satan, 'Whence comest thou?' Then Satan answered the Lord and said, 'From going to and fro in the earth, and from walking up and down in it.'" She crossed herself;

first her forehead, down to her heart, to the left of her chest and then to the right.

"See?" the evangelist wailed from the pulpit, "Catholics are going to bust hell wide open! They are praying to Mary and making the sign of the devil," she continued.

After that message, I viewed Catholics in a different light. On my way to and from school every day, I walked past St. Barnabas Catholic Church and its school. Every time I did, I felt sorry for those Catholics, who would burn in hell when Jesus returned.

As they attended mass day after day, I watched them. I watched the nuns, dressed in their black habits, and wondered if they knew they were all going to hell.

I especially felt sorry for the tall, thin, white priest, who was always cordial to my friends and me. He never made us leave the playground, even though he knew we'd climbed over the locked fence to get there. I couldn't look him in the eye anymore when he said hello to me. I felt sorry that he did not know Jesus as his personal savior.

Back in our room, Cynthia thought she heard the beast move again. Or maybe it was just one of us, she thought—Linda or I— stirring in our sleep.

"Debra, is that you?" Cynthia whispered. No answer. "Linda?"

"Linda?" he whispered, mocking her.

She heard his feet shuffle across the room in her direction and she felt his black breath move in closer.

"Satan, the Lord rebuke you," she prayed.

"Satan, the Lord rebuke you," he replied, mockingly.

"The blood of Jesus!" she shouted.

He froze. He hated those words. She was a dirty fighter.

"You old foul devil," Cynthia said. "Get out of here, in the name of Jesus."

"What is it?" Linda said with a start, popping up in her bed.

"There's an evil spirit in the room," Cynthia said, her voice raised an octave or two.

"Whaaa?" I had left my bed in the middle of the night to join Linda in hers, so I popped up behind her. "What did you say? Where?"

"Over there. In the corner," Cynthia replied.

I leaped over Linda and raced to the light switch. Linda grabbed her Bible from under her pillow and held it to her heart. The light went on.

"Where is he?" Linda asked.

Cynthia, who hadn't moved from under her covers, lay staring at the wall. Three sets of eyes were on her: mine, Linda's, and his.

Linda and I looked where Cynthia was pointing and saw nothing. Although we did not really believe her, we weren't taking any chances, because she was convinced she could see him. She even described him for us. He was a little old gargoyle, she said, hunched, black, and shriveled, and crouching in the corner. His hair was a gray, matted mass that hung down to the middle of his back. His fingernails, long, black, and curled, extended from his snarled dark-veined hands.

I stood in the middle of the floor clutching my Bible. I was terrified, just like I always was when Cynthia woke us up in the middle of the night claiming to see evil spirits. After all, she wasn't the only one who'd ever seen them in our house.

Those in our church who were "lucky" enough to have "the gift" felt compelled to give us regularly scheduled updates on the demon and devil population of our house on Fourteenth Street. According to their reports, it was not unusual for evil spirits to be lurking about our house. In fact, it seemed the demons were ever present. They hid in the closets, under the beds, in the bathroom, and in the corners of rooms. Sometimes they even sat boldly on the couch, just daring anyone to disturb them.

They came into our house along with all the many guests Mother brought in who might be angels: sundry spirits, witches, warlocks, demons, and the very devil himself. They entered just as casually as a fly or mosquito passing through an open door or a screen-less window on a hot Iowa summer's day.

I did not see them, but I felt their presence, and I was constantly afraid. In fact, Mother often reminded me how ironic it was that I was so evil during the day, but was too scared to sleep by myself at night.

"You're so tough," Mother would say. "Go on back in there and cast those demons out of your room."

But you're talking about spirits, I'd think, glued to the spot. *The devil! Demons! Whoever said I could defeat them? Whoever said I wasn't afraid of them?*

"You're going to be a whore when you grow up," she would continue. "You will have all kinds of men sleeping with you because you will always be too afraid to sleep by yourself."

If that is what it will take to get a good night's sleep, I'll take my chances, I thought, staring up at her, even though I knew she was at least partially right. Every night, I had to crawl into bed with Linda, because I was too scared to sleep on my own. I was even afraid to take a bath with the door closed at night, because I was terrified of what I could not see—even with the bathroom light on. Gift or not, I never wanted God to open my spiritual eyes.

And despite what Mommy imagined about the guests she entertained, angels rarely came to our house for a visit. At least, rarely did anyone report angel sightings. I rarely heard, "Oh, I just saw a beautiful angel standing over you, watching guard." No, it was always a demon or a devil, a little wrinkled old man or woman, or tiny goblins. I guess it was because we Roberts girls were always arguing and fighting. It was no wonder I couldn't sleep by myself.

We climbed out of our bed, and then Cynthia, Linda, and I joined hands and formed a circle in the middle of our bedroom floor. Mother and some saints she had staying at our house joined us. We all prayed and demanded that the demon leave. Then one of our guests went through the house, pleading the blood of Jesus. Finally, Mother went to the front door, opened it, and commanded the demon to leave and swept it out of the house using a broom.

"Now get out of here, in the name of Jesus!" she shouted, slamming the door behind him. Then she turned to look at us girls.

"He is gone now," she said. "But you girls better be good and stop that fighting and arguing, because if he comes back he'll bring seven more demons with him."

The thought of having eight demons living in my bedroom closet was more than I could take. Right then, I closed my eyes tight and prayed silently, *Jesus help me be good!*

But it was pointless. Two days later, Linda and I got into a fistfight when she accused me of cheating at Parcheesi. I was sure, when we'd finished, that the demon and his seven buddies were waiting eagerly at our front door—that is, if they had ever left.

The Curse

[I]f a woman has an issue . . . she shall be put apart seven days; and whosever toucheth her shall be unclean until the even be unclean.
—Leviticus 15:18–19

When I was eleven, Linda and I prepared to make our yearly trek back to New Jersey to visit Daddy for the summer. For seven years Daddy 's promise to join us in Iowa permanently and take over Mommy's church remained unfulfilled. Although he did visit us twice a year and we would usually drive back to Newark with him, I wanted Daddy to live with us. I wanted us to be a family again, like the other families who attended our church.

That year, Mother felt we were old enough to travel by ourselves. Linda would be thirteen in October and entering the eighth grade, and I was eleven and would enter the sixth grade in the fall. We were so excited.

Cynthia wanted to go with us, but Mother didn't think she was mature enough, even at fifteen, to go without an adult. So Mother and Cynthia, along with Sister Noble, would drive up and meet us at the end of the summer. Gloria, who was seventeen and long since left the madness at "Roberts Manor," hired herself out as a live-in nanny for a wealthy Jewish family. She was living a life that did not include us. Gloria was a phantom. I did not know where she was or what she was doing. Anyway, Mother's reservations about Cynthia stemmed from Cynthia's inability to take care of her feminine needs during "that time of the month." Cynthia had started her "curse" almost five years before, when she was just ten, yet she still didn't seem to understand how the whole process worked.

So once a month, Mother would sit us down and talk to us about our period, or what she called *'ministerating'*. (It was not until college, when some white girl laughed at my mispronunciation in a nice sort of way, that I learned that the correct term was *menstruating*.)

Our first lecture came when we were living in a tiny little apartment on the corner of Main and West Seventh Streets. Incidentally, this was also about the time she ordered us to start calling her Mother, rather than Mom or Mommy. Moreover, she told us that when she called us, we could not merely answer "What?" from the other room; we had to come to see what she wanted and respond by saying, "Yes, Mother?" And so when she called to us this time from the living room, that's exactly what we did.

"Debra, Linda, Cynthia, and Gloria?" she called.

My sisters and I filtered into the living room from all areas of the apartment. "Yes, Mother?"

"Sit down. I need to talk to you."

In front of Mother sat a box with the word "Kotex" written on it. She also had some sort of white flimsy belt with little hooks hanging from it and a stack of cut-up newspaper.

Gloria sat on the couch and I sat on the floor near her. (Although Gloria had started her period years ago and already had had "the talk" at Saints Junior College, each time Mother gave the talk, she made Gloria join us.) Linda, who was always smooching up to Mother, sat right under her feet, looking up at her with loving puppy-dog eyes. Cynthia stood in the entryway.

"Have a seat, Cynthia," Mother said.

Cynthia moved slowly across the room and sat at the other end of the couch.

Then Mother began the "curse" story. Mother always loved a good story, but a good scary story, Mother loved the best. She could make up a scary story about anything in life just to scare us into strict obedience. These stories all entertained our worst what-if curiosities.

"When you reach puberty," she began, "your body begins to undergo changes. You develop titties, and hair under your arms and down there between your legs. Your body is getting ready to have babies now. Boys will be trying to put their thing in you."

"You mean their ding-a-lings?" Cynthia asked.

Linda and I faked shock at the fact that Cynthia had just said such word. But then we couldn't help it—we burst into giggles.

"Yes!" Mother said, undaunted. "And you mustn't let them touch you down there. It can cause diseases and you can get pregnant and have a baby."

I imagined my Daddy putting his thing in Mother and getting her pregnant with my baby brother, whom Mother had aborted and flushed down the toilet. I wondered if it were possible that he was still alive and living in a sewer somewhere in Newark.

"Now when your body starts developing," Mother continued, "—and Cynthia, you are already starting to get titties—you will start *ministerating.*"

"Ministerating?" Cynthia asked.

"Yes. Blood starts flowing out of your body down there. It is called a period. Some people call it the "curse," because people can put a curse on you by squeezing the blood out of your sanitary napkin and putting it in your drink or something. So you must always be careful to wrap your used sanitary napkin in newspaper and throw it away. Once boys find out you have a period, they will be coming around you trying to get into your pants. Don't tell anybody about your period," she warned. "And don't leave your soiled napkins around."

I wondered whether some woman had stolen a soiled sanitary napkin from Mother and used it to put a curse on Daddy. Perhaps that was why Daddy was no longer with us. Perhaps that woman had been Sister Scott.

After three long days on the Greyhound, Linda and I met Daddy at the bus station in Newark. He was grinning and he showered us with big bear hugs and kisses.

"There she is!" Daddy said looking into my eyes as he lifted me into the air. "Ole Mosquito!" He laughed.

Daddy affectionately referred to me as his mosquito, because I been very small for my age, and whenever he'd turn his back to me, I'd run and jump up on it. He'd pretend not to know I was there. Then he'd look around himself and say, "What was that? It felt so light, it must have been a mosquito!"

It was good to be back with him.

He ushered us to an awaiting Checker Cab, where he opened the front-seat passenger door and told us to get in. It was a huge red cab, and the inside smelled of new leather. In the back was one large bench seat that could have easily seated four large adult males. There were also two leather-bound stools, which folded neatly onto the floor. When Daddy walked around the car and climbed into the driver's seat, Linda and I were astonished. It looked like a London Cab, except it wasn't red. It was a yellow Checker Cab.

"Is this your cab, Daddy?" Linda asked.

"Its *our* cab!" Daddy said proudly.

Several people were already shouting at him from the sidewalk. "Taxi!"

Daddy got back out of the cab. "Where you going?"

People shouted out various addresses.

Daddy paused a moment. "Sure. Get in."

Then he walked around the car to the curb, and with huge biceps bulging from beneath his short-sleeved shirt, he grabbed their suitcases and threw them into the expansive trunk.

My Daddy was so strong and muscular.

Then he climbed back into the driver's seat and started the cab. By the time we left the bus station, Daddy had five adult passengers in the back: two on the stools and three on the seat. Linda and I sat in front with Daddy. Daddy made small talk with all the passengers and witnessed to them about Jesus Christ and told them about his church. The passengers were impressed with him and promised to visit his church one day.

My Daddy was entertaining and a skilled conversationalist.

Little by little, he'd make money, dropping off one passenger and then picking up another. Finally, after the last passenger got out,

Daddy took a wad of bills from his front pocket. My slanty Chinese eyes grew wide with delight. I was teased unmercifully about my slanty eyes by the children in Iowa.

My Daddy was loaded.

Finally Daddy stopped in front of a large apartment building. Children were playing jump rope and hopscotch in the streets, under the watchful eyes of Negro adults sitting on nearby stoops.

"You live here?" Linda asked.

"No. Sister Scott lives here," Daddy replied.

"Awww," Linda and I began to whine. "We want to stay with you. We don't want to stay at Sister Scott's house.

"Now Daddy told you, I live at Sister Davis' house. And her house is small and Ray is visiting. There isn't enough room over there right now."

Ray was Sister Davis' oldest son, who was Gloria's age.

"That's okay," I said. "We won't take up much room."

"No, now, this is better. And Sister Scott's daughter Alice can't wait to see you. You and Linda are all she's been talking about since she found out you were coming. You don't want to hurt her feelings, do you?"

"When will we see you?" Linda asked.

"Every night. I promise," Daddy said woefully. Then he handed Linda and me each a wad of money, got our suitcases out of the trunk, and led us into the apartment building.

My Daddy was a liar.

Sister Scott and her family were excited to see us and fortunate for us, she was a beautician. Mother did not have any interest in maintaining our looks or our hair. As soon as Linda and I arrived, Sister Scott attacked our nappy heads. She washed it and dried it— well, sort of—because my hair was still wet when she began frying it with a straightening comb and smearing grease in my hair, which crackled and spat. I sat there flinching and getting burned.

"Hold still," she ordered.

"Ouch!" I yelled as tears began to form in my eyes.

"I'm sorry, honey. If you hold still, I won't burn you."

It was torture being black with short, fine, nappy hair.

The whole time we stayed with Sister Scott, Linda, Alice, and I lived at the local movie theater. We'd see the same movie over and over again. We especially enjoyed the marathon horror flicks. We stuffed ourselves on Jujubes, Chocolate Cows, and Good & Plenty, while watching hours and hours of horror movies.

At night we fought for sleeping positions in the same queen-sized bed. I always wanted the position next to the wall, and I could muster up enough tears at the drop of a hat to get it. Linda was a sucker for my tears and would always give in to them, which made Mother mad—she called them crocodile tears. Anyway, our first night together, Linda convinced Alice, Linda's best childhood friend and Sister Alice's daughter, to let me have the wall. After all, she said, I was the little sister.

When we weren't sleeping or at the movies, Alice kept Linda and me entertained the whole summer, telling us jokes and showing us Newark by bus and by foot. The three of us formed a particular bond. We called ourselves the three Musketeers.

I could already tell that this summer would be different. Daddy rarely made it over to Sister Scott's house even to see us. And after a while, Linda and I began to really complain about that. Seeing him for a quick second at church on Tuesday and Thursday nights and on Sunday mornings was not enough. So one Sunday morning, Linda, who rarely cried, and I double teamed him. We resorted to the crocodile tears trick. Crocodile tears or not, my tears always worked with Linda and Daddy.

"We want to come home with you," Linda cried.

"Why can't we come to Sister Davis' house with you? We won't take up much room," I said through sobs and tears. "And we want to play with Sister Davis' daughters."

Sister Davis' two older daughters were Linda's age and Cynthia's age, and we all got along well.

After quite a bit more prodding and begging, Daddy finally relented.

Sister Davis had a beautiful house, albeit small. It sat on a large lot with grapevines, apple trees, and peach trees, and it had a luscious lawn. It had one bedroom upstairs and a big bathroom, which the Davis girls shared. A second bedroom, which was downstairs, was very small and sat behind the kitchen. This was Sister Davis' room. The front room and dining room were one large room. Sister Davis' oldest son, who was visiting, slept in the front room. But normally he lived with his father.

The dining room area was divided by a curtain. Behind this curtain was Daddy's teeny-tiny room. He said he was renting this room from Sister Davis in order to save money and pay off the bills Mother had left him.

While Daddy was outside getting our luggage, Linda walked in and I followed her. There, sitting on the living room floor, were Sister Douglas' two sons. Ray was reading the newspaper, while his baby brother, Victor, who wasn't a year old, was chewing the corner of it.

Linda and I were delighted to see the new baby. We both loved babies and had gotten some experience taking care of babies at our church in Sioux City. Victor and I bonded immediately. That night when we called Mother, we were exuberant and could not contain our new-found discovery.

"Sister Davis had a baby," Linda told her.

"Really?" Mother asked, sounding surprised. "What's his name?"

"Victor," I replied. "He is soooo cute."

"Mmmm," Mother said, sounding distant. "Well, praise the Lord. Let me speak to your father."

The rest of the summer I spent climbing trees, eating grapes off the vine till I was cross-eyed, and waiting for my Daddy to come home at night. And then, as always, toward the end, Mother showed up with Cynthia and Sister Noble. We all stayed at a Howard Johnson Motel with Daddy, but there was no family outing this time.

On the way back to Iowa, I heard Mother say to Sister Noble, "Well, Elder Roberts finally got his son."

After that, Daddy never visited us in Sioux City anymore, and we rarely ever heard from him.

This May Be My Last Time

Sioux City
Fall 1965

*I saw the dead, small and great, stand before God; and the books
were opened . . . and the dead were judged out of those things
which were written in the books, according to their works.*
—Revelation 20:11–15

Now to the outside world and me, it appeared Mother was not the least bit concerned about the future of her marriage to Daddy. It was often suggested to Mother that she divorce Daddy and move on; after all, the affairs Daddy had had were with women who were supposed to be Mother's best friends and her sisters in Christ. But Mother was a stubborn Taurus the Bull woman who refused to throw in the towel and walk away. So she continued to pretend to believe Daddy when he denied everything. "The Niggahs are lying; them ain't none of my babies," he said. "I love you Frankie and I don't want a divorce."

While Mother was in Newark trying to salvage her marriage, some of the leaders of our church held a secret meeting about what to do with Mt. Sinai. Our congregation was growing and it had the potential for expansion if we affiliated with the Church of God In Christ (COGIC).

When Mother began her ministry in Iowa, she received a letter from the Bishop of Iowa, which said it was contrary to COGIC's official manual and the Holy Bible for a woman to be an ordained minister. The letter stated further she was in violation of the rules because she was a member of more than one church. The Bishop demanded her missionary's license and any other licenses she received from COGIC.

Mother and her congregation were ostracized by the local churches in Iowa and others who felt a woman's place did not include the pulpit. Sister Taylor, the leader of the rebellion, was of the same opinion.

Their long list of "thou shalt nots," which included smoking, drinking, Christmas trees, dancing, women wearing pants, fornication, adultery, movies, cards, and the like, also made it clear that it was a sin for a woman to usurp authority over a man. And Mother had gone way beyond that—she was a woman preacher. As such, those other Christians were of the opinion that Mother and her followers would burst hell wide open. Such irony.

One of those others was Sister Taylor, the leader of the rebellion. She said that it was time we move out of the storefront into a proper church building and become a legitimate church by having a man take over—someone who could be ordained and given the proper COGIC credentials.

Yet none of those other Christians asked Daddy for his credentials, even though he was a married man making babies with his parishioners. And no one from COGIC asked Sister Davis or Sister Scott to return their missionary licenses.

That's not to say, however, that our church denied the fact that Daddy was the father of Sister Scott's daughter and now Sister Davis' son. But the church had waited long enough for Daddy to get his act together and come to Sioux City to be our shepherd. And it was clear to everyone, including Mother, that this was just not going to happen. Even if Daddy wanted to accept Mother's former position, our church would not accept him; we could not be lead by a man who had flagrantly committed adultery with the members of his church or could we? After all there is forgiveness and the Church would blame the women for tempting Daddy.

And so it was that Sister Taylor found a church building that was both available and affordable to move into. It came as no surprise that Mother resisted the move. The vision the Lord had given her was to open a mission, a place that was not intimidating to the underclass and to lost souls. To her, a church building would not achieve that purpose. And no more than she wanted to move, did she want to turn over the reins of her church to a man.

As a result of this conflict, the church split. Sister Taylor's followers moved into the new building, and Brother Billie James, who was married to Sister Taylor's sister, would become the pastor of this New Holiness Church, under the auspices of COGIC.

Before the split, we'd had over one hundred and fifty adult members of the church; that was a large number considering we were nondenominational and our leader was a woman. We lost over half of them. Those who remained loyal to Mother were the outcasts of society. They were welfare mothers and people without jobs or education. They followed Mother unquestionably. They did whatever she said and sought her advice on everything. They would not have felt welcome at our rival's church anyway.

Brother Baker, Brother Billie James' brother, became our assistant pastor. And when the Lord said the time was right, he would become the pastor of Mt. Sinai Holiness Church #2.

Through all of it, I was embarrassed for Mother. But I was also embarrassed, mostly, for myself. We at Mt. Sinai were now the "despised few," the outcast. As a result, I was becoming ever more aware of myself and my family, and I did not like what I saw. In fact, if anybody had asked my opinion, I'd have told them I thought Sister Taylor and the others were right. If Mother hadn't been my mother, I would have left too.

Their pastor, Brother Billie James, could preach, and he wasn't long winded, either. On the other hand, Brother Baker did not have a clue about preaching. None of his sermons even made any sense. They were always about some fictional character named "Caldonyia" and her "snaggle-tooth mule." What did that have to do with the Bible?

I continued to hope that Mother would give up the church and return to Newark to work on putting our family back together. For over seven years, I had been praying that Jesus would bring my Daddy home, but it looked as though that prayer would never be answered, especially now since Daddy had a son.

Wasn't the Lord satisfied with the sacrifices Mother had made of her husband and children? Why couldn't we go back home now and be a family? Why couldn't she return full time to nursing, so we could be like other children and live in a nice home, wear nice clothes, and go on nice family vacations? Why did the Lord require us to live in misery?

Despite our consistent pleading with Mother to take us back to New Jersey, however, she wouldn't budge. Instead, she offered her children up like living sacrifices unto the Lord, like Abraham from the Old Testament had done with his son Isaac; she found a smaller storefront for us to move into—actually, a former nightclub—and it was even more in the public eye than the old building had been. It still had the bar in the back, with stools and places to store liquor. It had a jukebox and walls lined with smoky mirrors. But the rent was just right and it was on the main street of town, which Mother thought was the ideal location. People traveling up and down West Seventh Street on a Friday or Saturday night on their way to the nightclub across the street couldn't help but pass by and hear the saints praising the Lord in song and dance.

The increased publicity only made me grow more ashamed of both my religion and Mother, however. We'd open the church doors wide, allowing the music and prayers to overflow onto West Seventh, and I and the other kids would cringe and duck down in the pews as children we knew from school passed by and gawked at us.

It was particularly painful when we had tent revivals right there on the corner of West Seventh and Cook Streets. There, we had no place to hide. Our parents would get slain in the Spirit and fall to the ground like dead people. Some would lay still while others would roll all over the floor, foaming at the mouth and speaking in tongues. Grown men would start dancing in the Spirit, crying like babies.

The women were the most embarrassing. Big fat women would flop around, dancing in the Spirit, their large ample breasts bouncing. Then they'd fall on the floor, their dresses flying up, exposing meaty thighs and sometimes even underwear. Some women would flail so hard their wigs would fly off (wigs were no longer a sin at that point), and then, undaunted, continue dancing with nappy, matted hair.

And invariably, someone would be possessed by either demons or the very devil himself, prompting an exorcism that would scare the wits out of the children.

White people would stop their cars just to watch the sight. Sometimes they'd even park, get out, and walk in to see the spectacle up close and personal. And it was thus that I became ashamed of our church and of everyone associated with it.

The burgeoning shame I felt about my religion wasn't restricted to church, however. I did not invite friends home, either, for fear that someone there would try to witness to them and end up scaring them off with the rapture story.

I, myself, was always afraid of the rapture story—afraid of the devil and of dying and being thrown into the Lake of Fire when God discovered my name missing from the Book of Life. And this fear, and many others, seemed never more prevalent than when I was at home.

In fact, because I never knew what to expect when I got home, my confidence seemed to vanish the moment I walked through our front door. The greatest evidence of this fear might have been the way I spent my sleeping hours. Until I was twelve, I wet the bed and walked and talked in my sleep. And I could never sleep by myself. Fortunately, Linda didn't mind me crawling into bed with her in the middle of every night, but she did mind waking up in a puddle of my urine every morning. Often, I tried to hide my accidents from Mother by ripping the soiled sheets off the bed and hiding them in the closet. But this only made the problem worse, as the smell would escape the confines of the closet and seep into our bedroom.

And that's to say nothing about the shame I felt at home when I was forced to face our neighbors, for example, the time when Daddy stopped sending Mother child support. At the same time that happened, the Lord called Mother off her job, so we had to give up the house she was buying on Fourteenth Street and ended up moving next door to one of Sioux City's Negro social-elite family, the Carters.

The Carters were a beautiful family. They were quiet and respectable, and their duplex was small, but they kept it immaculate.

They had six children—four girls and twin boys—who were always well-dressed and found favor with white people. Their daughters were cheerleaders and in the school choir. Their twin sons were often called on in class, and all the girls, both Negro, Indian and white, were crazy about them.

All six of them were considered part of the in-crowd, popular with both the white school children as well as the Negroes. (Even if you were black, Iowa was a great place to grow up—that is, as long as you weren't a holy roller. Because, although I was not aware of any racial discrimination there, religious discrimination was definitely present.)

The oldest daughter befriended Gloria, and the one Linda's age somewhat befriended her—at least when she saw Linda coming, she said hi and did not look the other way.

The Carters' only flaw seemed to be that they were Baptists, which was too bad, because they were really nice people. But at Mt. Sinai Holiness, being nice and doing good didn't count. Our neighbors were not saved, sanctified, and filled with the Holy Ghost, and they surely did not speak in tongues. So they were doomed, on their way to the Lake of Fire.

In fact, one day, Mrs. Carter even knocked politely on our door and asked nicely if we could keep the noise down when we prayed. You see, Pentecostals are very loud; we can break into prayers and tongues at any hour of the day or night. It is unheard of to pray in a quiet voice so as not to disturb our neighbors. If we do, it means we are ashamed of Jesus Christ. On the contrary, the louder we pray, rebuke devils, and speak in tongues, the better we show our loyalty as his followers. After all, we are a peculiar people.

As such, the Carters' polite requests that we keep it down began happening routinely, until one day, apparently, they had had enough.

It was when one of our frequent freeloaders, Ma Harris, was visiting. She told my sisters and me to call her "Grandma."

Grandma Harris always used our kitchen as her own personal bakery to bake her infamous fresh bread, cinnamon rolls, and pound cakes from scratch. She would have Mother buy all the ingredients— butter, sugar, special flour, and other specific expensive ingredients, which she would keep a secret. (I always tried to hang around the kitchen, without her knowledge, so I could learn the recipes, but it never worked.) Then for hours, as she baked, sweet aromas would fill our house.

That all would have been fine if, after she had made them, she wouldn't have tried to sell the baked goods to my sisters and me for fifteen cents apiece, and then take what was left to church to sell after the service. I often tried to boycott her products, but whenever I saw my sisters eating one of her specialties, I couldn't resist. I thought Mother should have put her foot down and demand Grandma Harris give us at least one item for free or teach us how to make them, since Mother was the one who'd bought the ingredients and she was using our stove. But Mother never did, because she looked at it as a way to "give unto the Lord." She never made us learn anything practical that would have helped us survive this world; if it wasn't about God and the Bible, she wasn't teaching it.

Anyway, on this particular day, Grandma Harris was speaking in tongues and praying loudly with Sister Pat, a white woman who was also a recurring visitor at our house. Mother was away on one of her revivals.

When our neighbors came knocking, Sister Pat saw their request for quiet as a trick of the devil. The women did not take kindly to anyone trying to "quench the Holy Spirit" that way, so they walked throughout the house in a loud voice rebuking the devil that was in our next-door neighbors' house. Then Sister Pat went outside and began sweeping the foul devil out of the house and off the porch.

But while Sister Pat was sweeping, our neighbor was on the phone, reporting us to the landlord. The landlord promptly evicted us.

When Mother returned from her revival, she moved us back to the west side of town, where we had lived when we first came to Sioux City. I reluctantly had to return to Webster's School with zero Negro population.

Just a few weeks later, we caught news of the tragedy.

Mother Godfrey attended Mt. Sinai, and told us all about it. It was the worst tragedy in Sioux City history. It happened the week Mother Godfrey had witnessed to her son and invited him to give his heart to Jesus. Her son had just shrugged and said, "Nah, Ma. I'm not ready to give all this up."

Then a few Fridays later, after working hard all week at the local packinghouse, Mother Godfrey's son went on a drinking retreat with three other Daddies to Omaha, Nebraska, one of whom was our next-door neighbor, Mr. Carter. All of the men were hardworking providers and good fathers. Somebody had suggested they go to someplace in Omaha that weekend rather than the local nightclub— the one across the street from Mt. Sinai. Omaha was approximately one hour away (or two, if you drove like Mother).

As the story goes, one of the husband wives had begged them not to go that night, but they went anyway. So while the children of these Daddies slept soundly in their beds and while their wives paced the floors wondering when they'd be home, the Daddies drank and partied and played cards at the Pussy Cat Lounge in Omaha.

Afterward, too drunk to drive but too loaded to realize it, Mother Godfrey's son got behind the wheel of his brand-new, shiny black Cadillac. His three buddies poured in behind him.

The highway patrol man said Mother Godfrey's son must have been driving over one hundred miles an hour before he lost control of the car. The Cadillac had spun about wildly and crumpled into the cement pillar in the middle of the highway. There was nothing in particular in the road that caused the car to spin out of control. It just did. The Cadillac looked like an accordion. All four Daddies were killed instantly. The rescuers had to scrape them off Interstate Twenty-nine and peel any remaining body parts from the flattened car's interior. Then their remains were placed inside plastic body bags.

Mother Godfrey's Baptist daughter-in-law wouldn't hear of Mt. Sinai officiating at her husband's funeral. The four husband's funerals were held back-to-back—all closed-coffin, because there was nothing left of them to view.

That day, heaviness fell over the city, as we mourned the deaths of four young men cut down in the prime of life. Not only did several children lose their fathers, but none of the dead men had known the Lord Jesus Christ as their personal savior. After such tragic deaths, they would not find their names listed in the Book of Life, but would instead lift their eyes in hell, where there was weeping and gnashing of teeth.

The question that really plagued me was whether the tragedy was God's way of punishing our neighbors for, first, trying to quiet the Holy Spirit, and then, second, getting us evicted. That is when I began to fear God like never before. In fact, I became downright terrified of both him and Mother, equally. Because if the answer to that question was yes, then Mr. Carter was the third person he had struck down in the prime of life for crossing Mother and her church. It made me think Mother had a special connection with God and that I never wanted to get either one of them angry at me—there was no telling what they would do next.

The stories surrounding the tragedy served as good sermon material for Mother for months to come. Despite the fact Mother Godfrey attended our church, Mother's weekly sermons reminded her constantly that her son and his drinking buddies were anguishing in hell.

"It is a terrible thing to fall into the arms of an angry God," her voice would ring out in terror, damnation, and fear every Sunday, Tuesday, and Thursday, as she'd glare down at us from the pulpit, the holy place, wearing her cat-eye glasses and black minister's robe. I could never see her eyes when she was up there. I could only see the glare of her glasses. It was as if she had X-ray vision like Superman.

For many Sundays following the funerals, many people returned to Mt. Sinai. And many more—me included—found ourselves on our knees during the altar call, begging God to forgive us and to save us again, and making promises to him that we had no intentions of keeping.

BOOK II

Suffer! Little Children
1966–1974

*And they brought unto him also infants, that he would touch
them; but when his disciples saw it, they rebuked them. But Jesus
called them unto him and said, "Suffer little children to come unto
me, and forbid them not, for of such is the kingdom of God."*
—Luke 18:15–16

Who Shall Be Able to Stand?

Sioux City
1966

For the great day of his wrath is come;
and who shall be able to stand?
—Revelation 6:8, 13–17

While most Negroes were fighting for equal rights and education, standing up for equal access to drinking fountains, and struggling for equal choices in bus and restaurant seating, I was preparing for the end of the world.

What difference did it make to me where I sat on the bus or where I ate my food? Jesus was coming soon, at which point, the world, along with all of the people on the bus and in restaurants and at drinking fountains and schools, would be destroyed.

I completely missed out on the black power movement and on the civil rights marches, as well as on the notorious messages spread far and wide by Dr. Martin Luther King, Jr. I was somewhat aware of the Vietnam War, but only because several members of our church had a son or a spouse stationed there. Nor did I get to enjoy Motown or the Beatles or any other worldly music.

As a Pentecostal, I was to "be apart from the world and separated from sinners." A sinner, of course, was anybody who disagreed with our interpretation of the Bible and did not belong to a Pentecostal/ Evangelical church.

In general, white people were sinners and eternally doomed to hell-fire and brimstone. White people drank and smoked cigarettes.

And even though they went to mass, Catholics were the most hell-bound white people of all; they prayed to Mary, the mother of Jesus. And that's not to mention the white women. Since painting your face was a sin, and most white women—Christian or not—wore makeup, they were doomed to hell.

Jezebel painted her face. And then she met her death, climbing to a rooftop to watch the downfall of the prophet Elijah and falling to the ground where the "dogs licked up her bones." Moral of the story: don't paint your face.

Fortunately, though, I could read. And after reading the story of Jezebel, I realized that her painting her face had nothing to do with her dying. But many of the people who preached to me back then couldn't actually read the gospel; they always had to have someone read it for them. So they could only repeat the Bible stories as they were told to them—or as they remembered them.

Anyway, white people weren't the only ones on their way to hell. According to the gloom-and-doom preachers in Mother's church, even Dr. Martin Luther, Jr. was on his way there. He smoked, allegedly fooled around with other women, and drank alcohol. Even though he was doing a great work, he was still hell-bound. After all, First Corinthians did say, "Though I give my body to be burned, but do not have charity, it profits nothing."

It was at that point that I surmised that the only people worthy enough to go to heaven would be poor, colored Pentecostal/Evangelical people and the few whites who did not wear makeup or drink or were not Catholic. Suddenly the prospect of going to heaven became less appealing.

And yet, it was hard to believe that things could be any other way. Ministers and evangelist missionaries from all over the United States came to Mother's church to render their interpretation of God's Holy Word, and every one of them made it clear that we were self-appointed soldiers in the army of the Lord—that we were the true believers.

It gave us comfort and a sense of superiority to know that although we, the true believers, were also the poor, uneducated, and suffering in this world, in the sweet by and by, we'd be walking around heaven all day, living in our very own mansions, while the sinners burned forever in the afterlife.

Other sermons that visiting ministers gave in Mommy's church focused on how you should dress, where you could go and not go, who you were permitted to marry, and which holidays you were allowed to celebrate. And on that latter note, remember the disappointment my sisters and I had felt that first Christmas in Iowa? That turned out to be nothing compared to the following Christmas in 1960.

A visiting missionary came to Mother's church right before the holiday and declared, "Thus saith the Lord! No more Christmas trees!"

Of course, by then, many of the saints had already purchased their trees and decorated them. To those people, the visiting missionary said, "Get rid of them. God's people don't got no business with a Christmas tree. It is pagan worship. It is a sin."

I sat in my chair thinking that was the most ridiculous thing I had ever heard besides the Jezebel story. The pagans worshiped the tree; I didn't think anyone in our church was guilty of doing that.

Nonetheless, that evening, the members of our church who had trees (at least those who did not have unbelieving husbands at home) threw them out, decorations and all. Of course they did; they had no choice. If you disagreed with a woman of God, that clearly meant you were disobeying God; and if you were disobeying God because of a Christmas tree, then you had made the tree your god.

We hadn't bought our Christmas tree yet, so we went to the local five-and-dime store and purchased a cardboard red-brick fireplace instead. When we got it home, we decorated it with lights and paper ornaments that we had made at school.

Mother wrapped our gifts—toys from the Salvation Army, and shoes and gloves from the Goodwill—in colorful Christmas paper and set them in front of the cardboard mantel. Christmas never got any better than that.

The next year after that, an evangelist named Sister Jones came from New York City to run a revival at Mother's church. She preached, among other things, that women were not to wear anything pertaining to a man, for example, pants. She also said it was a sin to wear wigs. Now I'd heard everything!

Get real, I thought. I've watched enough Bible stories on television and at the movies to know that when the scripture was written, men wore dresses!

Sister Jones insisted, however, that God was displeased because we women wore pants. If we wanted to get to heaven, she said, the pants had to go. Even tomboy little girls like me had to throw away our pants and play in dresses. And if we refused to throw them away—thereby questioning the Word—then, of course, we had made the pants our god.

Sister Jones, whose hair was thick, long, and jet black, made the women in the congregation who were wearing wigs remove them. I felt embarrassed for Mother and the other women who hadn't had the time to comb their hair that day. They were forced to remove the wigs from their nappy heads right there in front of everyone.

Anytime someone came to our church and said, "Thus saith the Lord . . .," we had to follow what he or she said without question. We were damned if we asked questions or tried to reason and think for ourselves.

"Don't question God," was the 11th Commandment. The only exception to that rule was the "women are not supposed to preach" restriction. Visiting male ministers who wanted to take over Mother's congregation would ask a woman in the congregation to read that scripture and then remind us that God did not call a woman to preach. They reminded us that the woman's role in the Church is to obey her husband and to remain silent. That was one restriction we did not follow.

Loving a Son

Sioux City
Summer 1966

Chasten thy son while there is hope, and let
not thy soul spare for his crying.
—Proverbs 19:18

After we were evicted and moved back to the west side of town, I had to return to Webster School, a place I dreaded because only a few Negro children attended it. And by the end of that school year, the year of my sixth grade, I had lost all of what remained of my self-esteem.

That summer, however, my cousins came. In the middle of the night, after one beating too many, Cousin Rhoda and her four children—Peaches, twelve; Albert eleven; Samuel, ten; and Lynette, four—escaped their abuser. After her husband left for work, Cousin Rhoda and her children boarded a Greyhound in Newark for Sioux City. Unfortunately, she would soon learn that she had not escaped abuse, but had simply changed its location, along with the face of the abuser. She would fall victim again, only this time to religious abuse.

For me, however, the change was a good one. For the first time in my life, I had relatives. I was always envious of my friends who had grandparents, fathers, cousins, and aunts. When Mother left Newark, she cut off all ties with her relatives and Daddy's family.

There hadn't been much to her family when we lived in Newark though. Both her parents died before I was born. Uncle Percy, who was an alcoholic, was the only family she had left. He never attended any of Daddy's church services, but he'd pay us an occasional visit after Sunday school. We'd walk out of the church, and he'd stand there, waiting for us with a pocket full of quarters. I don't remember much else about him except that he was tall, dark, and handsome; he always wore a suit; and he always reeked of alcohol. Now when I think about it, I realize that he hadn't made it home from a Saturday night of partying.

On the other hand, Daddy came from a very large family. They all lived in New Jersey or down South. Daddy was not very close to his brothers and sisters, though, and his father died when I was about three. I remember going to the funeral home to view his body.

The fondest memory I had about family was of my Grandmother Cora, who'd fry up a mess of ham and make homemade biscuits that we'd slop in a big spill of molasses—and then eat without paying for it, like we had to do with Grandma Harris.

I barely got to know my relatives in Newark when Mother uprooted my sisters and me from the that fertile soil and "transplanted" us in—or, more accurately, tossed us aside on—the rocky ground of Sioux City, leaving us to fend for ourselves, without light, plant food, or water. How could she expect us to mature and blossom into healthy, well-rounded children? Looking back on it now, when we moved, we girls lost more than our Daddy. We lost our identity, our culture, and our roots.   When my cousins moved to Iowa, it seemed to help bridge some of that gap. But, then again, maybe it just helped me realize what was missing.

Cousin Peaches was a high-yellow pretty child trapped in a woman's body. She favored her mother and she was the oldest. Although Peaches and I were the same age, at twelve, she was more developed both physically and mentally. Peaches had breasts and legs. Let's face it—she was built like a brick house. When she walked down the street, men dropped whatever they were doing to watch her move.

She had pretty, jet-black hair, and although it was short like mine, she knew how to fix it. She made it okay to have short hair. Peaches would slick down her short bangs with petroleum jelly and then stick a big bow in the middle of her head that matched whatever she was wearing.

She also wore big round hoop earrings in her pierced ears. Mother would not let us pierce our ears. (And, incidentally, since the Roberts girls could not pierce their ears, neither could any of the other girls who went to our church. Mother said it wasn't the Lord's will for us to pierce our ears, and that meant it was a sin—well, sort of.)

But Peaches was a rebel and set the fashion standards in our church. Until Peaches came to Mt. Sinai, we had no sense of style. For instance, I couldn't for the life of me get my bangs to cooperate like hers did. Each night, Peaches would lay her bangs down flat, apply the grease to them, and cover her head with an old stocking cap. Even the stocking cap she wore at night looked cool. I mean, by the time I woke up in the morning my stocking cap would was coiled around my neck like a snake trying to choke me. But when Peaches woke up in the morning, her stocking cap was firmly in place, while she chewed the same piece of gum she'd had for days.

When I took the stocking cap off in the morning, my bangs would either stand straight up in the air or kink up on me, leaving my large forehead bare and greasy. And the big bow I tried to wear to look like her just overshadowed my head. In every way, my hair defied me, and no amount of petroleum jelly, Murray's Superior Pomade, or hair gel could convince it to do otherwise.

Peaches also taught me it was cool to shop at the Goodwill. Although everybody's mother shopped at the Goodwill, nobody ever admitted it. Peaches did. Peaches could walk into the Goodwill, and in a half hour come out carrying a bag full of exotic treasures. The next day, I'd see her dressed to the nines and completely coordinated.

"Oooh, that's cool! Where'd you get it?" I'd ask.

"The Goodwill," she'd say proudly. She did not care who heard her.

Peaches and her brother Albert could dance, too. They could do this thing with their heads and necks to the beat of the music. And they knew how to rap. They rapped things like "I know your hair is nappy, but I refuse to lend you my comb. If you have to beg and plead for my sympathy, I don't mind cause you need it more than me," to the beat of the Temptations' song "Ain't Too Proud to Beg."

Before my cousins came to town, we did not know how to dance. Dancing was a sin and so was listening to the music to which one danced. Sometimes my girlfriend Sally Mae and I would backslide, and since we were no longer saved that week anyway, we would buy worldly records, such as Motown hits. We'd sneak them into my room and listen to them. Although Mother never stopped me, she would preach about it in church and condemn me to hell. After listening to her sermon about the Lake of Fire, I would go home and throw away all my Motown records.

When my cousins came from New Jersey, though, they brought soul music with them. They knew about all the black entertainers. They knew all the Motown songs. They knew how to dance and sing.

But best of all, they knew all about being black. I never knew how cool it was to be black until my cousins came. "Black power!" they would shout, and tell us things like, "Black is beautiful." They brought black pride with them, and like a dried up sponge, I soaked it all in.

The coolest thing Peaches taught me was how to pop my gum. She knew how to turn her gum over inside her mouth and create this air pocket that made a cracking sound. She did it with such class and style. And she could make one stick of gum last forever.

"Do you have any more gum?" I'd ask, mesmerized by her popping gum.

"This is the same piece I had last week," she'd say. I swear, Peaches could make one stick of gum last for a month.

When the five of them showed up at our door that early summer morning, my sisters and I were so excited. It was perfect timing, as we were in between entertaining angels, and Gloria had just graduated from school and joined the Navy, so Cynthia finally had her own room. Although Linda and I shared a room, my section was in a cove and it was just like having my own bedroom.

The night before our cousins had arrived, without even knowing what was to happen the next morning, my sister Linda and I did this massive cleaning project. We hung pictures and rearranged furniture.

It was an omen. Every time Linda and I went into our cleaning frenzy, God would send someone to our home. In fact, I tried often to fight the urge to clean, just so God wouldn't send anyone else. It felt good having the place to ourselves.

We were shy with our cousins at first, but there is something about being related to someone that eases the awkwardness quickly. Right off the bat, Cousin Rhoda explained that Cousin Albert, Senior had beaten her so badly, she'd run out of the apartment in her see-through negligee with nothing underneath.

She said she ran to a local police station for help, but that the policemen did nothing but ogle her. They refused to get involved in a dispute between a man and his wife, and then sent for her husband. On the way home, Cousin Albert beat her again for embarrassing him.

So when he left for work the next morning, she threw what she could in a couple of suitcases, got Mother's address from Daddy, and left with the kids on the first Greyhound west.

"Well, praise the Lord," Mother said.

Mother welcomed their family into our house and laid down the rules: everybody had to go to church on Sunday, and to fast on Wednesdays and Fridays until three. Even the baby.

By the end of their first month with us, I realized I was too immature for my cousin Peaches. I still played Barbie dolls with the ten-year-old girl who lived next door. Peaches, on the other hand, was into boys, like my sister Cynthia was.

Cynthia also had an incredible body. She had an ant-sized waist and had very large breasts that jiggled when she walked. The men went crazy when they saw the two of them walking down the street.

Although my sister Linda was not into boys, Peaches and Linda had a lot in common.

And since I was a tomboy, Cousin Albert and I became inseparable when I was not playing with Barbie dolls. He taught me about all the exciting things boys did, like building racing go-carts. We played with walkie talkie, raced cars around a miniature track, and sold Kool-Aid at a stand we built together. In exchange, I showed him how to play the drums and the piano.

Albert and I fought a lot, though, too. One day, while I was trying to clean the kitchen, Albert and Samuel questioned my authority. They stood on the back porch, peering through the kitchen's screen door, teasing and taunting me. I would not let them in because I was mopping the kitchen floor.

"Go around and use the front door," I instructed them.

But they stood their ground, just peering through the screen door.

"Hold your peace and let the Lord fight your battle," I said to myself as I continued to mop.

I'd been on the altar the night before, asking Jesus to forgive me for my sins and to save me again. So I knew this incident was just the devil trying to tempt me into backsliding, and I was determined not to let the devil win. I did not want to have to get in the prayer line and ask for deliverance from my temper again.

"The blood of Jesus. The blood of Jesus," I chanted, while dipping my mop into the bucket of water. And then I struck up a gospel chorus.

I'm a soldier,
In the army of the Lord.
I'm a soldier,
In the army.

They stood on the porch, watching and whispering. I didn't care. I continued to mop and sing.

Got my war clothes on,
In the army of the Lord.
Got my war clothes on,
In the—

I heard the screen door fly open behind me. I turned and found them standing on my clean kitchen floor, their shoes covered in mud. Before I knew what was happening, I flung my mop threw the air and it landed with a thud on the kitchen table. I tackled both of them to the floor. Cursing and swearing, I pummeled their faces with my fists and sent them running out the back door, crying hysterically.

A week later Albert and Samuel tried to make it up to me by allowing me to play with a race car set they said they'd gotten from *this* boy who was moving out of town. According to them, his parents said they did not have enough room in their moving van to take the set with them. And in fact, they told me, *this* boy's parents didn't have room in their moving van for a lot of incredibly new expensive things, which included the walkie talkie set, a transistor radio, and some new sneakers, just to name a few.

I was outside playing with the walkie talkie, when Mother drove up. I was so excited. I showed her all the wonderful things *this* boy had given Albert and Samuel. Mother was just as surprised as I.

When Cousin Rhoda returned from work that night, Mother and the boys had a meeting with her. The boys gathered up all the gifts this boy had given them and gave them to Mother. It was only then that I learned they had actually snatched a lady's purse and used the proceeds to buy all the wonderful gifts .

First, Mother beat them with an extension cord. I heard them screaming in agony. Then she said that the Lord told her to put them in the basement and make them fast for three days as punishment for their sins.

I rarely went into the basement. I avoided it. Sometimes, it was where the demons would run and hide when Sister Sellers came over to cast them out of our house. Instead of going out of the door, they'd go down into the basement. She'd told us that once when we were fighting.

"You Roberts' girls better stop it," she said. "I was standing here, and the Spirit of the Lord showed me two evil spirits. One looked like a little old lady with gray, stringy hair and green teeth, and the other one looked like an old troll—short with a hooked nose. When you fight, they come out of the basement and go upstairs into your room."

Ordinarily, I wouldn't have believed Sister Sellers. It sounded like a ploy to keep my sisters and me from fighting. But Sister Sellers wasn't the only one who'd seen them come out of our basement on

Market Street. Their visits were not as frequent as those who had taken up residency with us on Fourteenth Street, however, those with the spiritual gift, including Cynthia and Mother, verified their existence.

The basement was cold and dark and it reeked of mildew. A single light bulb centered in the ceiling swung back and forth like a pendulum casting an eerie shadow over the pipes, water heater and furnace. Large, black water bugs and mice crawled and burrowed in the healthy layer of dirt that was the floor.

It was a good thing for my cousins that Mother removed the light bulb that night before she sentenced them to the basement. They did not want to see it. It was better to be in darkness.

As the boys descended to where Sister Sellers and others had seen the little old troll and the gray-haired lady, I prayed for their safety. After all, I'd been the one who had told on them. Mother closed the door behind them, while Cousin Rhoda stood nearby, trying not to cry, wringing her hands. Peaches and I cried openly.

For three days, they were confined to our basement, without food, water, or electricity. Visitors, God-fearing-saved-sanctified-Christians, visited our house. They knew the boys were confined to the basement in the dark without food or water. No one said or did anything to protect them.

Gloria's Payday

Sioux City
Fall 1967

For the wages of sin is death.
—Romans 6:23

Cousin Peaches and I slipped through the back doors of West Jr. High School and scurried down the adjacent alley. We emerged on West Seventh Street and raced toward home.

Time was of the essence. I didn't even have the chance to readjust the skirt I'd hiked six inches above my bony knees after I'd left the house that morning or wipe off the mask of pink lipstick and mascara I'd sneaked onto my face during second period study hall.

Cousin Peaches had an extension cord in her book bag and I had a leather belt in mine. We were loaded and ready to take on a fight if forced to, however, it was better to avoid one if at all possible. Rumor had had it that some of the Negro girls planned to beat us up after school because of a remark Cousin Peaches had reportedly made about Jessie McBeal's hair.   True, Jessie never combed her nappy, short hair, especially the part at the nape of her neck, her "kitchen," which curled so tightly it looked like little BB gun pellets. But in reality, Cousin Peaches hadn't said anything about Jessie's hair—at least not that week.

Because Cousin Peaches was the new kid on the block and because the girls were jealous that the Negro and Indian boys were so attracted to her, the Negro girls had been dying to get a hold of her.

Having grown up in the projects in Newark, she was used to street fights. But Cousin Peaches wasn't interested in fighting these girls because of the implementation of the new war tactics. Instead of trying to beat you up, the new fad was to rip your opponent's clothes off, leaving her standing in her bra, stockings, and panties—that's if she was wearing any.

Jessie McBeal had made the "rip and leave" fad famous after being forced to fight West Junior's school bully. Jessie, poor and on welfare, had once been our friend. Her family had attended our church for a while, and as were all the children from Mt. Sinai, she'd been ridiculed and chastised. But when Jessie's mother found out that she'd run home from school trying to avoid a fight with the school bully, her mother gave Jessie an ultimatum. Although Mt. Sinai's policy was taking the path of least resistance—pray for those who spitefully use you and turn the other cheek—Jessie's mother was having none of that.

"Don't bother coming home until you kick the shit out of her!" Jessie's mother had warned her. "Or I'll beat you myself."

Mother, on the other hand, did nothing about the children who teased us and beat us up.

"It is part of your walk with the Lord. If you want to be saved and go to heaven, you will just have to put up with it," she'd say, and explain that our reward would come after we were dead and in heaven. There, we could bask in the knowledge that our enemies were in hell, languishing in pain.

The day after her mother's "pep" talk, Jessie met her opponent head-on. Peaches, Becky, Sally Mae, and I had stood loyally by her side. Terror filled her eyes as Jessie surveyed her opponent—a large, black girl three times her size.

The girl spewed forth obscenities right before she punched Jessie in the face. Jessie hit the ground, tears welling in her eyes, and looked up at the girl towering over her, daring her to get up.

"Hit her! Get her!" The crowd of seventh, eighth, and ninth graders from West Junior High yelled as Jessie's opponent proceeded to kick her in the side.

Meanwhile, Jessie was flinching, tears gushing down her yellow face. As she lay there, defenseless, some of the spectators tugged at her short, nappy hair, while others kicked her in the sides. Peaches, Sally Mae, Becky, and I tried to keep the mob off of her, but without success.

Out for blood, the students fell into each other, laughing and taunting Jessie.

"Yo mama's on welfare!" they shouted.

"Yo mama shops at the Goodwill!"

They laughed.

"Holy roller!"

Then I imagined Jessie had heard her mother's warning in her head at some point, because before I knew it, she sprang off the ground and charged her opponent, grabbing her around the waist.

The bully's fist came crashing down on Jessie's head hard and fast, but Jessie would not let go. Instead, through tears and gritted teeth, Jessie let out a torrent of obscenities and then, with one fell swoop, she grabbed the bully's flimsy, psychedelic, orange-and-green polka-dot dress and ripped it off of her. The tormentor stood before the mob wearing nothing but a dingy white bra, large white granny panties, a garter belt, and stockings.

Then, like an afterthought, out flopped one of her breasts. The crowd gasped, held it, and then erupted in a convulsion of hysterical laughter. Jessie held the dress in the air in victory, a big grin spreading across her red, swollen, tear-streaked face.

The crowd roared some more, until, finally, the antagonist's sister covered her with a sweater. The treacherous teenagers, still shrieking with laughter, parted like the Red Sea to let the half-naked loser limp through, but not before the boys had their fun groping at her.

And with that, the mutineers embraced Jessie—and Jessie turned her back on us. After that, no longer forced to associate with us holy rollers, Jessie joined the in-crowd.

Now it was rumored that the in-crowd was after Cousin Peaches. And to show her loyalty to her cohorts, Jessie had to take on my cousin.

Peaches and I scampered out the back door of West Junior like the little terrified mice we were and ran in and out of alleys until we reached the safety of our home.

Linda, who was in the tenth grade at Central High School, was at the kitchen table eating dinner and reading a letter, with concern on her face. I ignored her apparent anguish. I had enough problems of my own.

"What's for dinner?" I asked, attempting to distract her as well as myself. I headed toward the pots cooking on the stove. It was every man for himself at Roberts Manor. We did not sit around the table the table discussing our day, as was seen on *Leave It to Beaver* or *The Brady Bunch*. We had to grab what we could, when we could, before it was all gone. Linda was attending senior high school and she had the unfair advantage of getting home before the rest of us. Linda did not respond, so I lifted the lid off of one of the pots and looked inside.

"Ugh! Again!" Slimy pinto beans swimming in red sauce stared back at me. I lifted the lid from the second pot.

"Rice!"

Then I peered in the oven and saw some catfish that one of the saints had brought us from a recent fishing trip. It looked promising. I piled some rice into a bowl and smothered it with butter and sugar. Then I grabbed a piece of cornbread and spread globs of butter and grape jelly on it.

Linda continued sitting, anguishing in a world of her own.

I walked to the cupboards to find another bowl for my fish, but there were none. All the bowls were in the sink, waiting for someone—namely, me—to wash them along with other greasy pots and pans and dishes.

There were so many dirty dishes because not only were our cousins still living with us, but also two more guests. Although there had been no more room at the inn, Sister Fat Pat and Sister Ross—two of our regulars—had taken residence in our small home, because, of course, Mother would never turn anyone away. One slept on the couch and the other on the floor in our living room, bringing the number of people in our three-bedroom, one-bath house to eleven.

Neither Sister Fat Pat nor Sister Ross worked. Both received some kind of assistance from the state. You'd think that since all they did all day was lie around sleeping, reading the Bible, and seeking God, that he would have told them to get up and clean the house and wash the dishes that were spilling over in the sink to the counter top. Since God did not reveal those needs to either of them, the house and the dishes waited for my sisters, my cousins, and I to do it upon our return from school.

I rinsed out a bowl and filled it with pinto beans and a piece of fried catfish. Then I sat down next to Linda, who now looked plain glum.

"What's wrong?" I took a bite of cornbread. The jelly and butter mixed so well, the cornbread melted in my mouth.

She did not answer. She just sighed and slid the letter she'd been reading over to me. Then she returned to the stove to replenish her bowl.

"Oh, it's a letter from Gloria!" I said. I began reading the letter as I stuck a large spoonful of beans in my mouth.

Gloria was quite a colorful writer, and I enjoyed reading the letters she sent us from the navy. Gloria had been gone for almost two years by now. She wrote to us often, and, at times, sent each of us a money order so we could buy clothes and school supplies.

Gloria's letter described her navy chief and some of the girls she was stationed with at Andrew's Air Force Base in Maryland. I was laughing when I turned the page, but then I stopped and almost gagged on my cornbread. My stomach became queasy and I immediately lost my appetite. At the end of page two, this had caught my eye:

Mary Jane is pregnant. And so am I.

Love,
Gaya

Looking up at Linda with disbelief, I pushed the letter away from me. Linda shrugged, dropped her head, and shoveled another spoonful of beans and rice into her mouth. I shoved my uneaten bowl of food to the other side of the table and then went upstairs, seeking sanctuary in the bedroom I now shared with my two sisters and Cousin Peaches.

I plopped down on my bed and stared up at the ceiling. Gloria had been my last ray of hope. If she could make it "in the world," I'd always thought, then so could I.

Tall and thin, with rich, dark, golden skin, Gloria was always like a movie star to my sisters and me. We had to worship her from afar, though, because Gloria would never let us near her.

I'd always wanted to be just like Gloria when I grew up. I admired her poise and self-confidence in adult situations. She knew who she was and what she wanted out of life. I had even eavesdropped on a number of Gloria's and Mother's grown-up conversations. They had a relationship that I envied. She wasn't afraid of Mother like I was.

For example, during her last year of high school, Gloria stood up to Mother and announced that she no longer wanted to be Saved. I was in awe of her defiance. Taking it a step further, Gloria also informed Mother she was going to her high school prom. This would be a first at Mt. Sinai. No young person at our church had ever attended the high school prom, though perhaps that was due more to the fact that everyone else had dropped out than it was to the fact that they hadn't wanted to sin.

The Roberts girls were unique in that respect; Mother insisted we all finish high school, although she never gave us time to study, because that would interfere with church nights, and, thereby, ultimately, with God.

I never really knew my sister Gloria. I remained moonstruck by her beauty and self-possession, although she never tried to hide the fact that she despised her younger siblings. Once, she'd even told my sisters and me that she was adopted, I guess just so she could avoid thinking that she was from the same gene pool as we were.

During a lot of my early years, Gloria was gone—away at private school or staying with Grandma Holmes, who spoiled her rotten. But when she was there, Gloria would spend time with me.

I remember one time when she was braiding my hair and telling me about life when Mother and Daddy had been together. She told me how babies were born, and how a man and a woman made babies. She also told me that Sister Scott's little girl, Frances, was our sister, even though Daddy denied her. She said that was why Daddy and Mother were no longer together.

Of course, I'd always known there'd been something between Daddy and Sister Davis, because I had caught them kissing once when she and her children lived with us. I'd gotten up in the middle of the night to go look for Daddy, and when I found him, he and Sister Davis were standing near the ice box, kissing. I told Mother the next morning, when she'd gotten home from her eleven to seven shift at East Orange General Hospital. Cynthia also caught Daddy kissing Sister Davis before, and Sister Scott, too.

That night, we were eating dinner around the kitchen table like a real family, when Mother confronted him.

"Daddy," Mother said sweetly. "Debra said she saw you and Sister Davis kissing."

I was embarrassed for Daddy. He denied it.

"Now, Debra, don't lie on your Daddy like that. I wasn't kissing Sister Davis." Daddy glanced in Mother's direction.

"Yes, you were," I said. "I saw you near the ice box."

"I saw you, too," Cynthia blurted out.

"What?" Daddy's hands flew to his chest, as if he were having a heart attack from the hurt of such allegations.

Soon after that, Sister Davis and her family moved out of our apartment.

Gloria tugged at my ends and corn-rowed my hair. "Mother left Daddy with a lot of bills, which is why he doesn't have any money. That's why we are so poor," she said. "Mother can make a lot of money as a registered nurse. I wish she would go back to New Jersey. That is where our family is and that is where colored people live."

Gloria knew all of our relatives back in New Jersey: our grandmother, our aunts, uncles, and cousins, even our godmothers and godfathers, who all loved us dearly. In Iowa, though, we did not have any family. And no one loved us, including Mother.

Gloria also told me that Mother almost died when she'd had an abortion.

"What's an abortion?" I asked. Gloria knew all the big words.

"When a woman is having a baby and she doesn't want it, she uses a clothes hanger to take the baby out," she said. "It would have been a boy, and Daddy had always wanted a son. But mother swore she would never have any more children for Daddy after he had sex with Sister Scott. You are lucky to be alive."

I didn't feel so lucky. Not today.

I wasn't so sure about that.

At seventeen, Gloria began to sin. She wore makeup, she listened to secular music, and she danced. She dressed in hand-me-down designer clothes she got from the Jewish woman she worked for. She went to school in style.

Gloria left for school earlier than I, and when she did, I'd steal into her room and put on her expensive clothes and perfume. The clothes were too big for me, but I'd pin them up or tie them around my waist using one of her leather designer belts. Then, before she got home, I'd sneak them back into her closet, reeking of the perfume I had poured all over them. When she would later ask who had been in her stuff, I'd deny it to the end.

Gloria also had worldly girlfriends. They came to our house to show her how to dance. She needed practice before she went to her prom. I would stand outside her open door, sopping it all in. Then a week before the prom, I overheard Gloria telling Mother how she had outsmarted the girls with whom she was supposed to attend the prom. Gloria had heard it through the grapevine that the girls were planning to steal her first date.

Wiley and shrewd, Gloria outsmarted them. She quickly formed alliances with some other girls and found a new date. On the night of the prom, Gloria wore a long, flowing, baby-blue taffeta dress, which her Jewish employer helped her purchase. A tall, handsome serviceman from the air base came to pick her up. He pinned a corsage on her dress and whisked her out our front door into a Cinderella coach—a big, shiny, black Cadillac.

The next morning, Gloria told me how she had danced the night away with her knight in shining armor and God had not struck her dead.

Then a few weeks later, the day after Gloria marched down the aisle to receive her high school diploma, she left on an airplane to Maryland to go join the navy. God did not make the airplane crash; she made it alive and well. So far, so good, I thought!

During boot camp, she sent us letters complaining about how tough it was, but said she was having the time of her life. Then, nine months later, Gloria returned home on leave with a tall, handsome, light-skinned man named Booker T.

Pleasant and personable, Booker T. was in love with our older sister. Booker T. promised Mother that he would not take advantage of Gloria; premarital sex was out of the question. But, then again, it was the late sixties, when "Make love, not war" was the pervading slogan. And by then, everybody was doing it.

I was especially impressed when I found a package of cigarettes in Gloria's purse. And she and Booker T. went to a nightclub while she was home on leave. Gloria had found the good life and it did not include Jesus, the Rapture, going to hell, demons, or Mt. Sinai Holiness Church. I couldn't wait until I turned eighteen.

Booker displayed his affection for my sister outwardly. None of the men at our church ever did that. They did not put their arms around their wives or kiss them in public. In fact, when Sister and Brother Taylor got married, she objected to kissing him at the end of the ceremony in front of everyone, so someone placed a toothpick between their lips, to give the appearance of a kiss.

Booker, on the other hand, wanted all of Sioux City and Mt. Sinai to know that he loved my sister. Sadly, though, eighteen months later, my dream came to a crashing end, when Gloria was discharged from the Navy for being pregnant. At the same time that was happening, she learned that Booker T. had forgotten to tell her he was already married and that his wife would not give him a divorce. He'd also forgotten to tell Gloria that he hadn't asked his wife for a divorce. And now he was on his way to Korea, which meant Gloria would have to return to Sioux City alone, as a failure and a disgrace.

Gloria arrived home in the fall of 1967, full of baby and hatred. She was four months along. I was ashamed of her and mad at her. She should have known better. Why did she have to get pregnant? More important, why did she have to come back home? As soon as she'd walked in the door, it was as if, suddenly, the light at the end of my tunnel had been turned off.

Mother put Gloria in charge of maintaining the house. Trained by the Navy on how to clean, Gloria treated us like lowlife enlisted slime. With her swollen belly, she ordered us to stand in formation and at attention, while she barked out duty assignments and instructions about how to clean and store our cleaning gear.

Several months after being drafted into Gloria's Navy, however, her war on dirt and chaos paid off. For the first time, our house was organized, spotless, and sparkling, despite its unruly inmates.

The troops, however, were beginning to show signs of fatigue. One night, after completing our duty assignments and our homework, we marched off to bed, exhausted. Just as I began to doze off, our commander-in-chief roused us out of our beds and ordered us to report to the chow hall. Befuddled, we dragged our tired bodies down the stairs.

At a little past midnight, Cousin Rhoda dragged her poor, tired body in after a full day of standing on her feet, changing bed pans, and passing out dinner trays. When she entered our impeccable kitchen, she was startled by a peculiar sight: a wild, swollen-bellied drill instructor ranting at six bewildered, pajama-clad, school-aged children, all standing in formation.

"This is not the proper way to stow a dish cloth! How many times must you be told?" Gloria screamed. She seemed happy to see Cousin Rhoda and to fill her in on Cousin Peaches' insubordination.

A puzzled Cousin Rhoda looked around the kitchen. Except for the dish cloth hanging askew over the sink, the kitchen was spotless.

Yawning, we continued to stand in formation, watching Gloria finish her rant, seemingly losing her mind by the minute. Finally, she dismissed us, at which point Cousin Rhoda spoke up.

"Peaches," she said weakly, "In the future, please show your cousin Gloria respect." Then she winked.

We left the kitchen single file, muttering several different things under our breath, but all to the tune of "Gloria has completely lost her mind."

The next day, Gloria wanted to punish us by making us fast until three P.M., but Mother wouldn't hear of it. Gloria gave us extra chores to do instead.

Gloria had the only working television in the house. It was a little colored portable she'd purchased when she had been in the Navy, living the good life. Now, the television sat on her nightstand near her bed. It was the Christmas season, and all the exciting holiday specials were on.

"Please, can we watch your television?" we begged nearly every night. "We promise to sit out here in the hallway. Just turn your television around to face the door."

"No!" Gloria would snap at us.

Once again, Mother had to intercede on our behalf. She forced Gloria to turn the TV toward the doorway, so we could watch *Magoo's Christmas* quietly from the hallway outside her door. *Rudolph the Red-Nosed Reindeer* was scheduled to come on after that, but Gloria turned off the television as soon as the credits began to roll, and slammed her door in our faces. She was mean and evil, but I loved her all the same.

It was obvious to all, especially Mother, that Gloria was not the least bit ashamed about her pregnancy. She was an unmarried pregnant woman, but proud of it.

"Gloria, you were supposed to be a role model to your younger sisters and the young girls in the church," Mother often reminded her. Mother also threatened to beat her for getting pregnant and bringing reproach on her ministry, but she never actually did. Though she said the Lord would surely punish Gloria for it.

You see, to Mother, we Roberts girls lived in a glass house, our every move watched closely by the members of her church.

"'If Sister Roberts' girls did it, then so can we.' That is what the young women are thinking," Mother fussed.

But women in our church had had babies out of wedlock well before we Roberts girls were forced to move to Sioux City. Their role models had been their own mothers and fathers. Take Sister Sellers. She'd had eight children without the benefit of marriage and didn't marry Brother Sellers until after she was Saved. And even then, she did not want to get married to Brother Sellers, who was a gruff and unaffectionate man. Mother had to force her.

And Sister Seller wasn't the only such woman in our church. The list of names went on and on. But Mother did not see it that way.

Still, Gloria remained unrepentant. She felt she had nothing to be ashamed about. She did not want to get married in the first place. This was the dawning of the new age woman. Women were throwing away their bras, using birth control pills, and making their own way in life.

Booker T. still loved Gloria. He wrote to her and Mother and told them so. To prove it, he sent her money each month. He said he was excited about the son Gloria was carrying for him and told her that as soon as he could muster up enough leave, he would come to see her and the baby. Then everything would be all right. Gloria said they would get back together after he did his tour in Korea.

As the time for her delivery neared, however, Gloria's confidence began to wane. In a few weeks' time, a van would come pick her up and take her to Iowa City Hospital, the place where young doctors honed their skills before going out into the real world. It was where the indigent women and Gloria went to have their babies.

About that time, news spread of a young black girl, someone whom Gloria knew from high school, died in Iowa City during childbirth. It was tragic.

Mother forced us go to the funeral to see what happens to young girls who sin. We went to the Baptist church and saw her lying in a shiny brown coffin. Her eyelids were stretched over her eyes. Her mouth looked as it if it had been glued together. She did not look peaceful or natural, as described by the mourners who filed past before me. She looked like an unmarried sinner who was being tormented. Meanwhile, somewhere else, the father of her child, the man who'd gotten her pregnant, was living it up, looking for his next victim. The stillborn child was said to have been placed in the coffin at the young girl's feet, but we couldn't tell, since the bottom part of the lid was closed.

It's what I thought would happen to Gloria. And Gloria must have thought so, as well, because by the time the van came to pick her up for Iowa City, she was terrified. She begged Mother to come with her, but Mother refused.

When Sister Cee-Cee had given birth to her first daughter in Iowa City, Mother had accompanied her and held her hand. But Sister Cee-Cee had been married when she'd gotten pregnant. Sister Cee-Cee was also saved, sanctified, and filled with the Holy Ghost. Gloria wasn't. Mother refused to go.

But then I remembered that I had seen Mother hold the hands of many women—married or not—during labor. And afterward, I had seen her nurse these women in our home while forcing my sisters and I to help take care of them and their babies.

Still, Gloria left on the van to Iowa City all alone. About a week later, she called us.

"Hello?" I said.

"Is Mother there?" Gloria was crying.

"What's the matter? Is the baby all right?"

"Where's Mother? Let me speak to Mother," Gloria demanded.

Mother picked up another receiver, so I listened in from my end. Gloria was panicked and wanted Mommy by her side.

"The baby isn't turning! It is breached! I'm scared! Please, can you come?"

"You'll be all right," Mother insisted.

"Mother, please. I'm scared. I don't want to have a baby. I want to come home."

"Calm down. Everything will be all right," Mother assured her, though rather coldly.

"Will you pray for me?" Gloria asked.

As I listened to Mother pray over Gloria and her baby, I kept thinking about the young girl who died during child birth, and I was extremely fearful. Now already several weeks past due, the baby apparently still resisted coming into this world. I did not blame the baby, but I was scared for Gloria.

By the time Mother hung up, Gloria sounded a little calmer.

Mother wasn't working and didn't have anything else to do. But she wasn't going to Iowa City. It was Gloria's punishment for her pregnancy.

Finally, however, Gloria gave birth to cheery-faced little girl. She was beautiful. Gloria named her after our sister Cynthia. The disappointment and shame I felt for Gloria disappeared suddenly when I held "Ladybug"—a nickname Gloria give her—in my arms. She was perfect.

Gloria had escaped the wrath of God yet again. I looked down the tunnel and saw a dim light flickering. Perhaps there was hope for me after all.

Make a Joyful Noise

Sioux City
March 1968

Make a joyful noise unto the Lord, all ye lands. . . .
[C]ome before his presence with singing.
—Psalms 100:1–2

Y a'll sing!" Brother Roy shouted, snorting at us through his large, brown nostrils. I swear I could look straight up his nose and see clear to his tonsils.

Brother Roy was our new choir director. He'd been stationed with the Air force in Sergeant Bluff, Iowa. After joining our church he'd moved off base to share an apartment with Sister Gretchen and her two children, Matthew and Leah.

He and Sister Gretchen hit it off well. It was a purely platonic relationship. She was now the assistant choir director after her annual backsliding binge. She was back in the church, wearing no makeup and long dresses with slits up the side that Ma Harris said "talked when she walked." She was living a pious life.

Sister Gretchen had a large afro and resembled Angela Davis, except that Sister Gretchen was pretty and soft. No matter what she wore, she was sexy.

Brother Roy, who was also saved, sanctified, and filled with the Holy Ghost, did not date and showed no interest in women. For a long time, it had been rumored by the teenage boys in our choir that Brother Roy did not like girls anyway.

He did seem to be very effeminate to me, but then most COGIC and other Pentecostal/Evangelical men appeared to have a little "sugar in the tank" perhaps because Pentecostals were just generally emotional people. We cried, hugged, and danced in the Spirit unabashedly.

So the fact that Brother Roy possessed qualities more typical of a woman than a man raised no eyebrows. The gossip, even from the teenage boys who knew Brother Roy on a more personal level, was not taken seriously by Mother and the other Mt. Sinai grown-ups.

Then, when Brother Roy and Sister Gretchen started hanging out together, we gave him the benefit of the doubt and mistakenly chalked up his lack of chasing skirts to his deep devotion to the church and fleeing fornication.

I'd first met Sister Gretchen back when we lived on Fourteenth Street in the big scary house where the demons came in and out like the place had a revolving door. She'd been a young, pretty girl with an infant. And she'd lived in Minneapolis, where her in-laws were from. She was the daughter-in-law of Elder Russell, who had a large nondenominational church in Minneapolis, and his church and ours would fellowship with each other two to three times a year.

Elder Russell's church had the finest gospel choir I'd heard by far, well-stocked with talented drummers, organists, pianists, and soloists. His church would come down by busloads and run revivals at Mt. Sinai that lasted until midnight, after which we'd stay up all night, eating soul food and partying for Jesus.

Elder Russell's son, who was Sister Gretchen's husband, had long since come to know the penitentiary as his permanent address. And his parents, Elder and Mother Russell, never thought much of Sister Gretchen. Sister Gretchen had a lot of untamed wildness in her. She had been in and out of juvenile courts and foster homes most of her life.

So one summer, when Elder Russell's buses loaded with saints to return to Minneapolis, Sister Gretchen and her baby Matthew stayed behind. And from that point on, they became permanent fixtures in my family's life. Mother told Sister Gretchen to call her Mom.

Sister Gretchen never did get a home of her own. Unemployed and supporting herself and her children on welfare, she always lived with us. But I liked her—at least at first. Her outspokenness and zest for life made her fun and exciting to be around. She was sexy and feminine, but in a mannish sort of way; Sister Gretchen could drive a car and fix them better than any man I knew.

As the young girls in our church matured, however, we began to resent Sister Gretchen, because her crazy sense of humor attracted men to her like moths to a flame—and the teenage boys in our church were no exception to that axiom. Yet, while we were extremely jealous of her, we secretly vowed to be just like her when we grew up.

Sister Gretchen found it hard to stay "in the way," and her walk with the Lord was unsteady. She would backslide often and when she did, it was usually by taking off and leaving her young children (now there were two) for Mother to raise. Of course, the child-rearing duty ultimately fell on my shoulders, because Mother worked and because I loved children. (I always felt more comfortable around them than I did around adults, because they were not judgmental.)

Sister Gretchen left her children behind with Mother when she was really on fire for the Lord. An Evangelist Missionary from Los Angeles ran a two-week revival. When the evangelist missionary left, she took Sister Gretchen with her, against Mother's advice. Sister Gretchen did not return until nearly a year later. By that time, Matthew and Leah were calling me Mommy. At thirteen years old, I had single-handed potty trained both of them.

When Sister Gretchen finally returned, she was pregnant with her third child. Mother told us that it was the work of a warlock—that while Sister Gretchen had been away, he had impregnated her and put a spell on her. Then, to make matters worse, as if that were possible, Sister Gretchen learned that her legal husband, Elder Russell's son, had just been released from the state penitentiary.

The following Sunday, during the evening service, Sister Gretchen sat in the back row with her two children, one on each side of her. She had become a wretched sinner, full of shame and baby.

"Come up here, Sister Gretchen," Mother called to her from the pulpit. Mother's eyes were dark with her spiritual X-ray vision.

All heads turned to the back of the church, as we watched Sister Gretchen struggle to lift her pregnant self from the pew. You see, at Mt. Sinai, anybody's business was everybody's business. If you sinned, you had to stand up before the congregation and confess.

Sister Gretchen waddled to the front of the church, leaving her two children alone on the bench. I went to them. I sat between them and placed my arms around them.

"Turn around!" Mother commanded.

Sister Gretchen did as she was told and turned to face us. I dropped my head, embarrassed for her. She began to cry as she stood in front of everyone and confessed her sin of adultery, which resulted in her pregnancy by a man other than her prison-bird husband.

"Do you want to be saved?" Mother asked her.

Then one of the Sisters in the church retrieved the blessed oil and made the sign of the cross on Sister Gretchen's forehead. The church began to pray for the deliverance of Sister Gretchen's soul. For the church—or, in other words, Mother (after all, they were one and the same)—was convinced that Sister Gretchen was still under the spell of the warlock.

"Loose her, devil!" the saints commanded. "You can't have her. Satan, the Lord rebuke you. You come out of this girl!"

Sister Gretchen's swollen belly began to stir and she began to struggle with those praying over her. Her yellow face became beet red and contorted in pain. She groaned and moaned, as if possessed by something terrible, and all the while her young children watched her.

"Loose her, devil!" the saints commanded.

I grabbed my Bible and held it tightly against my heart, while embracing Sister Gretchen's children in my arms. But Leah and Matthew were used to this. Watching their mommy puke up foamy white stuff while people stood around her shouting at the devil did not seem to disturb them. This was business as usual at Mt. Sinai Holiness Church.

After the demons were cast out, Sister Gretchen got down on her knees and asked God to forgive her again and to save her. The saints tarried over her well into the night, until she was finally delivered.

But just because she had been redeemed didn't mean our church had been. A disgrace and an abomination in the sight of God, Sister Gretchen's actions, according to Mother, had also brought reproach on Mt. Sinai.

"The Bible says, 'Let *it* not be named among you,'" Mother said. "Maternity clothes should be worn only by women who carry something they could be proud of."

Of course, Sister Gretchen did not fit into this category. Furthermore, when one of the saints tried to throw a baby shower for Sister Gretchen, Mother was adamant that it couldn't happen.

The ultimate sacrifice, however, was for Sister Gretchen to give up her baby for adoption. Otherwise, Mother said, Sister Gretchen was not saved, and her attending Mt. Sinai further would be out of the question. After all, we were a holiness church and this kind of behavior was not to be named among us. This would be Sister Gretchen's true test of faith to the Lord and to Mother. This ultimate sacrifice would determine whether Sister Gretchen was truly repentant. Sister Gretchen was torn.

But alas, when the baby was only a few days old, Mother, accompanied by another saint, took her from her mother's arms. It reminded me of the time Mother took our pet Cocker Spaniel and drove away with her. When she returned, Candy was no longer with her. I repeatedly asked her where our pet dog was, but every time, Mother would just smile and change the subject.

It was the same with Sister Gretchen's baby. Nobody talked about her whereabouts. I just knew that one day when I left for school the beautiful baby girl was there, but when I came home that evening she was gone. And so was Mother.

Sister Gretchen stayed sad and despondent for months after that. But Mother kept reminding her that if she wanted to be saved, sanctified, and filled with the Holy Ghost, this is what the Lord required. Mother kept saying that she did not want the warlock to come looking for Sister Gretchen and his baby. And so Sister Gretchen had to forsake all, including her child, to follow Jesus, and Mount Sinai, and Mother. And so that is exactly Sister Gretchen did. It's just too bad she didn't remember before she allowed Mother to talk her into giving her child away that she could never fully commit to the holy-roller life.

To recover from the loss of her baby, Sister Gretchen began taking night classes at the local community college and joined the Army National Guard. Later, after she received permission from Mother, she divorced her prison-determined husband and moved with her small children, Leah and Matthew, to a subsidized luxury apartment in Morningside.

Sadly, she could not afford furniture on her monthly welfare check. Brother Roy's contribution made it possible for Sister Gretchen and her children to live in a luxury apartment with furniture.

Brother Roy's presence at the apartment made the young men in our church all the more comfortable hanging out at Sister Gretchen's pad. The young girls in our church were green with envy. We'd watch from the sidewalk as Sister Gretchen, Brother Roy, and a carload of teenage boys took off to do fun and exciting things, like bowling, drive-ins, roller skating, and just plain joyriding.

There was never enough room in the car for the girls; especially the Roberts girls. After all, who would watch Sister Gretchen's children? Mother never allowed her daughters to go anywhere or do anything, anyway. And even if Mother did, nobody wanted my sister Linda around because she was such a blabbermouth—she told Mother everything! And if Linda wasn't welcome, then neither was I.

Although Brother Roy did not sing well, he had the acumen of reining in others to sing. He was dedicated, and Mt. Sinai Holiness Church was lucky to have him.

Holiness churches never paid anyone to do God's work. Your pay came from God after you died and went to heaven. So Brother Roy donated all of his free time to Mt. Sinai's choir. And his devotion and dedication to excellence paid off. Our more-than-forty-voice choir—a mixture of adults, teenagers, and youth—became one of the best in

Iowa, at least in the Pentecostal circuit. We traveled by bus to Des Moines, Waterloo, Davenport, and the state fair. Once, we even went all the way to Cleveland, Ohio.

On this particular night, as Brother Roy tried to teach us a new song called "Kept on Searching for the King of Kings," his patience was wearing thin.

"No! No! Listen to the way I'm singin' it. Ya'll ain't singin' it right!" He slammed his hand down on the top of the organ. "It's like this . . ."

For hours, it seemed, we sucked air through our teeth and rolled our eyes as Brother Roy continued shouting at us to sing it louder, sing it softer, sing it like this, or sing it like that. The youth in the choir had a habit of pissing Brother Roy off. Especially me—I was confrontational to say the least.

"Sing!" he yelled.

We hung our heads down low and mumbled the verses:

A long, long time ago,
my heart was troubled with sin
my head—

"That don't sound nuthin' like the way I just showed you," he said, interrupting us. Sister Gretchen stood by the empty organ, shaking her head in disgust.

Brother Roy now resorted to his old tactic of threatening to tell our parents. These were idle threats, though, because every other time he'd told our parents on us, the only thing they'd done was tell us we had to stand up and apologize or else fast the next day.

On this portentous night our organist wasn't there. I wish she had been there, because, as it was, Brother Roy was trying to teach us a new song without the benefit of music. We would have done a much better job if our organist had been there to help us find the right key. Although Brother Roy was a great choir director, he always sang off key.

"Okay, sopranos," yelled Brother Roy, looking at me. "Sing it like this . . ."

Then, Brother Roy threw his head back, opened his mouth and nostrils wide, and began to sing in an off-key falsetto voice: "He changed my feet so I could walk . . ."

I tried not to focus on his gold front tooth and his large nose, now smashed by his glasses, which had slipped down his face when he'd thrown his head back; or his wide rounded nostrils; or his seriously off-key singing, but I couldn't. I got the giggles and I couldn't stop laughing.

"That's it, Sister Debra," he glared at me. "I am telling Sister Roberts when she gets here."

But his threat also seemed funny to me. Especially because when I looked up Brother Roy's nose, I swear I saw smoke coming out of his large, round nostrils. Sally Mae must have seen it too, because then she started to unsuccessfully suppress her giggles. It was contagious. Before long, the whole choir, including the adults, were snickering.

Brother Roy did not see the humor. And the fact that he wasn't laughing only made it more hilarious. The laughing grew until snorts and chuckles emanated from everybody. I think I even saw Sister Gretchen crack a smile.

Just then, our parents began to filter in for the evening service, including Mother. (Our choir rehearsals were held on one of the two regularly scheduled church nights, Tuesday or Thursday, before the service.) Mother looked weak and frail from the twenty-one-day fast she had begun a week ago for Linda's healing. Linda had been sick in the hospital for two weeks. The doctors did not know what was wrong with her.

When Brother Roy saw her, he began his complaints anew, turning his attention to me. "Sister Debra doesn't respect me . . .," Brother Roy trailed off.

Sister Gretchen, still standing next to the organ, nodded in agreement.

Mother took a deep breath and let it out slowly and deliberately. "Come up here, Sister Debra," she ordered.

By now, I was used to Mother calling me out and humiliating me in front of my peers. The last time had been just a couple of Sundays ago. The choir had been right in the middle of a tambourine-playing, drum-beating, organ-tickling gospel jam. Mother had been sitting quietly in the pulpit in her black pastor's robe, obtrusively observing the choir from behind her cat-eye glasses. A couple of the saints had just begun to break out into a holy dance, when Mother stood up.

"Stop the music! Stop the music!" she'd commanded, waving the music to a halt.

The music hung in the air as she approached the podium.

"Come up here, Sister Debra," she directed.

All eyes were on me as I approached the altar.

"Now turn around."

I did as I was told, while all one hundred pairs of eyes were on me.

"Lift up your arms."

I complied.

"Now, saints, I want you to look at Sister Debra's dress."

I looked down to see what she was talking about. I was wearing a one-piece dress. (Our choir did not wear robes). The hem stopped just above my knees, but when I raised my arms, it hiked up, revealing about four inches of flesh over my bony knees.

"This is a sin and an abomination. We are not going to have it at Mt. Sinai."

The congregation tisked and feigned shock for Mother's benefit.

"Now, you go home right now and change your dress. Show the Lord some respect."

I walked down the long aisle and out the front door of the church as all eyes followed me. It was not as if I had deliberately picked a dress that was short and revealing. I just did not have any other clothes to wear. I had finally begun to grow, my dresses were getting shorter, and Mother did not have the money to buy me any new ones.

Besides that, this was the late sixties. While the Pentecostal girl wore her dresses two inches below her knees, her worldly counterparts were wearing miniskirts—even micro-minis.

So I was used to her calling me up before the church, but on this particular night, I wasn't prepared for what she had in store for me.

"Come on up here, Sister Debra," Mother called again.

I sucked air through my teeth and slowly got out of my seat. I sighed heavily as I took my sweet time getting there. I figured she would make me apologize or repent.

"Get on your knees," she said.

I knelt in front of the altar, my butt facing the choir, Brother Roy, and Mother.

"Brother Sellers, get an extension cord," Mother said.

Brother Sellers found one and handed it to Mother.

Now, I know she is NOT going to beat me in front of everybody for something Roy said I did, I thought, just as she cracked the extension cord down on my butt.

Whack!

The extension cord seared my flesh.

"Didn't I tell you?"

Whack! It lashed into my naked legs, but I refused to cry or even utter a sound.

Whack!

"Didn't I tell you?"

I hate you! I seethed, as the cord caught my flesh once again, ripping into my back.

Whack!

"I'm sick and tired of hearing . . ."

Whack!

"I'm going to beat the devil out of you!"

Whack!

I was fourteen years old. There were young boys in the choir, whom I'd been trying to impress. But, by now, my skirt must have been hiked up over my butt and thighs, and the exposed areas covered in gashes and welts.

Didn't I tell you?" She kept going, on and on, and wouldn't stop.

I wanted to get up and run away and never come back. I hated her so much. I hated her till it hurt. I hated Mt. Sinai. I hated Sister

Gretchen. And I could have killed Roy. But most of all, I hated God, because he allowed this to happen. What kind of craziness was this? Wasn't this against the law or something?

From a lifetime of beating experiences, I knew the only way I could get Mother to stop was to show defeat. So I began to whimper. It was all I could muster; I was too embarrassed and too mad to cry. When she heard me, she gave me two more lashes, and then forced me to stand and face my accusers, Brother Roy and Sister Gretchen.

"Now get up with your evil self and apologize to them!" she yelled.

I stood up and slowly turned to face the enemy. When I did, I was surprised to find that my face was flushed in tears. I'd thought I wasn't crying. Brother Roy and Sister Gretchen looked at me. I glared back at the two of them, and they dropped their eyes.

"Apologize," she commanded.

"I'm sorry." I sniffed. "Please forgive me."

Brother Roy shook his head slightly and said, "That's okay, I forgive you." Sister Gretchen just nodded. I detected smirks in their eyes.

"Now go sit down, and I better not hear—" Mother said as I stumbled back to my seat. I could barely sit down.

Pastor Baker seemed elated. He wore a sardonic smile on his face. He could smell blood. He took the extension cord from Mother and with that the beating frenzy began.

"Come on up here, Junior," he said to his sixteen-year-old son.

Junior, who was in the back row where the altos stood, came to the altar and knelt.

Whack!

The extension cord slashed across Junior's back. He buckled like a bucking horse. Pastor Baker aimed for the unprotected areas.

After he beat his eldest son, he called his second son, Mark. Shaking his head in disbelief, Mark submitted himself to his father and knelt before the altar. Pastor Baker beat the fifteen-year-old with elation and vigor.

Then he called Sally Mae, who began to cry before she could reach the altar.

"Kneel down," her father commanded.

"Please," Sally Mae pleaded as she slowly approached the altar. "I'll be good. I promise."

"It's too late for that," her father responded, waving the extension cord around. "Come on up here, Sally Mae."

Sally pleaded with him some more. "I will be good. Please don't beat me."

Pastor Baker did not listen. But when he was through with Sally Mae, he did not call up his oldest daughter, who was seventeen and sickly.

So it was Brother Sellers' turn. He called his four sons: Ralph, who was seventeen; Jeff, sixteen; Ricky, Jr., fifteen; and Len, fourteen. One by one, he had them kneel at the altar, where he made sure to beat them on their backs, where there was little, if any, protection.

After that, for those children who weren't lucky enough to have a father there to beat them, Pastor Baker and Brother Sellers took it upon themselves to do the honor.

"Come on up here," Pastor Baker called to my cousins. Albert and Samuel did not take it lying down. Both ran for cover. Brother Sellers ran after Albert and caught him. He picked him up like a sack of potatoes and hung him upside down, while Pastor Baker beat him. Then it was Cousin Samuel's turn.

Finally, when it was time for Cousin Peaches to go up, she was too cool to cry and acted as if her abuser were taking beating requests.

"Please," she begged, "don't beat me in the same spot." Her only request went unmet, however, as Brother Sellers whacked her repeatedly on her back, legs, arms and thighs.

When the beating frenzy was over, the parents made us get on our knees and ask Jesus to forgive us for being disrespectful. Brother Roy was finally happy again and agreed to stay on as choir director.

That night, most of us thought of running away from home. I wanted to get adopted or go to a foster home. I also thought about calling Daddy and asking to go live with him. It had been almost two years since I'd seen him, but though he'd called me from time to time, he no longer seemed interested in me. I had been replaced by his other children. I was no longer his baby.

And so I had nowhere else to go but home. After school the next day, I did not go directly home. I roamed the streets, trying to think of somewhere else, anywhere, I could run to. But there was nowhere. So finally, I headed for home. When I got there, I circled the block one more time, postponing the inevitable. As I walked, deep inside, I promised myself that when I grew up, I was going to be the biggest sinner this earth had ever seen.

Mark Baker was the only one brave enough to carry out what the rest of us only dreamed about. He was not there that Sunday when the choir powerfully and harmoniously delivered our newly learned hymn:

A long, long time ago
My heart was troubled within
My head bowed down in sorrow
You know, the devil had me wrapped in sin
But I started out to seek salvation
I had a hard time resisting temptation
But I kept on searching till I found the King of Kings

His family did not know of Mark's whereabouts and did not hear from him again for a very long time. In fact, they didn't hear from him until five years later, when they found him in the Illinois state prison. He was serving time for armed robbery.

Touch Not My Anointed Cynthia

Sioux City
Summer 1968

*[W]o unto him through whom they come! It were better for him
that a millstone were hanged about his neck, and he cast into
the sea, than that he should offend one of these little ones.*
—Luke 17:1–2

There was a new black man in town. Ronnie Taylor was six foot two, twenty-something, and gorgeous. He had smooth jet-black skin, black wavy hair, and a perfect set of pearly white teeth, which he loved to flash at the ladies. He was well mannered and from the South. Ronnie said things like, "Yes, ma'am" and "No, sir."

He was a well-bred, well-hung, eligible young bachelor, and all of the black women and white women, including my eighteen-year-old sister Cynthia, were crazy about him.

Ronnie was Brother Taylor's baby brother. I heard he had been in trouble with the law down South, so Brother Taylor sent for him to keep him from going to jail. Sioux City was supposed to give Ronnie a fresh start. Unfortunately, it was the wrong move.

That summer, God was inundated with prayer requests from single women at Mt. Sinai and several other churches to the tune of "Lord, please give me Ronnie for my husband." Ronnie had already talked many of these women saints out of their panties.

Then he set his sights on my sister Cynthia. Although her mind still had not caught up with the rest of her, Cynthia had developed into a beautiful young woman. Her 36DD-sized breasts sat above her twenty-six-inch waist. She had long legs and a firm, round butt that swayed when she walked down the street. Her large front teeth had finally settled into her pretty mocha face. The men who were attracted to Cynthia did not seem to notice her learning disability and her lack of conversational skills.

One summer evening, Cynthia and I were walking home from choir practice when a long, lean, red Coupe de Ville slithered up alongside us, and the horn sounded, startling us. We turned to see Ronnie sitting in the driver's seat.

"Hi!" he said, flashing his dazzling white teeth at Cynthia.

Cynthia and I stood on the sidewalk and peered into his car.

"Hi!" he said again. "I'm lost. Can you tell me how to get to Hamilton Boulevard?"

Ronnie had been in Sioux City for a long time. He lived with the Taylors. I knew he knew where Hamilton Boulevard was, because that's where the Taylors lived. He was definitely going in the opposite direction.

"Um-mm," Cynthia responded coquettishly, pouting her lips like she had seen Marilyn Monroe do. "Let's see.

Impatient and in no mood for his foolishness, I jumped in. "You need to turn around and go back down West Seventh. You can't miss it." I overheard many ugly stories about Ronnie from women who had come to Mother for advice and sympathy after being spurned by him. And by the way he was scanning my sister up and down, I knew he had more on mind than directions to Hamilton Boulevard.

"Wha's your name," he asked in his sexy Southern drawl. He ran his large hand over his black wavy hair and tilted his head slightly so that he could get a better look at Cynthia's legs through the open passenger window.

Cynthia was wearing a tight red skirt that fell slightly below her knees. Ronnie's thick, massive biceps strained underneath his short-sleeved plaid shirt, demanding to be set free. His black, smooth skin was shiny from the hot, humid Iowa summer.

"Cynthia," my sister responded.

I looked at Cynthia and then at Ronnie. She, it was clear, was enamored with him—his good looks and his smooth talk. He, on the other hand, never took his eyes off my sister's body.

"Cynthia," he repeated. "That's a pretty name. Cynthia what?"

"Cynthia Roberts," she said.

"Roberts . . . Roberts?" I watched as his puzzled eyes grew dark before the light bulb in his head went on. "Oh, no! Are you Sister Roberts' daughter?"

"Yep." Cynthia giggled.

Ronnie mulled this over. I could tell he was thinking, *Is she worth the wrath of Sister Roberts?*

"Oh, no," he sighed again. "Sister Roberts' daughter, huh? Do you think your mother would mind if I called on you?"

Yessssssss! I thought. Both Cynthia and I knew Mother would not approve of her meeting up with Ronnie, or any other boy, for that matter.

"I don't know. Why don't you ask her?" Cynthia giggled some more.

"How old are you?"

"Eighteen."

"Really." Ronnie strained forward to get a better look at Cynthia's breasts. "Ummm."

"How old are you?" Cynthia licked her lips seductively.

"Twenty-four. Am I too old?" He licked his full lips in response.

Cynthia giggled again and shook her head, which caused her large breasts to jiggle. Ronnie's eyes widened with interest.

I was feeling totally left out of the situation by now, not to mention jealous. At fourteen, I was short, thin, and ugly, and nobody ever noticed me. Cynthia always got the looks. Sometimes, even Linda caught the eye of an admirer. But I never got so much as a glance. Irritated by this, I grew testier.

"Come on, Cynthia!" I demanded. "We have to get home."

"Oh. And who is this?" Ronnie asked, as if just noticing that I was standing there.

I did not respond. I folded my arms over my chest and stood defiant.

Cynthia looked over at me. "Oh, this is my baby sister, Debra."

"Hello, Debra," Ronnie said. Even the way he said my name was sexy.

I grunted.

"Come on, Cynthia," I said again.

Cynthia and Ronnie exchanged numbers and then he drove off. Cynthia floated home. Mother wasn't home. But then, she hadn't been there for most of the summer.

Right now, she was away at a twenty-one-day revival in Waterloo, Iowa. She'd left us with Gloria, Grandma Harris, and Sister Gretchen, who had been evicted from her luxury apartment and had returned to Roberts Manor with her two small children—which meant we had virtually no supervision. Gloria and Sister Gretchen both worked full time, and Grandma Harris was always too busy with her cinnamon rolls and pound cakes. Cousin Rhoda and her family were also gone by now. Mother had made them move out into a home of their own some time ago.

That entire next week, Cynthia began to disappear every day after she got out of school. Cynthia was now in tailoring school. She had gone as far as she could with adult special education, receiving her certificate of completion, so Mother decided to send her to trade school.

When Mother called at the end of the week, I immediately told her about my suspicion: that Cynthia was sneaking off every day to go be with Ronnie. Turned out I was right.

Mother got on the phone with Cynthia and strictly forbade her from having anything to do with Ronnie. But by then, it was too late. Cynthia had fallen for him. It would take more than Mother's stern rebuke to get Ronnie out of that girl's system.

Mother returned home two weeks earlier than expected, right before school was about to start for Linda and me. She brought a lady named Sister Barbara with her. As Mother introduced Sister Barbara to the family, it was clear to me that our new visitor was heavily medicated. She just stood there, catatonically rubbing her hands together.

"The Lord told me to bring Sister Barbara to live with us," Mother said.

I wondered where the Lord had decided Sister Barbara was to sleep, since our house was already overflowing with people. Moreover, I was afraid of Sister Barbara. She looked and acted just like a stone-cold zombie. Her movements were slow and her eyes were glazed over. I did not like being around her one bit.

Mother said she was that way because she had been disobedient to the Lord, and he had caused her to have a nervous breakdown. She said that when Sister Barbara was a young girl, she had had an affair with the pastor of one of the COGIC churches in Waterloo, Iowa. The affair had taken its toll on her and given her a nervous breakdown. She had been institutionalized for years, but the institution had finally released her.

The pastor, a married man and much older than Sister Barbara, went unscathed. He remained the pastor and stayed with his wife of twenty-some-odd years. However, Sister Barbara was no longer welcomed at his church and her family needed to relocate her. Mother volunteered.

Now, Mother always had to tell her what to do.

"Sister Roberts, should I put on my pajamas, now?" Sister Barbara would ask Mother. "Sister Roberts, should I wash up now?" Then Mother told her to call her Mother, as she did with all the women who lived with us. After that, it was, "Mother, should I eat now? Mother, should I go to sleep now?"

She was weird.

Of course, by now, my sisters and I were used to Mother dragging home all kinds of off-the-wall people, but that did not make the situation any better. I still longed for the day when we would have our home and our Mother to ourselves.

Sister Barbara ended up sleeping in our dining room, so we had to tiptoe around her. I avoided her like the plague.

In addition to bringing Sister Barbara with her from Waterloo, Mother brought a good deal of fury. She was on the warpath when she returned.

I filled Mother in on Cynthia's strange activities. Cynthia had come back just the day before, her top lip swollen and red. I guessed Ronnie had bitten her lip while they were kissing. Then Grandma Harris and Sister Gretchen gave Mother an earful on Gloria's behavior. Gloria hadn't been keeping up with Ladybug's soiled diapers and dirty milk bottles. Also, Gloria had been going out to the club and staying out late. When she came home, she reeked of cigarette smoke and alcohol. Mother was furious.

That night, when Gloria returned at eleven from her job as a nurse's aide, Mother let her have it.

"I told you I was going to whip you if you came home pregnant, didn't I?" Mother yelled at the top of her lungs. "And what did I tell you about those nasty, smelly baby diapers? Who do you think is going to clean up this mess?"

Then, our twenty-one-year-old sister stood stoically, as Mother lashed out at her with her favorite—the brown extension cord.

From the front room, Grandma Harris, Sister Gretchen, a comatose Sister Barbara, Cynthia, Linda, and I had ringside seats at the attraction. Ladybug was sitting on my lap, drooling. We watched as Gloria fumed, towering over Mother. Smoke billowed from Gloria's head and her face was black with anger. Gloria submitted to Mother's wrath without so much as a grunt.

Then it was Cynthia's turn.

"Quit it, Mother!" Cynthia said as the extension cord caught her by surprise on her thigh. Then she sprang from the couch. "I am not playing with you now."

After Mother beat Cynthia, she called the Taylors and demanded a meeting with Ronnie. This I had to see.

The next day, I opened the door and escorted Brother Taylor and Ronnie into our front room. Ronnie flashed me a dazzling bright smile. I felt my checks turn red.

"Mother," I called, "Brother Taylor and Ronnie are here to see you." Then I took the stairs up, two at a time. There was not a moment to waste; I needed to get to my favorite eavesdropping spot as quickly as possible so that I wouldn't miss a word.

On my way up the stairs, I saw Mother walk into the living room, dragging Cynthia behind her. Brother Taylor stood up and shook Mother's hand.

"God bless you, Sister Roberts," Brother Taylor said nervously. He motioned for Ronnie to stand up. Obeying his older brother, Ronnie stood.

Brother Taylor tried to make small talk, but Mother wasn't hearing any of it.

"I understand that you have been seeing my daughter. Is that true?"

"Yes ma'am," responded Ronnie, in his sweet Southern drawl. I liked the way he said "ma'am."

"Well, I must ask you to stop," Mother said.

"With all due respect, Sister Roberts," Ronnie said, "Cynthia is old enough to make up her own mind."

"Cynthia has the mind of an ant."

"Mother!" Cynthia wailed.

"Hush, Cynthia, and don't talk back," Mother snapped. "Cynthia has the body of a grown woman but the mind of a child. I am asking you, as your sister in the Lord, to leave my daughter alone."

Ronnie did not respond. He dropped his head.

"See, Brother Ronnie, the Bible says, 'Touch not my anointed and do my prophet no harm.' You have been here for six months and you have been messin' with a whole lot of the anointed—the saints and the saints' daughters. But, you see, the Lord is not going to stand for it. He said it is better that a millstone be tied around your neck and you be dumped in the lake, than to mess with his little ones. And Cynthia belongs to the Lord. You had better straighten up and live right, or God is going to get you."

"Well, I didn't force any of those women to be with me," he said, in his deep, rich Southern drawl.

"Shut up, I'm talking," Mother warned.

Mother loved to order grown men to shut up and do other things. I feared for her life every time she did, because one of these days one of them was going to let her have it.

Ronnie fell silent as Mother continued.

Mother pointed a crooked finger in his direction. "The Lord said to tell you to leave the saints and the saints' children alone. There are plenty of women in the bars and on the streets for you to have your pick. But the Lord said to tell you to leave his children alone."

The room fell silent.

Brother Taylor cleared his throat several times and stood up. "You have a good day, Sister Roberts. The Lord bless you."

"You too," Mother said sweetly.

And then they were gone.

Cynthia did not speak to Mother for weeks after that. And then months after that, Mother informed us that Ronnie and Beverly Green had become an item. In fact, we found out later that while Ronnie was messing around with Cynthia, he'd also been pursuing Beverly.

Ten years older than Ronnie, Beverly had repeatedly rebuffed her paramour's advances. But now, apparently, she was madly in love with him.

When we found out, Cynthia was seething with jealousy and hatred. And every time Beverly visited our house after that, Cynthia made a big production of stomping out of the room in Beverly's presence.

Beverly was a backslider, on her way to hell. But she did not care. We knew that about her because she had once lived with us on Fourteenth Street. Beverly was married to a man who was stationed in Vietnam. She often complained about sex, how she didn't like it, how she couldn't understand all the fuss about it. But now, it seemed, she couldn't get enough of it with Ronnie.

By that time, Beverly and Ronnie had been dating over a year, and Beverly no longer attended our church, but she still stopped by our house occasionally to ask for Mother's advice. Every time she did, I made it a point to listen to them through the heat vent on the second floor.

Beverly also dropped by occasionally to pick up Linda to baby-sit her daughter. Sometimes, Linda would let me come along, though on one particular night, I wished I hadn't.

That evening, Linda and I were watching television and Beverly's active daughter, when Beverly returned home with a very pregnant Sister Cee-Cee. Sister Cee-Cee, who was about to give birth to her second child, had said the Lord had given her a message for Beverly about returning to him and Mt. Sinai. Linda and I fell asleep on the sofa bed while the two of them talked into the night.

Suddenly, at some unknown hour in the morning, the front door blew open and a gush of cold air filled the room. I sat straight up and looked around. Beverly and Sister Cee-Cee were standing in the entryway to the living room, staring at a blank wall across from them.

"Do you see him?" Beverly asked.

"Do you?" Sister Cee-Cee responded.

"The tall black thing in the corner of the room."

I scanned the room. I didn't see anything.

Linda was sitting up now and looking around the room as well.

"Yeah!" Sister Cee-Cee said nervously.

"What is he doing here?" Beverly asked.

"I think he is the death angel," Sister Cee-Cee responded.

Linda and I leaped from the sofa bed and ran to Sister Cee-Cee and Beverly. My heart raced with panic.

"What does he want?" Beverly asked.

"I don't know," Sister Cee-Cee said. "But I'm gettin' outta here!"

Grabbing her sleeping daughter and throwing a blanket over her, Beverly led the race of terror out the front door, leaving it wide open. We piled into her car, and she took off, driving like a bat out of hell, taking the corners on two wheels.

Barely had we come to a halt in front of Mother's house when all four doors flew open, and we leaped from the car and ran to the front door, fearing that the angel of death was closing in on us.

Suddenly realizing we had no house key, we began banging, pleading, screaming for someone to come to our rescue. We thought surely our frantic knocking would break the glass pane from the front door and get someone's attention.

"Let us in! Help! Let us in!" Our chorus cried in unison.

Through the door, a figure appeared at the end of the hall. Help was on the way—or so we thought. But then the figure remained stationary, and our panic increased.

"Let us in! Hurry!" we continued at the top of our lungs.

After what seemed like forever, the solitary figure began to move toward us as if in a slow-motion trance, until her face became illuminated by the porch light streaming into the house. To our dismay, it was Sister Barbara, in her zombie-like, medicated state. In her unconscious daze . . . Sister Barbara inched her way . . . toward the front door . . . eventually arriving . . . at her destination . . . oblivious to the frantic faces . . . on the other side of the glass.

"Hurry! Open the door! Now! Please, hurry up!" We stared in disbelief, as Sister Barbara *slooowly* reached for the lock, *slooowly* grasped the handle, and painstakingly turned each one.

We burst into the house, almost knocking her over, and raced upstairs to Mother.

"Praise the Lord!" Sister Barbara called after us.

Mother was not sympathetic. "Go back there and order him, in the name of Jesus, to get out of your house," she commanded.

"But Sister Roberts . . .," Beverly and Sister Cee-Cee protested.

I scurried past Mother's bedroom and jumped into my bed and under the covers before Mother tried to make me go back with them. I hadn't seen anything, I didn't know anything, and I wanted to keep it that way.

Finally, in the wee hours of the morning, I fell asleep in the glow of my trusty night-light.

In the meantime, God had added two new members to our church: Pop and Mrs. Samson. An old man and legally blind, Pop Samson wore tinted yellow glasses, thick as the bottom of pop bottles. In order to read, he had to hold whatever he was attempting to read under his one good eye and squint really hard. He had a white cane to help him see where he was going when he walked, but he refused to use it. Pop Samson was always running into walls, closed doors, and chairs. He was a stubborn old man.

And his wife was older than he was. Their house smelled of mildew and urine. Even though Mrs. Samson had gone to our church for some time, she didn't accept the Lord until she was on her deathbed.

She had sent for Mother and some saints to come pray for her, so Mother took Grandma Harris, Sister Pat, and Sister Barbara across the bridge which separated Sioux City from South Sioux City, Nebraska. The ride wasn't very long. The two cities were separated by the Missouri River. They went to her house every day to pray for her deliverance.

They lived on a five-acre farm, which had several barns and a large orchard that consisted of apple, pear, and plum trees. This was where I stayed while they went into the house. I went into the house once but was driven out by a heavy, dark feeling. I was also afraid of Mrs. Samson. She had a evil presence. She lingered on her deathbed for several months, while Mother and the saints continued to visit her daily.

Mother said God wasn't letting her die yet because he was giving her a chance to get "her house" in order before he took her. Although the old woman had accepted the Lord, Mother said, she did not have peace with God, because there was something she still had not given up.

Eventually, they learned that Mrs. Samson had been practicing witchcraft. After finding a voodoo doll with pins stuck in it, Mother and the saints went through her house rebuking the witch craft devil and clearing it of all the voodoo stuff. Then Mrs. Samson confessed her sins and died.

Pop Samson, as it were, was now an eligible bachelor. He received a pension and owned property—a good catch by Mt. Sinai's standards. In addition, the state of Nebraska was interested in Pop's property. It had plans to build a highway through some of his land.

Pop Samson accepted their offer; he was looking forward to a change. He wanted to move to the "big city"—Sioux City—and find himself a new wife, specifically, my Mother.

Was he kidding? Pop Samson had one foot in the grave. He smelled old, he looked old, and he was blind. Linda and I immediately let Pop Samson know what we thought about his intentions. Besides, Mother was still a married woman.

After Mrs. Samson died, Pop's son Tony came to live with him until Pops got himself situated. Tony had grown up in the same hometown as Ronnie. In fact, Tony and Ronnie had been best friends, and after Tony moved to town, they hooked up again. They hung out and chased women together quite often.

That is, until one fateful evening. Nobody really knew what the argument had been about, but apparently it involved Beverly's brother, Buddy, and made Ronnie and Buddy mad enough that they insisted on driving to South Sioux City, Nebraska, to confront Tony about it in person.

Both Buddy and Ronnie had been drinking heavily. Their women tried to get them to go home and sleep it off, but the men insisted "this thing" had to be resolved tonight. Buddy was driving. His girlfriend, Susan, sat in the front seat. Ronnie and Beverly rode in the back.

It was ten o'clock and very dark. After all, it was the country. Out there, there weren't any street lights. Tony must have heard the car coming before it reached his place, because as soon as they pulled up, he slung open the door, his father's shotgun in hand. Pop was right behind him.

A drunken Ronnie staggered up the porch, yelling at Tony. Pop told them to leave or he would call the police.

"Go ahead and call 'em!" Ronnie shouted as Buddy joined him on the porch. Beverly and Susan stood at the bottom of the steps, pleading with Ronnie and Buddy to forget it and go home.

"No!" yelled Ronnie. "We are going to settle this right now."

"You better leave, man, before I shoot you," Tony said.

"Go ahead! Shoot me!" Ronnie took a step backward, arms raised at his sides, as if opening himself up to the gun.

Tony raised the shotgun and cocked it. The explosion took everyone by surprise.

Ronnie looked down at where his muscular stomach had been and saw a hole, gushing blood. He looked back up at Tony and stared into his eyes with bewilderment.

"You shot me, man!" Ronnie moaned.

Tony looked at the hole in Ronnie's stomach and then at the gun. He dropped it as if it were searing hot. Tony rushed to Ronnie's side just as he began to crumple to the floor.

"You shot me, you shot me," Ronnie whispered over and over again.

Beverly and Susan screamed and ran around in circles. They were too hysterical to help Ronnie, let alone themselves. Pop went in to call an ambulance. While they waited, Tony cradled Ronnie in his arms, trying to assure him everything would be all right.

"I'm sorry, man," Tony wept. "I didn't mean to do it. The gun just went off."

"You shot me, you shot me. Now, I'm going to die," were the last words Ronnie spoke.

And all of it was Beverly Green's fault. She was a backslider. Having once been saved, though, she had been responsible as her brother's keeper. Now, Ronnie's blood would be on her hands forever.

She came to our house to get comfort from Mother. Mother did not sugarcoat her words. Mother had to cry loud and spare not. Yes, she agreed, it was all Beverly's fault.

Neither Cynthia nor I attended Ronnie's funeral. By then, I had boycotted funerals. Mother did not make me go this time either, because there was no lesson I needed to learn from it. Ronnie's mother said he'd given his heart to the Lord when he'd been a young boy. But in Holiness, that didn't count; you had to be saved on the day you died.

It went without saying that Ronnie lifted his eyes in hell. Cut down in the prime of his life, Ronnie was in his early twenties when he died. Mother's warning to him came true. It confirmed my belief that she had a direct line to God and that God was mean and vengeful. I was terrified of both of them.

I heard Ronnie's funeral was fit for a king, though. The mourners spilled out the door of the church. And for some time after the funeral, Ronnie's death caused many sinners to run back to the church momentarily.

Cynthia became depressed as well. So she and Gloria moved to New Jersey to live with Daddy and start a new life. Gloria had been planning her escape ever since Mother had beaten her with the extension cord, and she saw this was the perfect opportunity. Mother insisted that she leave Ladybug with us, however, until she got herself settled.

A week after Gloria left, I found a letter to her from Booker in our mailbox. Gloria had been depressed for several months before she'd left for New Jersey, because she hadn't heard from him and was afraid he had dumped her for another. From the return address on the envelope, I could see that he was still in Korea.

I handed the letter to Mother and watched as she ripped it open. Mother read the letter and shared it with Sister Gretchen. Then, after Gretchen read it, Mother ripped it up and threw it in the trash.

I gave Mother the evil eye, which luckily for me she did not notice. Then I walked toward the back door, passing a catatonic Sister Barbara, who was humming and rocking at the kitchen table. Outside on our back porch, I planned my escape as well.

At fifteen, I only had three more years to endure the madness. I hoped I could hold onto my life and sanity for just a little while longer.

The Casualties of War

Sioux City
Fall 1969

And [God] said [unto Abraham], Take now thy son . . .
whom thou lovest . . . and offer him for a burnt-offering.
—Genesis 22:2

Not a dry eye was in our crowded little church that Wednesday evening, as the nephew of Sister Barbara sat at the organ, playing and singing. (Yes, that's the same Sister Barbara who'd been sleeping in our dining room, although she wasn't catatonic anymore; I'll get to that story in a bit.)

Evangelist Calvin was singing

In a mansion
Made of stone
In a castle
All alone
He cares
He cares
He cares
He cares
God cares—he really cares for you.

Although Calvin was a dark, obese man with three chins, a face smashed like a Pekineses, and large, Jell-O-y belly, he always dressed impeccably and smelled of expensive men's cologne. He was a skilled

146

pianist and had an awesome voice. He was as good as, if not better than, anyone I had ever heard in the entertainment business. His talents made up for his homeliness.

That's probably why, despite his appearance, the young women in our church who'd been bugging God to send them husbands were enamored with Evangelist Calvin.

However, I'd overheard Calvin tell his Aunt Barbara over several pieces of fried chicken and some collard greens that he was not looking for a wife. You see, after church each week, Calvin and Sister Barbara had begun preparing a big spread for us. We would feast on fried fish, fried chicken or fried pork chops, greens, sweet potatoes, and potato salad. Then, to top it all off, we'd eat peach cobbler, apple pie, pineapple upside down cake, or Ma Harris' lemon pound cake (which she'd charge fifteen cents apiece for, but it was worth it). It was at one such feast that Calvin told his aunt that he was having the time of his life as a traveling evangelist and that he wasn't ready to give that up for a wife and a family. Bachelorhood suited him to a tee, and the single women at Mt. Sinai knew it. Regardless, they continued to bombard the Lord for his hand in marriage.

Calvin was a young college graduate, too, with a master's degree in music or something. This was highly unusual, because most of the people in our church had been directed by the Lord to quit working or give up their educations so they could fully devote their lives to doing the Lord's work.

Like Sister Joe. For the past three years, Sister Joe had been a frequent guest at our home after the Lord had called her off of her nurse's aide job. She depended on the kindness of those whom the Lord had laid on their hearts to give her free "room, board, and donations."

At twenty, Sister Joe was also asking God to bless her with a husband. She was torn between Calvin and Harry, Pastor Billie James' son, though neither man had any interest in her.

Early one afternoon, when I returned from school, I found Sister Joe in the same spot as she'd been when I'd left that morning, wearing the clothes she'd slept in the night before. Loud gurgling snores emanated from her open mouth, filling the living room. My entry startled her.

"Oh! Did I wake you?" I asked.

"Nah, baby. I wasn't sleeping, I was mediating on the scriptures," Sister Joe yawned in a heavily sedated voice.

My eyes dropped to her Bible, which lay closed on its side on the floor next to the couch, and back up to meet her gaze.

"Umph," she smiled sheepishly. "I guess I must have dozed off."

That night, Sister Joe was dressed to the nines, her hair neatly pressed and curled, and she was sitting in the front pew so that Evangelist Calvin would be sure to see her.

"Ooooh, sweet Jesus," Sister Joe cried. "Bless him, Lord," she said piously.

"Seekimsha-na-na-ya!" She began speaking in tongues and leaped from her chair, dancing in the Spirit toward the front of the church to where he sat, playing the organ and singing. He closed his eyes and pretended not to see her.

Somehow, I had the feeling Sister Joe's dancing had less to do with the Holy Spirit than with Calvin's performance. If you closed your eyes while listening to him play and sing, you'd almost think he was the lead singer for the Temptations or even Marvin Gaye.

Anyway, Calvin had been in Sioux City several weeks when Mother decided he should run a young people's revival in conjunction with a fast. He did as Mother asked, of course, but Evangelist Calvin modified the way we fasted. He allowed us to drink anything we wanted on our fasting days, including milkshakes, soda pop, and juice. After all, he realized, we were full-time students. We couldn't study or pay attention in school on empty stomachs.

Evangelist Calvin was different like that. Although he claimed to be saved, sanctified, and filled with the Holy Ghost, he did not speak in "Pentecostalese" every time he opened his mouth. He joked with the young people in our church. He enjoyed going to movies, roller skating, and gossiping about entertainment celebrities. When preaching, he actually spoke proper English and understood the Bible from an intellectual perspective. His sermons were brief and to the point. He used an outline and talking points.

Evangelist Calvin was young and alive. He didn't think it a sin to have fun and enjoy life, and I admired him greatly because of that. He seemed to be a genuine Christian.

The third night of Evangelist Calvin's revival, Sister Barbara and I left the house for church. We turned the corner, followed Sixth Street down to skid row, and turned right.

Skid row was right around the corner from Mt. Sinai. It consisted of two large, rundown apartment buildings, each with a large front porch and lawn, where weeds and trash mingled together. Winos, stone-cold drunks, and the dregs of society cascaded from the front porches and down onto the street at all hours.

Most of them had staggered into our church at one time or another, asking for prayer or dancing to the music that spilled out of our church and filtered around the corner of West Seventh Street. Sometimes they would even volunteer to solo us. I remember whenever a wino would wander in and serenade us with "Amazing Grace" or some other hymn he probably remembered from childhood how hard it was to sit there and watch him without cracking up. Even Mother would start laughing and tried to hide it behind a fan.

Anyway, on this particular night, as Sister Barbara and I walked past the buildings, a light-skinned drunken man jumped up and swayed in front of us. He blocked Sister Barbara when she tried to walk around him.

By this time, Sister Barbara's medication had been tapered substantially and she was no longer catatonic. She had regained her complexion and her personality, although she always remained serious, as though she felt it was a sin to joke or laugh. Eventually, her true self was revealed through her amazing singing voice, which she often used for the Lord by soloing at our church.

She was also now gainfully employed at Iowa Beef Processing, where she worked in one of the coldest sections of the plant. That meant that, surprisingly, every morning, she was up and out of the house before the rest of us even dared to stir. She worked the seven

A.M. to three P.M. shift, but had to leave the house by four in order to get there on time.

On our fasting days, I felt compassion for Sister Barbara because a lack of food made her job even tougher. Meanwhile, the majority of people in our church slept through fast days because they did not work. Though I knew this was unfair, I dared not voice my opinion.

"Hi," the drunken bum said now, slurring his words.

"Hello," Sister Barbara said curtly, trying again to walk around him.

I clutched my Bible to me tightly. I wished Sister Barbara hadn't insisted on walking past skid row. We should have turned on Sioux Street like I had suggested.

"Where ya' goin'?" he asked.

Frowning, Sister Barbara stared him up and down. "To church."

"Can I come with you?"

Always the missionary and witness for Christ, Sister Barbara responded, "Sure. We'd love to have you."

"Can I sit with you?"

"Umph!" Sister Barbara responded, a smirk on her face.

I turned up my nose. He reeked of alcohol.

"What is your name?" he asked.

"Sister Barbara," she replied.

I cleared my throat and looked at my naked wrist, as if there were a watch on it.

"Ah, we better get going or we'll be late," I said.

The drunk turned and stared at me. Then he turned back to focus his red eyes on Sister Barbara. "How can a man like me get together with a woman like you?" He almost lost his balance.

"You got to be saved, sanctified, and filled with Holy Ghost," Sister Barbara responded quickly.

The drunk was taken aback at first, but then continued. "If I get saved, can I have you?"

"Well, I don't know about that," Sister Barbara said, laughing. "But at least you will know where you are going when you die. That's more important than getting me."

"I don't know about that." Then he stretched out his right hand toward her.

Sister Barbara hesitated a second and then placed her dark brown hand into his large yellow one.

"My name is Jack Moore," he said. "And one of these days, you are going to be my wife."

Sister Barbara quickly retracted her hand. She shook her head in disbelief and laughed mockingly. "I don't think so!" Then she abruptly ended the conversation and brushed past him. I had to run to catch up with her.

When we got to church, Mother and Linda were there. We helped lay out the prayer pillows. Shortly thereafter, the rest of the saints slowly filtered in.

After prayer, Evangelist Calvin asked Sister Barbara to lead a testimony service. Sister Barbara stood in front of the church dressed in a matronly, flowery dress, looking tired, but singing in her incredible voice. With her nephew accompanying her on the organ, Sister Barbara began to stir the congregation. When she hit one of her high notes and held it, we couldn't stay in our seats any longer. We jumped up and began to praise the Lord along with her.

Just as she was starting the second stanza, Jack Moore staggered in. He stood at the back in the open doorway, just staring, as if afraid to come in. But then he tottered down the center aisle, never taking his eyes off his "wife-to-be."

Sister Barbara was singing with her eyes closed and her head tilted back, so she did not see him. But when she finished her song and opened her eyes, there he stood—in the middle of the floor, only steps away from her, grinning from ear to ear. Sister Barbara frowned. Finally, a deacon escorted Jack to a seat.

"Testimony service is about over," Sister Barbara said as she grabbed her Bible from the podium. "Is there anyone out there who would like to say something for the Lord?"

Jack's hand flew up. Then he dragged himself up off of the pew. "I'd like to say something," he said, slurring.

"Praise the Lord," the congregation responded.

"I know I am a sinner, but I believe Sister Barbara is my wife."

A hush fell over the church, except for among us teenagers, as we were snickering quietly.

Sister Barbara was frowning and shaking her head. Then, because Sister Barbara had been fasting and praying for a husband, she looked away from Jack and an expression crossed her face that seemed to say, "God has got to be kidding."

Mother stood and moved to the podium to address the new guest.

"You see, Sister Barbara is saved, sanctified, and filled with the Holy Ghost. God is not going to give her to you unless you are saved as well. She is God's daughter. If you want Sister Barbara, then you will have to clean up your life and give your heart to Jesus. Would you like to do that today?"

"Well, I dunno. I want to be saved, but—"

"No buts," Mother interrupted him. "The Bible says, 'The day you hear my voice, harden not your heart.' This may be your last chance. You don't know. You could walk out of here tonight and get hit by a semi-truck or have a heart attack. Tomorrow or the next day is not promised to you." (There it was again, the old scared-straight tactics.)

Mother has to be joking, I thought. *God is not going to give Sister Barbara to that red-eyed, reeking-of-alcohol, dirty-breathed, filthy-clothed wino from skid row. And another thing: if that is the best God can do, then I don't think I'll be asking for his help when it comes time for me to marry. Thanks, but no thanks. I'll find someone on my own.*

Jack seemed to be considering what Mother had said as he stood swaying in the middle of the floor, looking back and forth from Mother to Sister Barbara, who was now wide-eyed with fear.

Finally, Jack came to the altar and gave his heart to the Lord. And for the next two weeks, Brother Jack returned to our church, clean and sober. But after that, we did not see him for a while. I breathed a sigh of relief for Sister Barbara. I am sure she did the same.

Later, after Evangelist Calvin left without a wife, Mother made Sister Barbara move into her own apartment. Of course, that freed up room in our house for another masquerading angel. Enter (again) Brother Jack.

Out of nowhere, it seemed, Brother Jack came staggering back into the church one night, reeking of urine and alcohol. He fell down on the altar and asked the saints to pray for him again.

As it turned out, Brother Jack wanted to be saved; however, he found it hard to live for Jesus on skid row. The temptation was too great. There was too much free alcohol, drugs, and sex.

Finally, though, Brother Jack gave his heart to Jesus for good after a man he occasionally worked for, called Big Boy, died in his sleep. As with most winos who lived on skid row, Brother Jack did not have a steady job, so Big Boy would hire him to skin cattle hides only when he was sober enough.

Big Boy was so named because he weighed over three hundred pounds and was short. Half Negro and half Indian, he was also as generous as he was big, helping all the skid row winos earn money the way he did with Brother Jack, even though none of them could maintain full-time employment. Big Boy came to our church one night and gave his heart to the Lord. The next day, they found him dead. He had died in his sleep. His death stirred up a lot of emotions and fear among the winos on skid row—including Brother Jack.

So after Brother Jack gave his heart to Jesus for the umpteenth time, Mother decided it would be best if he moved in with us.

What? I wondered. *It doesn't matter that several men in the church have homes that Brother Jack can squeeze into, does it? Mother just has to make the ultimate sacrifice and bring him into her home with her two teenage daughters.*

Mother, who worked as a registered nurse on the night shift again, would leave Linda and I alone with the drunk from skid row. Worse, Brother Jack had a bad case of the D.T.'s, which meant that all night long, I could hear him groaning and moaning, tossing and turning. Not to mention vomiting; I'd hear the stairs creaking, as a hacking and coughing Brother Jack climbed to the top to use our only bathroom, which was right next to my room.

Mother said he was detoxifying.

"When an alcoholic can't get anything to drink, his body begins to crave it," Mother said. "His body is purging itself from alcohol."

"Great!" I said. "But what if he tries to do something to Linda or me?"

"God will take care of you," Mother told me.

I wanted to reply, "What about you taking care of me?" but I didn't. As with any war, there are casualties, and when it came to Mother's personal war against sin, I began to think of myself and my sisters as the casualties of war.

My sisters' and my needs always came second to those of the lost souls. Mother always had a larger picture and we weren't in it. I wasn't in it at all.

To his credit, Brother Jack never made any passes or even showed any questionable behavior toward Linda and me. All the same, I was terrified of him.

For many more years, off and on, Brother Jack would suffer from the demons of alcohol, until the day he no longer touch the stuff again. Brother Jack and Sister Barbara eventually married and lived happily ever after for about six months.

Mortify Your Members

Sioux City
Summer 1970

*Mortify therefore your members which are upon the
earth; fornication . . . for which things sake the wrath
of God cometh on the children of disobedience.*
—Colossians 3:5–6

My childhood church friends and I had come of age. The
girls were developing into young ladies and the boys were
growing facial hair, their voices deepening. Puberty was
as certain as the Sun rising each day. Our hormones were raging,
and there was a lot of talk about the dos and don'ts of sex. Little did
I know at the time that there was a whole lot of *doing* going on at Mt.
Sinai Holiness Church—by everybody, it seemed, except for my sister
Linda and me.

Linda was Miss Goody Two Shoes and still a virgin. She was also
sick. As for me, I probably would have been doing it too, except that
nobody asked me.

At fifteen I was still short, skinny, shy, and unattractive—or at
least that's how I saw myself. I hadn't even started my period. The
teenage boys in my church didn't know I existed, or if they did, they
were too afraid of Mother to do anything about it. They, like I, had
begun to think that Mother not only had a direct line to heaven but
could be the Lord himself. So no boy dared mess with the preacher's
daughters, especially after Ronnie's death.

During the summer of 1970, then, while the other youth at Mt. Sinai were doing it, I was next door playing Barbie dolls with my twelve-year-old neighbor. Otherwise, I was pretty much on lock down at Roberts Manor.

As for poor Linda, she was in and out of the hospital. At first, the doctor said she was pregnant, and Linda believed him, even though she'd never had sex, poor child. Later, she was diagnosed with irritable bowel syndrome, which would eventually be diagnosed as Chrohn's disease.

Constant diarrhea forced her to run to the bathroom what seemed like fifty times a day. Unable to make it to the bathroom many of those times, Linda would soil herself and have to come home from school to clean herself up. After a while, she began taking a change of clothes with her and then to Beverly's house, who lived near Central High School, to wash herself and change her soiled clothes.

My Rock of Gibraltar was crumbling before my eyes, but instead of feeling pity for her, I felt only panic and anger. I had no tolerance for her illness. The sicker she got, the meaner I became. I despised her.

"Linda, how dare you even think about dying on me and leaving me in this craziness to deal with all this Pentecostal crap?" I'd often said to myself.

Meanwhile, Linda was literally living in her own crap—in more ways than one. Miraculously, through her heartache and humiliation, she seemed to have an indestructible private line to God that *no one* could disconnect. It's a good thing she had that, since there was little else for her to hang on to.

Especially now, ever since she heard it through the grapevine that her first love, Jeff Sellers, was doin' it with another—as if she needed one more obstacle to overcome. Linda had fallen in love at first sight with Jeff when she'd been seven years old, and though it had gone unrequited, Linda had held on to that love all these years.

Tall, handsome, and a real ladies' man, Jeff was well spoken and confident. To top it off, he was also resourceful and hardworking. He was very resourceful. He had been a paper boy, had bagged groceries at a local supermarket that refused to hire Negroes, (somehow he'd been able to pull that off) and had worked at the Sioux City, Iowa Bakery. He was even a Boy Scout.

He also played basketball for Central High School. And it was around this time when his picture began appearing in the *Sioux City Journal* and on the ten o'clock news almost every night. Everyone loved him, even though he was, by definition, a holy-roller and attended Mt. Sinai.

We couldn't go to watch Jeff's basketball games if they were on church nights. You'd think someone from our church would have at least organized a basketball night, so that we could all go support Mt. Sinai's rising basketball star. But at Holiness, his athletic talents were considered a waste of time and a distraction from God.

Linda always dreamed of being on the basketball court, wearing a Central High School cheerleader's uniform and cheering Jeff on to victory. But Mother told her cheer leading was a sin. So instead, Linda formed a group called Cheerleaders for Jesus at our church. On youth night, she'd stand there in her long dress, yelling, "Two, four, six, eight! Who do we appreciate? Yeah, Jesus! Yeah, Jesus!"

It wasn't quite the same. Poor Linda did not stand a chance of becoming a cheerleader or Jeff's girlfriend. Especially since Jeff had met Becky, a young, high-yellow, half-Indian-half-black girl with hair that ran the length of her back. Because of the color of her skin, Linda's nicknames were "black-sco" and "tar baby." Her hair was long but nappy and unmanageable. And her deep voice made most people think she was a man when she spoke on the phone calls.

Because of constant teasing about her voice, she worked on it by cultivating her voice. She spent hours and days practicing. It worked. People on the other end of the phone couldn't tell she was black. People then accused her of trying to sound like a white girl.

Becky came from a hardworking middle-class family. Their neatly furnished home was just up the street from the Sellers' and the Bakers'. Becky wore beautiful clothes. Her mother made some of them and purchased others on accounts at Sears, J. C. Penney's, and Yonkers. Even after Becky's parents divorced, her mother and siblings remained in the family home, nothing changed about the way she dressed and carried herself, even though her father was no longer there. Just another hard-working middle class family. There was no magic too it.

There was no way Linda could compete with Becky. Even amid the sixties social revolution, Linda remained faithful to the Pentecostal establishment. In tenth grade, when others were donning the fashionable mini and micro-mini, Linda obediently wore the only two dresses she owned on alternating days—one blue-and-white striped and the other pink-and-white striped.

As she grew taller, however, the hemlines became shorter, so in turn, Mother cut each dress two inches above the hem and added tacky, four-inch-wide, flowered remnants. Even realizing the disastrous fashion statement she would be making at school, Linda nevertheless smiled politely at Mother's finished product. And then, in her endless desire to please Mother, Linda meekly wore the chaotic combination of fabrics, the outer symbol of her inner turmoil.

And while Linda held tightly to her submissiveness, I held firm to my rage at my Mother's dressing my sister like the school idiot.

Why must we be held hostage, when we are blossoming young women, I wondered. *Just because the Pentecostal doctrine dictates the protection of the male predator from his own evil concupiscence?*

"That's okay, Debra," Linda assured me. "I don't mind."

I hid my favorite dresses from Mother. I wasn't taking any chances. I would bide my time for two more years, and then I would make my own revolutionary fashion statement. But until then, Mother would not even let us out of the house. We went to school, church, and home, and that was it. Mother was often out of town, but even when she was out of town, we had to stay home. And, of course, when she was in town, we had to stay home. She ran a tight ship.

Eventually, Jeff introduced Becky and her little brother to our church and to the Lord. Later, he introduced her to sex. And when they consummated their love, she got pregnant.

Because Cousin Peaches was dating Ralph, Jeff's older brother, she and Becky became close friends. That's how she found out about the baby. Unfortunately, Cousin Peaches made the mistake of telling Linda. It was a well-known fact that Linda was a blabbermouth.

So although she was sworn to secrecy, Linda told Mother everything. As soon as Mother returned from her most recent out-of-town revival, Linda was right there, filling her in on all the sordid details and giving her enough sermon content for about another year. Mother didn't hesitate starting in on the subject, either. The following Sunday, she called the sinful affair to everyone's attention.

"Come up here, Brother Jeff and Sister Becky," she said before the service had barely even started. We held our breath as we knew what was coming next.

"You've been fornicating," Mother said.

"Everybody makes mistakes," Jeff said as he stood tall and proud. His mother, Sister Sellers, began to weep. Her daughters, Rita and Rene, quickly closed in on their mother. One on each side, they grabbed her arms and began to comfort her. Brother Sellers, who always perched himself in the row directly behind his wife, sat stoic and solemn-faced. Sister Sellers always took up for her babies, no matter what they did or how old they were. She loved her children and her husband, and I envied them.

"You must get on your knees and ask the Lord to forgive you," Mother directed. Mother had been known to call fornicators to the front of the church and exile them. Sister Becky, surprisingly, did not seem upset about the disclosure. Although barely fifteen and in her first semester of tenth grade, she'd been out looking for an apartment, and had even found one around the corner from the church on skid row. She was now working on decorating tips. Becky was fantasizing about becoming Mrs. Jeff Sellers.

Brother Sellers would have no part of a shotgun wedding for a son whose future he surely fantasized would be a hell of a lot better than his own. Brother Sellers had never finished elementary school. And as father to four of Sister Sellers' eight children, he never saw the need to marry her until they both got saved—and that didn't happen for five years after Sister Sellers had her eighth child by yet another man.

I looked at Brother Sellers; he was shaking his head no. I imagined him arguing to himself, *My son has promise. I want him to go to college and pursue his dreams of becoming a basketball star with the NBA.*

"Everybody makes mistakes," Jeff said again, not backing down.

Sister Becky, who wore a wry smile, looked like the cat that had secretly swallowed the prized canary. "I've alweady asked the Lowd to fowgive me, Sister Wobbets," she said. She had a cute little speech impediment which sounded something like a female version of Elmer Fudd, as she stood there wearing her hand-made, blue-polka-dot maternity top, her hands folded gingerly over her flat tummy. The five-foot mother-to-be was dwarfed by the six-foot-four father-to-be. She wore a matching polka-dot bow perched atop her long, black, wavy hair. She looked like a little china doll: sweet, innocent, and undefiled.

But the Lord—well, Lord Mother—had a plan. Jeff Sellers would be forced to marry Sister Becky, but only if Sister Becky did what she was told and followed Mother's every command. This, however, Sister Becky could not do. And as such, Mother—well, the Lord—let Brother Jeff off the hook.

A few weeks later, while the congregation was away in Omaha, Nebraska, preaching and singing the Word of God, Sister Becky and Brother Jeff remained behind. Brother Jeff had a basketball game or work or something that weekend, and Sister Becky continued to experience morning sickness. Well, as it turned out, neither of them really must have been sorry that Sunday when they had asked the Lord and the church to forgive them for their sin of fornication. Because as soon as the congregation was away, they were back at Becky's house fornicating again.

"Silly girl" is what Mother called her. "That's it. You just won't listen. Now, you'll never be married."

Brother Sellers and Jeff breathed a sigh of relief. When Becky's mother, however, realized there would be no wedding for her pregnant daughter, she placed her in a home for unwed mothers. Becky would have to sit out the tenth grade. After Becky gave birth, her mother forced her to give the baby up for adoption. Brother Jeff, on the other hand, continued to free-throw and slam-dunk Central High School to victory.

At some point along the way, my body began to develop without my noticing it. And out of the blue, Junior Baker noticed me.

I didn't realize it, though, until the time I was sitting next to him on a chartered bus ride back to Sioux City from a choir performance in Omaha, Nebraska. Someone had dared him and so he did it: he kissed me on the cheek and put his arm around me. Me! I couldn't believe it, and neither could my Cousin Peaches.

In fact, as soon as Junior Baker started showing a slight interest in me, she could not decide whether she wanted to continue to be Ralph Sellers' girlfriend or start anew with Junior Baker.

When it came to Ralph Sellers, there was no doubt about it—everybody wanted him. He was the best-looking guy in our church and had been the subject of most of the young girls' nightly prayers: "Lord, if you delay your Second Coming, could you please fix me up with Ralph Sellers?"

But Cousin Peaches was just plain greedy. She wanted them both. A few days later, when the church took us on a roller-skating outing, I saw Peaches green with envy as she watched Junior and I round the rink, arm and arm, during the couples-only skate. Actually, we made it only partially around the rink, because I kept falling and couldn't keep up with him. So, finally, he left me sprawled on the floor, and he skated off in the direction of Cousin Peaches. I was seething.

Not long after that, my sister Cynthia wrote to tell us she was getting married and asked us to come to Newark, New Jersey.

"It is not the Lord's will for you to marry Robert," Mother had informed the bride-to-be. But in Cynthia's usual defiant manner, she went forward with her wedding plans anyway. Cynthia used her mental defect to her advantage, to manipulate others and get her way. She would pretend that she was confused and didn't understand whatever directions she was given. She would agree as if she did understand, then do the exact opposite. Afterwards she'd say, "Oh, is that what you meant. I didn't understand that that was what you meant."

So Mother, Sister Gretchen, Linda, Ladybug, and I set off for Newark, New Jersey, but not before I left strict instructions with Cousin Peaches: "Leave Junior alone. He is my man." She was experienced and I wasn't. I knew if she gave him some, it would be all over for me.

It took three days to get to Newark.

"Look at all the Niggahs," Sister Gretchen quipped as we drove down Clinton Avenue in Newark.

"Sister Gretchen!" Mother scolded, pretending to be shocked at her language.

"Well, look at them," she laughed. "This place looks like a war zone. These Niggahs, excuse me, Negroes, have destroyed their own stuff. Look at this place."

It was true. The Negroes had set their stuff on fire to protest the death of Martin Luther King, and the city of Newark didn't bother to clean up the mess the rioters left. Burnt buildings were deserted and boarded up. Graffiti was everywhere. Trash piled high in the middle of sidewalks, spilled onto the streets. People walking past just ignored it, pretending it wasn't there. I couldn't understand why Daddy, Gloria, and Cynthia, or anybody, for that matter, would want to live in this mess.

We continued down Clinton Avenue to go to Gloria's apartment first. Gloria asked mother to stop by her house before she went to see Daddy. Gloria said she had something very important to tell Mother.

As Gretchen pulled the car to a stop in front of Gloria's apartment complex, we saw Booker coming down the stairs wearing his United States Postman's uniform. Tall, light-skinned, and handsome as ever, he smiled and waved at us.

Mother was reluctant to return the greeting. Despite Mother's attempts to keep them from each other, Booker had given up his career in the military to be with Gloria. But Gloria did not want to marry Booker. It was the Sixties; they didn't need a marriage certificate to legitimize their love, Gloria said. Gloria was free-spirited and she wanted to keep it that way. She had a good job. She worked for Prudential Insurance Company in downtown Newark. She sent money home to cover Ladybug's expenses and a little something for her sisters. But to Mother, that meant that now Gloria and Booker were living together in sin.

As we walked up to Gloria's apartment, we stepped around the trash on the ground along with the overhanging flies feasting on it. When we walked through the door, we found Gloria in her bedroom, sitting on the bed, smoking a cigarette.

Gloria had a beautiful sixties pad, and she was more glamorous than I'd remembered. Her hair was in a short Afro, and she wore large hoop earrings, makeup, and a mini skirt. She had incense burning and a soul music streamed from the radio station playing the Jackson Five in the background. As I listened to Michael Jackson and his brothers crooning "I Want You Back," I thought about Junior and our budding relationship.

When Linda carried in our two-year-old niece Ladybug, Gloria put out her cigarette and grabbed her baby. She showered her with kisses and began to sing to her.

Later, after we settled in, the conversation became serious.

"I am going to leave the baby here," Mother said, to everyone's surprise.

Linda and I protested. We had fallen in love with our little Bug, and the thought of her not returning home with us was unbearable. Mother kept other people's babies, while they were off finding themselves, so why not her own granddaughter? Linda and I were the ones the responsibility fell on. We did not mind. Gloria, however, said she wasn't ready to take the baby. She said she wished Mother had given her warning, because she and Booker needed time to prepare for a baby. Both of them had full-time jobs and, together, a full-time life. And their apartment was too small for a baby.

But Mother insisted. "If you and Booker are going to play house, then you need a baby to help complete your happy family," she said.

Then Gloria let us in on a surprise of her own.

"Daddy made an announcement in church a couple of Sundays ago," she said. "He told the congregation that the Lord said Sister Davis is his wife."

Mother showed no emotion. Gloria continued.

"Sister Davis is calling herself Sister Roberts now."

Still no reaction from Mother.

"That is not all." Gloria sighed. "Daddy has two more children."

Mother held her breath.

"Both Sister Davis and Sister Scott have had another baby by Daddy. Sister Davis had a little girl and Sister Scott a son. The babies are the same age."

I tried to picture two women walking around in Daddy's church, with big bellies, full of his babies. It was embarrassing. Daddy's life was a mess. No wonder we hadn't heard from him.

Sister Gretchen picked up a magazine and rolled it tightly. "Niggahs and flies!" she slammed the rolled magazine down on the coffee table. Then she lifted the magazine and looked underneath. "Gotcha!" She picked up the dead fly and tossed it in the wastebasket. "Excuse me. I mean Negroes and Flies. Ump! Ump! Ump!" Her words hug in the air, as it filled with silence.

Finally, Mother sighed, "Well, praise the Lord."

"Mother, you can't sleep with him . . ." Gloria said.

She, like the rest of us, knew Mother was a fighter. We knew Mother would go to Daddy just to prove to the other women that she could still have him if she wanted him.

"It is time to let him go, Mother," Gloria said.

"Get your father on the phone," Mother said.

Mother ended up sleeping with Daddy anyway and pretending nothing happened. In fact, she, Sister Davis, and Sister Scott all pretended that everything was normal. Daddy told Mother he still loved her and that she was still his wife. He told her he did not want a divorce.

"Niggahs is always lying," he said. "Them is none of my babies," he swore.

That was the last time I saw my parents together as husband and wife, though, legally, they would remain married for the rest of their lives.

As for Cynthia, Mother told her to hold off on the wedding and it wasn't the Lord's will for her to marry Robert. Cynthia listened to Mother and read along in the Bible where Mother showed her it wasn't the Lord's will. Cynthia asked questions, which Mother answered. Sister Gretchen confirmed it wasn't a good idea to marry someone she hardly knew. Finally Cynthia agreed with Mother, Sister Gretchen, and the Lord.

The next day Cynthia returned to Gloria's apartment carrying a beautiful, elaborate, white wedding gown with a long train and a set of wedding rings for her and Robert.

"Cynthia, what is this?" Mother asked in disbelief. "I thought we talked about this yesterday and you agreed this was not the Lord's will. I told you—you are not ready for marriage," Mother said as she rubbed her head in exasperation

"Oh, is that what you meant? I didn't know you meant not to buy the wedding dress and the rings," Cynthia said, while trying to play the retarded card.

Cynthia had a full-time job in Newark and made good money, which she saved while living with Daddy in the crowded house with Sister Davis and her family.

Robert was a black Muslim who sold newspapers and bean pies on the streets of Newark. Daddy said Robert was a Niggah and that he did not want his daughter marrying a Niggah. Especially a Black Muslim Niggah.

Both our parents agreed the marriage was not the will of God. In an effort to nip the whole thing in the bud, Mother told Cynthia to come to Sioux City, and she would throw a big wedding for her there—that is, if it was the Lord's will. And it would be the Lord's will if Robert followed Cynthia back to Sioux City, got saved, sanctified, and filled with the Holy Ghost, and got a job. Robert agreed.

We returned to Sioux City figuring Robert would be a no-show. We were wrong. Mother would marry them months later.

Back in Sioux City, I had returned to my own relationship problems. I left my potential man alone with my Cousin Peaches, and she had sexed him, and all was lost. So on my first day back to school, during first period, instead of listening to the boring biology teacher, I took out a piece a paper and began to pour out my feelings in a letter I wrote to Cousin Peaches. I wrote:

Dear Cousin Peaches,

> I hate you. I am crying, but not because I lost Junior
> to you. Rather, you were supposed to be my friend.
> You are my cousin. I asked you not to go after Junior
> because I am in love with him . . .

As I continued to pour out my heart and soul into the letter, I found it hard to hold back the tears. Finished, I folded it and wrote Cousin Peaches' name on the front. Then, with teary, blurred vision as well as blurred judgment, I handed the letter—and little did I know, my dignity as well—to my only confidante: my sister Linda. I trusted that she would, in turn, give the letter to Cousin Peaches, who would read it privately during the third-period study hall they shared.

What unfolded for me thereafter was what I have since deemed the Ten Cardinal Acts of Public Mortification:

First, Linda took it upon herself to open the letter and read it. Second, after reading it, instead of giving it to Cousin Peaches, Linda—who was then eighteen and in the twelfth grade—kept it the whole day, as she thought it would be necessary to first get Mother's approval to give the letter to my cousin. Third, Linda left school and walked two blocks over to Beverly Green's house, where, for the purpose of getting that permission, she called Mother and read it out loud to her in front of Beverly and her four teenage sisters.

Fourth and fifth, Mother directed Linda to give the letter to Cousin Peaches, which Linda did in front of the entire Baker family—all twelve of them, including Junior. Remembering his days as a lady's man before giving his heart to the Lord, Pastor Baker was proud to know his son was following in his footsteps. He boasted that women had always fought over him; now they were fighting over his sons.

Then, somehow, the Bakers' next-door neighbors, the Sellers, became apprised of my romantic entanglement. That was number six.

Seven: eventually, every member of Mt. Sinai had either read the letter personally or had heard about it.

I was so embarrassed I could have died. That made eight.

Nine: Mother never spoke to me about the letter—well, until much later. Of course, by the time she did, Cousin Peaches and I had already made up.

I had apologized to her in private for writing the letter. After all, I'd had to! It was a sin to be angry with anyone; you see, we were not supposed to express any of the emotions God gave us. And although Jesus had delayed his Second Coming, we were still under the impression he'd be back any day. If Jesus would return while I was holding a grudge against my cousin, I would burn in hell forever. So, if I wanted to go to heaven, I had to apologize, and I had to forgive her.

A month or two after the letter incident, Peaches and Junior became engaged, and a wedding date was quickly set. Peaches and Junior were sexually active and thus they had to get married. Peaches flaunted the engagement ring Junior bought her. I was green with envy and suffering from a broken heart. I smiled and acted like I was happy for them. During Sunday afternoon service, after the happy couple had announced their wedding, with the embarrassment of the letter far behind me, I found myself dancing in the Spirit beside the newly engaged couple.

In my euphoria, I was wonderfully out of control. I wanted to sit down, but the Spirit wouldn't let me. Perhaps I was dancing to let them know all was well within me. That I had now logged in the back of my subconscious mind the pain that came from knowing I had once loved Junior but he had not returned my affection. That I was hurt, but would get over it. Eventually. I was still pretty hurt but trying to pretend it didn't bother me.

As the music played, the saints stood dancing in the Spirit, praising the Lord. Mother sat in the pulpit, frowning down on us behind her cat-rimmed eyeglasses. Then she rose.

And that was number ten.

"Stop the music!" she commanded, with outstretched arms.

My heart began to race. I knew what was coming. I was dancing right out in front for everyone to see. I wanted to run out the door, but it was too late.

"Stay where you are, Sister Debra. Brother Junior and Sister Peaches, I want you to come up here."

I was becoming angrier by the second.

"This ain't right! It ain't right!" Mother announced. "You wrote that letter to Sister Peaches and now, here you are, dancing in the Spirit! It ain't right, and you aren't saved! Saints do not have any business writing trash like that. You aren't saved until you ask her to forgive you."

"I asked her to forgive me," I said, through gritted teeth.

"Don't talk back!" she screamed.

Cousin Peaches shook her head in affirmation. "She did apologize, Auntie. It's all right. We made up."

Both she and Junior looked painfully embarrassed for me.

"Well, that is not enough. She has to apologize to the church for her behavior."

Why do I have to apologize in front of the church, to the church, for something I did to Peaches? I wondered. Everybody was looking at me, even Linda, and I felt as though they were laughing at me. I looked like a fool.

"I am sorry," I mumbled to Junior and Peaches.

Both gave half-disconcerted smiles. Then the saints watched as I emotionally limped back to my seat and sat down. I hung my head low, totally humiliated.

At that moment, I both despised Mother and hated Linda. Linda was always after brownie points with Mother.

Why didn't Mother tell Linda to bring the letter home so we could have a mother-daughter talk about my feelings? Why didn't Linda say something to me? I sat thinking, massaging my black and blue emotions.

Next time Linda is on the toilet after crapping all over herself and asks me to get her a new roll of toilet paper, I am going to dunk it in water and throw it at her. I hope it lands in her poop! It will serve her right! Niggahs, flies, and wet toilet paper. Three things I can't stand! Ump! Ump! Ump!

The People of Nineveh

Sioux City
Christmas 1970

[B]y decree of the king [of Nineveh] . . . [l]et neither man nor beast, herd nor flock, taste anything: let him not feed, nor drink water . . . let them turn every one from his evil way, and from the violence that is in their hands. Who can tell if God will turn and repent, and turn away from his fierce anger, that we perish not?
—Jonah 3:6–9

The best Christmas I can remember was when I was sixteen years old. This was the first time Mother actually went out of her way to make it a merry one. Mother, Linda, and I decorated the house and the red cardboard chimney. We even hung lights in the window.

It was just the three of us. Cynthia was an old married lady (her fiance followed her to Sioux City and got saved), Gloria was still in Newark with Booker and Ladybug, and our house was free of guests.

The first week of Christmas break, I baked all kinds of goodies: cookies, fudge, colorfully decorated Christmas treats, and Rice Krispie bars. Cynthia dropped by and made her famous apple crisp. Mother went all out baking a turkey with all the trimmings.

At that time, two suitors were pursuing mother—Pop Samson and a middle-aged white man who owned a farm. Mother had no interest in either man.

The white man was a farmer. He would bring Mother fresh vegetables and fresh eggs and chickens. Then Pop Samson took us all to the movie *Oliver* and to dinner at the Biltmore. Before we got to the Biltmore, Mother told us they served smorgasbord.

"I don't like smorgasbord, Mother," Linda said adamantly. "I've had smorgasbord before. I don't like it. Can't we go somewhere else to eat?"

Mother humored Linda. We walked into the Biltmore to find buffet dining. We laughed at Linda, and she did too. It was obvious Linda didn't know what she was talking about. At eighteen, this was Linda's first introduction to buffet all you can eat dining—and mine too. I felt like we were a regular family then.

The next day was Christmas. I'd bought myself a new coat with a faux fur collar and had wrapped it and placed it under the fireplace. Mother actually purchased gifts for Linda and me too. She wrapped them, topped them off with brightly colored bows, and placed them at the base of our cardboard hearth. Linda's was an electric typewriter and mine was a record player.

The next night, we sat around watching television, eating leftover Christmas goodies, turkey, and dressing.

And then they showed up. Linda and I stayed in the living room, while Mother left to go answer the door.

"Praise the Lord, Sister Roberts," said the strange woman in our doorway.

"Come on in," Mother said, smiling. "What are you doing here?"

"The Lord sent us," they replied.

It turned out to be a minivan full of folks from Minnesota. These people hadn't called us first; they just dropped in out of the blue on their way back from Miracle Valley, a religious combine in Arizona. Miracle Valley was a Evangelical sect lead by Reverend A. A. Allen. People always returned from his meetings thinking God could raise the stone-cold dead from the cemetery. (I always wondered why anyone would want to raise someone after he or she had been buried.) Reverend Allen also was famous for casting out demons which he recorded and sold copies of the Exorcism and faith healing.

The lump of turkey lodged in my throat refused to go down, as the saints filtered into our living room. I was watching the *Flip Wilson*

Show, and he had just gotten to the funny part when they stood in front of the television and introduced themselves. I already knew Evangelist and Sister Dumpling and Sister Joe. Then there was Sister Diana, and two other people I had never met before.

"Well, praise the Lord," Mother said. "This is a surprise." Then she turned to Linda and me. "Get up, girls. Ya'll go fix up your rooms. Looks like the Lord sent us some company."

Fuming, I rolled my eyes.

Mother caught it, gave me that look, and then said,

"Debra, give your room to the Dumplings. You can bunk in the room with Linda and the girls." By "the girls," Mother meant Sister Diana, a woman I had never met before, and Joe.

Then Mother called Sister Barbara to see if she could take the other two women.

Little did I know then that that was only half of it. That night, I dreamed about eating the chocolate chip cookies I had baked, and so, naturally, the first thing I wanted to do when I woke up the next morning was to go do that very thing.

Unfortunately, though, while I had been sleeping, it seems Evangelist and Sister Dumpling had been conferencing with Mother, telling her that the Lord laid it upon their hearts to run a seven-day revival in conjunction with a seven-day fast. The Dumplings had several children of their own, who were in Minneapolis enjoying Christmas and eating whatever they wanted.

But for me, that meant no more Rice Krispie treats, no more chocolate chip cookies, no more rich dark-chocolate fudge, no more turkey sandwiches with dressing topped with cranberry sauce. No more eggnog. No more Christmas celebration. No going to the movies or visiting friends over the holiday. No! We had sinned and God was pissed off at us again for whatever it was we had done.

It was painful to watch Mother wrap all of the Christmas food in plastic and place it in the freezer.

In addition to the sins that we had committed and weren't aware of, we were also fasting for husbands. Sister Martie Baker and Sister Joe didn't have husbands yet, and Sister's Barbara's husband, Brother

Jack, had returned to the bottle not long after they'd been married. She kicked him out of the house because he'd tried to choke her. She told us that when it had happened, she said, "In the name of Jesus," and then proceeded to hit him in the head with a frying pan so hard that *she* saw stars swirling around his head. Then he'd staggered out of the apartment and down the stairs and disappeared. She hadn't seen him for months.

Then there was Sister Gretchen's husband, who we also had to pray for. When we returned from Newark after our most recent visit, Sister Gretchen was married off to a big ill-tempered dark man who hung around skid row. He wasn't an alcoholic, he was gainfully employed, and was saved long enough, by Mother's standards, to marry Sister Gretchen. He promptly move his new family to another small town in Iowa to get them away from Mother's controlling nature. Then he backslid and became abusive to Gretchen and her two children.

Before they'd moved, Gretchen's new husband had attacked Mother. He was the only man I'd ever known to strike Mother after she'd told him that "the Lord said" something unpleasant. No one else dared question whether the Lord really said what he said to Mother or not. If Mother said that the Lord said it, we accepted it as fact, and that settled it. We simply followed orders without question. After all, who were we to question God's word and the woman through whom he spoke it?

Anyway, God picked a fine time to be angry with us and proclaim a fast. Now I'd have to spend the rest of my Christmas vacation starving, in sackcloth and ashes, along with several other women and teenagers, in Sister Barbara's two-bedroom apartment.

I stocked up on breath mints and Juicy Fruit gum, eating them like food as we prayed around the clock and walked to church in the freezing cold every evening. In the shut-in for seven days and nights, we prayed at six A.M., noon, three P.M., six P.M., midnight, and three A.M., before a new cycle would begin again at six A.M.

The week of the revival, Evangelist Dumpling claimed he was led by the Lord to pray for people who had one leg shorter than the other.

Most of the people he prayed for were not even aware they had one leg shorter than the other.

I must admit I was skeptical at first. But when Evangelist Dumpling felt led to pray for hair growth, Sally Mae and I weren't taking any chances. We had always wanted long, flowing hair, and, now, what did we have to lose? Besides, I wanted to give God another chance to prove himself to me, since he still hadn't answered my "send my Daddy home" prayer.

When it was my turn to receive prayer, Evangelist Dumpling, who was tall and lanky, bent over close to me and whispered in my ear, "What do you want the Lord to do for you?"

"I want the Lord to bless my hair to grow," I said, feeling somewhat embarrassed.

"Raise your hands toward heaven," he said, as he took the bottle of olive oil from his wife, who was wearing a wig. (It didn't dawn on me until later that she didn't have any hair either.) He dipped his crooked right index finger into the bottle, like a quill into ink, and used it to make the sign of the cross on my forehead. Then he rubbed both hands in the remaining oil and raised them toward heaven.

"In the name of Jesus . . ."

Whomp! He smashed my head between his big, oily hands.

"I command you to loose her hair . . . and let it grow!" He pushed my head back.

Sally Mae stood patiently behind me, waiting her turn.

After Sally Mae was my cousin Peaches. Although Cousin Peaches had one deaf ear, this was not the reason she was seeking prayer. Not yet seventeen, the young wife of the man of my dreams—Junior Baker—was facing having a baby alone and getting a divorce. After they were married, Junior dropped out of high school and enlisted in the army. After finishing boot camp, he refused to send financial support to his wife and refused to have anything more to do with her. I suspect that he really did not want to marry Cousin Peaches in the first place but had been coerced by the church to do so. Now that he was outside the reach of Mother and Mt. Sinai, he could do as he pleased. Cousin Peaches had already gained twenty-five pounds or more, even though she was only a couple of months pregnant. She had gotten pregnant when she went to visit him after he completed boot camp. A few days of fasting would probably do her good.

When the evangelist asked Cousin Peaches about her prayer request, he noticed she had to tilt her head in order to hear him.

"Glory be!" he seemed to say to himself. His eyes widened with exhilaration. "She's deaf in one ear!"

This was Evangelist Dumpling's favorite thing to pray for in addition to the "one leg shorter than the other" healing. He did not ask her what she wanted prayer for.

He poured a glob of blessed oil in his hand, and then, without even taking the time to make a cross on Cousin Peaches' forehead, he rubbed his two hands, dripping in oil, together before smashing them down on poor Cousin Peaches' head. Then cupping her face, he stuck the long second finger of each of his hands in Peaches' ears.

He screamed in her good ear. "In the name of Jesus, I command you, you fowl devil, to loose this woman's ear and let her hear!"

I thought I saw Cousin Peaches squirm.

Then, in her religious fervor, Sister Dumpling, halitosis and all—we were fasting, and everybody had a bad case of halitosis—joined her husband in the "name of Jesus" chorus. Peaches crinkled her nose in distaste as they yanked and pulled on her head, his left finger acting like a cork in her right ear. Reeling and rocking, Cousin Peaches tried to keep her feet firmly planted on the ground, while they tried to push her body down to the floor. Finally she gave in and went down to the floor.

After the faith-healing service, the evangelist, who was a notoriously bad, long-winded preacher, failed miserably to deliver a message.

As an important side note, the evangelist's wife was a better speaker than he was—she had more insight, could tell a more interesting story, and wasn't long-winded—but, of course, God did not call women to preach. It was the same with most of the other wives. They were good preachers. They captured our imaginations. Sister Cee-Cee, for example, made the Bible downright fascinating. However, Sister Cee-Cee recognized her role as a wife, as did Evangelist Dumpling's wife and all the other sanctified wives—all except my mother.

My stomach growled while the evangelist preached. Then at some time during his two-hour sermon, my head begin to itch. This was a good sign, I thought. A sign that the miracle was working. I just knew that when I awoke the next morning, I would have a long, gorgeous, thick head of hair.

Later, after church, Sally Mae told me that her head had begun to itch, too. We carefully walked along the ice-slicked sidewalks to Sister Barbara's house, dreaming of the various new styles that we'd wear with our long, luxurious hair.

The next morning, however, I awoke to find my hair just as short and nappy as it had been the night before. I did not give up hope though, just as I had never given up hope that God would put my parents back together.

Finally, on the seventh day of our fast, at three P.M., we had a foot-washing service, after which we were allowed to eat soup and drink warm honey milk. I was happy to see the minivan fill up with the "saints of the most high" that evening and head out of town.

Sister Diana, Goddess of Love

Sioux City
Christmas 1970

[T]he temple of the great goddess Diana should be despised and her magnificence should be destroyed . . . when they heard these sayings, they were full of wrath and cried out, saying, "great is Diana."
—Acts 10:24–28

S ister Diana was a beautiful, high-yellow Creole woman. She wore no makeup on her flawless face. She had large, brown eyes and perfect, naturally arched eyebrows, which complemented her thick, jet-black Afro.

Purity, virginity, and Christianity were the virtues she epitomized. Her obvious destiny would have been to become a nun; however, because she knew all Catholics went to hell, Sister Diana had found "the right door and entered therein." When the Lord had called her, Sister Diana had been on the verge of graduating from law school and living in sin with her boyfriend.

Originally from New Orleans, Sister Diane taught me how to cook. French toast, French-quarter style, and Southern fried chicken were her specialties. (Mother never taught us how to cook. What I learned about cooking, I gleaned from our house guests.)

Sister Diana adorned herself in white nurse dresses and shoes. She frowned on women wearing pants. She never watched television, read the paper, or read any books except the Bible.

But I was never intimidated by her holier-than-thou-ness. She was like a mother to me. Her gentle, caring spirit comforted me and encouraged me as I would have expected my own mother to do.

On the other hand, Sister Diana was also weird. Very weird. Many times, I'd walk in on her and find her in the trance I'd seen the night Sister Joe had been full of the devil. This scared the daylights out of me.

She would lay prostrate on the bed or the floor, her hands folded across her chest and her eyes wide open, staring at the ceiling without blinking. Her breathing was shallow; I could barely see her chest moving. She almost looked dead. A couple of times, I was tempted to place a mirror under her nose to see whether I should call the coroner.

She would stay this way for a long time and then, when she would awake, she'd say the Lord had given her a vision or had told her to do something.

The weirdest of these trances, by far, however, happened the day she awoke and said the Lord had told her to call Mother her husband and had said that Mother was to call Sister Diana her wife.

"*What?*" I, of all people, knew that Mother desperately needed someone to look after her. She had a full-time job and a full-time ministry. Mother definitely needed help. But why this? Why give room to the devil? Why give people something to talk about?

It was weirder still when Mother accepted Sister Diana's message from the Lord. What was Mother thinking? Especially when she knew the rumors that had floated around about her all my life—those rumors that Mother was a lesbian.

Even Daddy had said that she didn't like men. He'd said that she had wanted to be a man. He'd said he'd thought she was a man. Why on earth would Mother add fuel to the fire by allowing this beautiful young woman to call herself Mother's wife and my own Mother her husband?

And as if that weren't bad enough, Sister Diana began combing Mother's hair every day and setting it in rollers, as Mother had never known the first thing about styling hair—hers or ours. Then every night, Sister Diana helped Mother dress for work and sent her off with a hug and a kiss on her cheek. She made sure the uniforms Mother wore were cleaned and pressed. She even made Mother take her vitamins and eat properly.

I was all for Mother finally having someone, but I was also very jealous of Sister Diana. Mother had never had time for me or my sisters, because she'd been so busy with her ministry. Now, Sister Diana monopolized Mother's time, and, in turn, Mother monopolized Sister Diana's time. I felt more left out than ever.

In my heart, however, I realized that Sister Diana really loved my mother and took very good care of her. And I realized that Mother needed desperately to be loved that way.

Just as I began to accept that and to think that everything was well and good, however, Sister Diana scooted together the twin beds in Mother's room to create a single bed for the two of them.

I went into shock. *What the heck is this?* I wondered.

Then to top it all off, the two of them exchanged gold bands. Now what was I supposed to think? The word *confused* doesn't even begin to describe it. My mind was zooming in circles like a race car at the Indy 500.

The only thing I knew for sure was that not only didn't it feel right, but it didn't look right either. I mean, what would other people think? Didn't the Bible say something about "avoiding the appearance of evil"?

And what would happen to Mother and Sister Diana if they died right then? That is, if fornication and adultery were sins that sent you to the Lake of Fire, then what would God do to you if you were a lesbian?

"Lord, correct me if I am wrong," I began to pray often. "And forgive me for thinking evil."

After a while, I would no longer allow myself to think about it. I carried on, pretending I did not see or hear anything—that is, if there was anything to see or hear. The point was I didn't know and I didn't want to know. I just went to school and worked full time and kept myself busy, because the more I avoided the situation, the better. And yet, as hard as I tried not to think about it, somewhere deep inside, I still did—constantly.

One day, as I past the closed door to their bedroom, I heard soft whispering. I knew the doorknob to that room had a large keyhole through which you could see, because I'd used it on many occasions to spy on my sexually active sister Cynthia. I wanted desperately to look through the keyhole now to find out the truth for myself.

I paused at the door and studied it, debating what to do. *What if what they say is true?* I thought. *What if what Daddy has been saying all these years was right? But do I really want to know? What would I do if it were true?* Then, something inside me said, *You don't want to know! You don't want to know!* I raced down the stairs and out the front door.

Some things are better left alone, I thought, *and this is definitely one of them.*

The Making of a Harlot

Sioux City
Spring 1972

[T]hou didst trust in thy own beauty and playest the harlot.
—Ezekiel 16:15 (KJV)

By the twelfth grade, I began to realize just how shallow my faith was. It seemed contingent on material things like clothes, makeup, and my high school prom.

Maybe it was because it was 1972, and manufacturers were producing beautiful imitation designer clothes. I remember walking into Lerner's and seeing rows and rows of short skirts, miniskirts, micro-minis, hip huggers, and see-through blouses—none of which I could wear because I professed to be saved, sanctified, and filled with the Holy Ghost.

I also wanted to wear wigs and makeup. Through a bit of secretive experimentation, I had discovered that with a little bit of makeup, the curly Afro wig Linda had sent me from Los Angeles, and modern clothes that fit me, I was pretty.

But you can't be pretty and live for God, I thought, as I reached for the miniskirt and then headed back to the dressing rooms. I thought God was forcing me to make a choice. *Look cute or be saved? Do I want God or the miniskirt?*

I looked at myself in the mirror. I was slim, and I had a nice, round butt, long legs, and small, perky breasts. The miniskirt was six inches above my knees—too short by Mother's and Mt. Sinai's standards, but too long for the rest of the world.

"Oooh, that looks cute on you," said the store clerk, peeking through the curtain. "I know just the blouse to wear with it," she said, as her head disappeared.

I must admit, I did look good in the skirt. I stared back at my reflection until she returned with a see-through white blouse.

"You wear a camisole underneath," she said, handing it to me.

It was a little white slip of a shirt, and I knew there was no way Mother or Mt. Sinai would approve of it. Still, it looked good.

As I handed the clerk the money for my new ensemble, bells and whistles were going off in my head to the tune of *You can't wear that! God is going to get you! You're sinning!*

I fought back. *It's okay to wear this and be saved. Get thee behind me, Satan!*

But the condemning voices kept shouting at me, telling me I was sinning and that Mother and Diana would certainly not approve.

When I got home, I hid the bag in the back of my closet, where it sat for two weeks before my conscience got the better of me and forced me to return the items. For the next month, I thought about the clothes I had almost worn and about how I was tired of the list of restrictions. What was the point of even trying? It seemed I could never please God, Mother, and Mt. Sinai anyway. Nothing I did, no matter how well intended, was ever right.

I was not alone in feeling guilt, insecurity, and hopelessness. By that time, most of my peers at Mt. Sinai had fallen by the wayside. They had become weighted down with the guilt that came from trying to live a saved, sanctified, and filled-with-the-Holy-Ghost life and then, inevitably, failing miserably at it.

We were torn: we were terrified of God and what he might do to us should we cross him, yet we knew that there was nothing we could do to please him anyway. God, we had learned, was impatient, short-tempered, and judgmental. He sat on his throne, with his notepad and that pencil with a big eraser on the end, watching our every move, just waiting for one of us to mess up, so he could erase our name from the Book of Life. Just waiting for one of us not to repent and turn from our evil ways, so that one of these days, he could let something horrific and deadly happen to us.

And meanwhile, in the process of our trying to be perfect, we had all somehow missed our youth. We had been sent into the adult world equipped only with the knowledge that there was no pleasing God, and therefore, most of us just threw in the towel and walked away—all of us, in fact, except for Linda, Martie, and Cousin Peaches. Martie and Linda were too sick to sin.

At sixteen, my best friend Sally Mae dropped out of school and ran away from home after one beating too many. For a long time no one knew where she was.

Becky left the Lord too. For a while after her baby was born, Becky returned to the Lord, to Mt. Sinai Holiness, and to Central High School as a sophomore. This was about the time Sister Diana took her and Martie Baker into our house, right before Martie got married.

But then Becky began to date my Cousin Albert. Sister Diana forbade the two of them to date. Once, right before Valentine's Day, Sister Diana even forced Becky, against her will, to return Albert's tokens of affection—a box of chocolates and a romantic card. Albert was crushed.

Becky left our house, however, and the two of them left the church. Right away, Becky became pregnant with Cousin Albert's child.

By that time, Cousin Peaches was an old married lady and a mom. Junior had long since escaped from his wife and Mt. Sinai by way of the army, and he no longer wanted to be saved or married. When he came home on leave he wanted nothing to do with his wife or his son. He also didn't want to go back to the army. He became a deserter and a pimp. Cousin Peaches remained loyal to the church anyway, hoping that God would return her wayward husband.

By the time I was a senior; all my friends and acquaintances were gone. At first, it didn't matter because I was too busy to notice. In the morning, I attended school. After school, I worked full time as a nurse's aide at Gordon Memorial Hospital. I had to walk ten miles to get there from school and, after completing my shift at eleven P.M., walk five miles home, unless one of the other aides offered me a ride. I hardly studied because I didn't have time.

I could barely stay awake in class either. Taking No Doze in the morning and sleeping pills at night helped me maintain my school routine. After working full time for eight months, my hours were reduced because one of the regular nurse's aides needed more hours after her husband died. I finally had some free time and money in my pocket. But I didn't have anyone to hang out with because all my friends were dropouts or pregnant. I wanted my freedom, but I did not want God to be angry with me for having it or enjoying it. The conflict was driving me crazy—literally. But as fate would have it, I wasn't the only one.

Len Sellers, like me, had been told he had a calling on his life. At least that's what the saints all said. They had said God was calling him to be a preacher, and both Mother and Sister Sellers had confirmed it.

Thereafter, Len Sellers had tried to live "the life," but he blew it. Len was a junior in high school, same as me, when he confided in Mother that he felt he was losing his mind. (I had also felt I was losing my mind, but I did not confide in Mother.) Mother had told him that the Lord was calling him to come higher, which meant more prayer, more fasting, and more church. Meanwhile, Sister Diana had felt led by the Lord to invite him to move in with us.

Len had slept on a twin bed in our dining room because Linda had still been at home and Martie hadn't been married off to Brother Clyde yet.

Len had only been staying with us for a week or so, when Becky and Sally Mae and I ran into Cynthia on our way home from school. Cynthia, although married and living with her husband in a small one-bedroom apartment, spent most of her time at Mother's house; she and Robert Houston were having intense problems. Cynthia was waiting for us at the corner of Market and Sixth, and when we got there, she immediately started complaining about Len's behavior. Len had said something out of line to her. She was rambling on about it when he suddenly appeared out of nowhere.

"Hi, Debra," Len said. He had a strange look in his eyes and he was sweating profusely. He seemed agitated and hyper; Len was usually shy and reserved. Fear suddenly gripped my heart and a sickly feeling took over my stomach. I had seen that look before.

I had seen that look a few years before, when Brenda Jackson had burst into our house, sweating profusely and wearing the same strange look in her eyes. Brenda was a white country girl, shy and introverted. She never spoke two words to anyone.

"Have no fear! Jesus is here!" Brenda shouted as she entered our house. She blabbered so much that no one could shut her up.

"Look at my hands," she had said, as she held her palms out to me. "See where the nails were? Do you see the blood?"

Later, Brenda had been heavily sedated and sent to Iowa City Mental Hospital.

"Hi, Len," I said cautiously.

He began to quote strange scriptures from the Bible. Cynthia immediately took the defensive and began to argue with him.

"Cynthia!" I tried to give her the eye and I shook my head. But Cynthia would argue with a tree. She refused to drop the subject.

"And another thing, Len . . .," she went on.

Len did not seem to hear what Cynthia was saying. He skipped off down West Sixth Street, yelling something like, "The end is near!"

"Cynthia!" I shouted. "I think Len has had a nervous breakdown!"

I kept trying to get Cynthia's attention, but she was on a rampage. Just then, Mother drove up in her gold Plymouth. Sister Diana was sitting in the front passenger seat.

I ran over to the car and shouted into the window. "Mother! Len is crazy. He is acting strange!"

"Oh," Mother said with low affect. "Well, praise the Lord."

"He went down that way!" I pointed in the direction that I had last seen Len hopping, skipping, and twirling around.

Mother turned off the engine and removed the key from the ignition, as though nothing were happening. I thought it strange that she did not even perk her ears up, let alone go after him to make sure he was okay. So I continued, just in case she had not understood what I was trying to convey to her.

"He just went down West Sixth Street, shouting, 'The end is near!'"

Mother opened the driver's door and stepped out. So I looked at Sister Diana. She just sighed demurely, with a pious, angelic countenance, and walked into the house. Then it dawned on me: they didn't care because it was church night. They didn't have the time to care. They had to go straight in and get changed so they wouldn't be late.

Nothing ever, ever, ever stopped church night at our house—not even the fact that the teenage boy who lived with us had just suffered a nervous breakdown and was last seen wandering down the street screaming.

When Len finally found his way back home in a delusional state, Mother and Sister Diana told him to get dressed and meet them at church. As soon as I saw him, I darted out the back door.

Len showed up late for church. He floated into the sanctuary in a world of his own, smiling, sweating profusely, and greeting the congregation. I immediately grabbed my Bible and placed it over my stomach.

Mother hadn't bothered to tell the Sellers that their son had suffered a nervous breakdown or was possessed by demons. But if they hadn't already suspected as much, they were sure to soon find out.

As the service progressed, Len's demons got the better of him. In the middle of the sermon, Len got out of his pew, lay on the floor, and began to slither across the floor like a snake. Sister Sellers gasped in horror and threw her hand up to her mouth. Rita and Rene Sellers began to cry. Brother Sellers and Rickie Jr. sat there stone-faced. Len's older sister, Sister Cee-Cee, began crying, "The blood of Jesus," as did the rest of the congregation.

Hissing like a snake, Len's tongue darted in and out of his mouth. Then, using his mouth for suction, he continued his journey across the floor. Sister Sellers could not take it anymore. She jumped up to leave. Rita and Rene were right by her side.

"Sit down, Sister Sellers," Mother ordered from the pulpit.

Except for Len's hissing, the church was silent. Sister Sellers and her two daughters stood frozen.

"You think we want to watch your son, and you get to leave? I said sit down!"

Sister Sellers and her daughters held their ground. Brother Sellers rose to be by his wife's side. Together, the Sellers stood in the exact middle of the church, halfway between the pulpit and the door, ready to make their escape but afraid to do so.

Mother was glaring at them and pointing a dark finger in their direction. "Both of you sit down now."

I saw Rita and Rene trying to convince their mother to leave. I saw everyone crying, except for Mother and Sister Diana, while Len continued his reptilian rendition, hissing and slithering underneath the pews.

It was too bad about Len. He was the handsomest boy in the church and the smartest. From the moment I had first met him, when we were both six, I had been secretly praying that God would bless me with him as a husband.

Len Sellers was brilliant. He made straight A's throughout school. And he was tall—six foot five—with jet-black, silky straight hair. I just knew our babies would be gorgeous and they would never have to ask God to bless their hair to grow.

And despite what the saints said about his calling into the ministry, Len was planning to become a doctor. He was half Indian, and, as such, his college education would be free. I had always looked forward to becoming a rich doctor's wife. I did not want to be married to a man who crawled on the floor, hissing like a snake.

Finally, Sister Sellers fell onto the pew crying inconsolably. Her family stood by her trying to comfort her.

The deacons gathered Brother Len off the floor and sat him down on a chair. The saints who were not afraid of Len and his demons formed a circle around him and began to pray.

Len's demons were much stronger than their faith and God's power that night. When church let out two hours later, Len left the church still thinking he was a snake and threatening to kill his brother, Rickie, Jr., if he caught him alone. The Sellers went home; Mother and Diana left in Mother's gold Plymouth with Candy, who needed a ride home; and I, who would've ordinarily walked home with Linda, Becky, and Martie, dove into the backseat just as the car was pulling away from the curb. Linda, Becky, Martie, and a very pregnant Cousin Peaches stayed behind to make sure Len got to our house all right.

"*Our* house?" I shouted to Mother in the car. "Why can't Len go to his own house? Shouldn't we call somebody?"

I wondered why no one would call the paddy wagon or something. Brenda had been hospitalized and medicated, and now she was fine. Why didn't they do the same for Len?

Mother was too cool and calm. After dropping off Sister Candy, she drove to our house. Just as we pulled up to the curb, I saw Len walking through our front door, followed by Linda and the gang.

Sister Diana opened the door and got out while the motor was still running. Mother stayed put.

"Aren't you coming in?" I asked Mother. I was glued to the backseat.

"Honey, I've got to go to work." Mother was looking straight ahead with both hands on the wheel.

"But . . . but . . . I don't want to go in there with Len. He's crazy!"

The situation, as I saw it, was this: Len was either possessed by the very devil himself or Len had suffered a nervous breakdown. Either opinion led me to the same conclusion: I was terrified of Len and didn't want to be in the same house with him.

"Get out of the car," Mother commanded. "I'm running late and I have to go."

"But, Motherrrr," I whined, staring at the back of her neck.

"Listen. Get out of the car. You are so brave during the day. Now get out of my car with your evil, mean self!"

"Mother, I am afraid to go in there." I was stalling as I tried to think of somewhere to go. Mother was getting frustrated by the minute.

Sister Diana, still standing outside the car waiting for me, could see it. She opened the back passenger door and reached for my hand. "Come on, Debra. It will be all right. God is with us."

I didn't know about that. God hadn't been able to deliver Len at church earlier. How was he going to take care of me now?

As I got out and watched Mother drive away, I was in tears and my stomach was in knots. When I got into the house, I ran quickly upstairs, past my own room, and into Linda's bedroom, which she then shared with Becky and Martie. Cousin Peaches and Sallie Mae were there as well. They were all sitting on the beds in shock. No one said anything.

Then, down the stairs, we heard Len start up again.

"Debraaa!" he called to me. "Debraaa!"

Terror struck me.

Then he continued chanting my name in a husky voice. "Debra! Debra! Debra!"

Sister Diana emerged from the room she shared with Mother. Hearing her, we opened our door to peek out and see what was going on. We found Sister Diana peering over the banister down the stairs.

"Len?" Sister Diana called. "Len, what do you want? Stop calling Debra."

Len did not answer. He just kept chanting my name in that voice.

"Jesus, help us," Sister Diana prayed as she disappeared down the stairs. For a moment, there was silence. Then we heard her scream.

"Oh my God, Len! Stop that right now! Put your clothes back on. The blood of Jesus! Satan, the Lord rebukes you! Len! Len!"

Then we heard Sister Diana come flying back upstairs. When she was about mid-flight, we ducked into the room and slammed the door shut. A few seconds later, Sister Diana burst through the door and closed it behind her, resting her back against it. She was breathless. I had never seen her excited.

"Wha-wha-what does he want?" I asked. "Wha's he doin'?"

Sister Diana took a deep breath. "He's naked and he is masturbating."

"Masturbating?" I asked.

188

"Ecck!" Linda said, frowning.

"He is playing with himself and calling your name," Sister Diana replied.

Everybody looked at me like I had something to do with it. As far as I knew, Len never noticed me. I had no idea he masturbated, let alone the fact that he thought of me when he did. I would have been flattered if it had been under different circumstances and wasn't so terrified.

"Well, don't let him come in here," I said. "I don't want to see him naked."

I had never seen a naked man before. But having been attracted to Len's fully clothed body, I have to admit, I now wondered what he looked like without them.

We could now hear him calling to me from the bottom of the stairs. He was moving closer. Linda, Martie, and I sat on the floor, silent and nervous. Becky sat on the bed crying.

Finally, I pleaded, "You've got to stop him!"

"I can't stop him by myself," Sister Diana said.

"Cousin Peaches, since you've seen a man naked before, you go help Sister Diana get him back in his clothes," Linda suggested.

Becky had seen a naked man before, as well, but she appeared to be too overwhelmed with the situation. Cousin Peaches, on the other hand, was calm. And so it was decided.

We squeezed Cousin Peaches and Sister Diana out the door and closed it quickly behind them. Then I began to panic and cry. I was about to be raped, and there was no way out unless I jumped out the second-story window.

I was angry with Mother, to say the least. She should have been there to protect me or, at least, should have called the hospital and had Len committed. Not to mention the fact that Len had a big father and big brothers who could have watched him that night.

But instead, Mother felt it best to leave a crazy, six-foot-something, two-hundred-and-something-pound, deranged teenage boy alone in the house with her teenage daughters, one of whom was about to be raped.

After what seemed an eternity, Cousin Peaches and Sister Diana knocked lightly on the door.

"It's us," I heard them say.

Linda reached to open it.

"Don't!" I snapped. "Ask them where Len is."

Linda opened the door partially.

"Don't," I begged through clenched teeth.

"Where's Len?" she asked. Then she nodded and opened the door.

I was ready to jump out the window the minute I saw Len's face. They said they had subdued him and prayed over him. He wasn't asleep, but at least he was fully clothed.

I did not sleep that night or the next couple of nights, until Len was put on the paddy wagon and sent to the mental hospital in Iowa City.

Later, assuming that Len's breakdown was God's punishment for his past bad deed, I shared everything I knew about him with Mother. I told her about the time Len, my cousins, and about six other boys pulled a train on a twelve-year-old white girl. I told her that it had happened years ago, but felt that God had been patiently waiting in the wings to get even with him. After all, God may forgive you, but he certainly would not forget. No bad deed goes unpunished.

"What's a train?" was Mother's only response.

"Each boy took a turn with her. There were about ten of them."

"Did they rape her?" Mother asked.

"No! In fact, after they were through, she invited Len, Cousin Samuel, and two other boys to her house to do it to her again."

"Ummm," Mother mulled that over.

For the next year or so, Len was in and out of the mental ward. When he came home, heavily medicated, he looked nothing like the Len Sellers I had secretly fallen in love with.

I admit my religious convictions were shallow. If I betrayed God would he allow the 'crazy demon' to take over my soul? I was already starting to feel as though I was losing my mind.

But fashion statements aside, I was also having a tough time backsliding because Gloria had returned home, the epitome of the prodigal son: a beaten, dejected, wretched sinner.

Early one February morning, she and four-year-old Ladybug showed up on our doorstep just like that. It was evident something was troubling Gloria before she even said anything. Then she told us she had felt as though she were going to die or lose her mind.

So in the middle of the night, she had slipped out of the house with her daughter and boarded a plane to Sioux City, looking to Mother for guidance and to Mt. Sinai for the Lord. She deliberately did not tell her husband where she was going.

Once she found the Lord, Gloria was never the same person I'd known as a child. She was passive and timid. She asked Mother for direction in everything from what to wear to what to eat and where to go.

On Thursday evening, during the testimony service, as Gloria described her life of sin to the people sitting in church, my heart filled with excitement. If she was trying to deter me from backsliding—forget it! She had done just the opposite. Gloria testified about the illegal abortions she had had and how the second one had done something to her uterus so she could never have children again. She described the wild parties, the orgies, and the drugs.

I sat there drooling. I couldn't wait till I turned eighteen, joined the navy, and got away from Sioux City. But I would be different. I would not get pregnant by a married man on purpose, as Gloria had done. Gloria told us she told Booker not to use a condom when she had gotten pregnant because she had been sick of the navy and pregnancy was her only ticket out.

She also testified that, once, she'd smoked what she thought was marijuana, but someone had spiked it with LSD. She woke up in the middle of the night, hallucinating, seeing visions of skeletons, demons, and witches. Then another night, when she was at a party, she said she'd heard herself saying, "Woe! Woe! Woe!" But she hadn't known why. It frightened her so much that she felt it was God's way of calling her and telling her to come back to him before it was too late.

One of the deepest fears of the Pentecostal backslider is not only that you will die before you have a chance to return to God, but that God will call you back to him just before the time of your predetermined death. We felt God knew we could not live a saved, sanctified life on earth, and so he would call us to return to him just before our death. Then, as soon as you were re-saved, God would kill you off before you had a chance to backslide again. We had seen it happen many times before, especially with the winos.

Now just twenty-five, Gloria did not want to die. It was a typical Pentecostal sentiment; we always talked about going to heaven, but we didn't want to die to get there. We were afraid of death. In Gloria's case, after she became saved, sanctified, and filled with the Holy Ghost, she stopped living because she was afraid of dying.

To pay penance for all the wrong she had done, Gloria began wearing dresses two sizes too big, which she had purchased from the Goodwill, and a mismatched Aunt Jemima scarf on her head. She put away her makeup, her jewelry, and her zest for life.

Then Mother told Gloria that her marriage to Booker was not right in the sight of God, and she made her get it annulled.

"But Mother," I said, trying to reason with her. "What about the couples you married who were already married to someone else? How is it different?"

Mother did not have an answer, and Gloria did not have the strength to fight. She simply went with Mother to her lawyer's office and did as she was instructed. I tagged along out of curiosity.

After discussing the annulment, the lawyer had just started in on the topic of child support and visitation rights, when Mother interrupted him with, "We don't want any."

Gloria shot a quick glance in Mother's direction.

"No. I mean, yes. I want child support," Gloria responded, timidly.

"No," Mother said adamantly. "We don't want anything to do with Booker."

I shook my head as I watched my big sister cave in yet again.

I had to say something. "Why wouldn't she want child support?"

"The Lord said don't ask for it," Mother replied.

Anytime Mother wanted things to go her way but did not have a good explanation for it, she blamed her position on the Lord, because no one would dare argue with what the Lord said. Except for me.

"Why would the Lord tell you not to accept child support?" I asked.

Mother ignored me. Gloria hung her head low. What could she say? She had already made a fine mess of her life. Perhaps she thought that if she listened to Mother, this time things would turn out better.

After that day, Mother intercepted all letters and phone calls from Booker. I was angry with her for everything she was doing to my big sister. I was ashamed of my big sister for letting Mother do it to her. I vowed that when I turned eighteen, I'd show them how to live the life of a sinner the right way and be good at it.

It was April 23, 1972, and I had just turned eighteen. Only two more months and I would graduate from high school. I had big plans. I was determined to get away from Mother and Mt. Sinai.

After cashing my paycheck, I returned to Lerner's and gathered the new line of spring fashions. I paid for two sheer blouses, three miniskirts, and several pairs of bell-bottom pants. I stopped by the local grocery store and picked up a package of Kool's cigarettes, which I stuffed into my shopping bag along with the other contraband of sin.

When I got home, Mother, Sister Diana, and Gloria were sitting in the living room. Sister Diana was reading the Bible, while Mother and Gloria were watching television.

"Mother," I said. My stomach was in knots. "I do not want to be saved anymore."

There, I'd said it.

Sister Diana's hands flew to her mouth and she began to cry softly. I think I saw Gloria's eyebrow flinch.

Mother shook her head slightly. "Okay. But you still have to go to church on Sundays."

"Okay," I said. Then taking the stairs two at a time, I ran to my bedroom and closed the door behind me. I climbed into my bed, pulled my bedspread over my head, and fell into a deep sleep.

The Evangelical's Daughter

Sioux City
Summer 1972

*Therefore, said I, "Look away from me; I will weep bitterly, labor not
to comfort me, because of the spoiling of the daughter of my people."*
—Isaiah 22:4

B. J. Green, Cookie's older sister, had a bad reputation. She had had two children out of wedlock, and most people believed her to be a prostitute. Her house was decorated to the nines with colorful throw pillows and love beads. Black and psychedelic lights strewn throughout added to the ambiance. The sounds of Motown filled her house, as did the aroma of soul food. B. J.'s crash pad was a magnet, especially for outcasts like me. After I had decided to backslide, her place had become my hangout when I did not have to work or go to church.

B. J. always had money. She had the uncanny ability to stretch her monthly welfare check as far as it would go. And she was as generous as she was large. I knew she would have made someone a great wife. And I knew for a fact that B. J. was not a prostitute.

Sally Mae, my best friend, dropped out of school and ran away from home when she was sixteen after her father beat her for something she said she did not do. She was living with B.J. and her two children. She was a live in babysitter. B. J. treated her like a younger sister. A couple of months after Sally Mae disappeared, and no one knew where she was, B. J. called Sally Mae's parents and assured them that she was all right and was living with her.

I understood why Sally Mae went to live with B.J. Her home was the only place I felt comfortable being by myself or finding myself. And besides, her older brother Jason was usually there.

I hadn't seen Jason since I'd been ten, and back then I hadn't known that he was B. J.'s brother. I was standing in B. J.'s kitchen talking to her and Sally Mae. We were drinking Boone's Farm Strawberry Wine, smoking Kool's cigarettes, and listening to the Dells. B. J. was standing over a hot stove, frying pork chops.

I could smell him before he entered the room, the sweet, musky aroma of Brut—my favorite.

"B!" he called out. His voice was soft in a manly sort of way.

"In here, Jason," B. J. replied.

I could hear the clickety-clack of Jason's four-inch platform shoes approaching. When he entered the room, he took my breath away, just like he had eight years before.

The first time I'd met him, I'd been lying on the couch watching television, nappy-headed and covered in dirt and sweat from a day of playing. He'd knocked on the door, and Linda and I had both run to open it. We found Jason standing there in his green army uniform. He greeted us with a warm, sexy smile that revealed a gold front tooth.

"Hi," he said. His voice was soft with a hint of a Southern accent. "Is Beverly here?"

Beverly Green had been living with us at the house on Fourteenth Street at the time, along with several other married women whose husbands were away in Vietnam. Beverly's baby was his niece and she had just been born.

"No, she is at church," Linda replied. "Do you know where the church is?"

"No. That's okay. Just tell her Jason Green dropped by to see her."

Only, when he said Jason, Linda and I both heard James. Beverly's husband's name was James Green, and he had been stationed with the army in Vietnam. Once a month, he'd send a government savings bond and a support check for his wife and daughter.

When Jason left, Linda and I couldn't contain ourselves. We thought Beverly's husband was finally home from Vietnam. We raced out of the house and down the hill ten blocks to our church. We slipped in the back and, right in the middle of the service, sneaked up the aisle to find Beverly.

"Your husband is home," we whispered excitedly.

Beverly was calm.

"Really?" she said. "Are you sure?"

"Yes!" Linda said, trying to keep her voice low. Mother was looking over at us. "He just left the house."

"What did he say?" Beverly asked.

"He said to tell you he was home and that he'd be back," I replied.

"Did he tell you his name?"

"Yes!"

"Did he say James or Jason?"

Linda and I thought about it for a moment.

"I think he said Jason," I finally said.

"Oh. That's what I thought. My husband's name is James. Jason is his twin brother," Beverly said, smiling.

"Oh," Linda said.

We felt foolish. We were also stuck. Mother ordered us to sit down and stay until the service was over.

During the ensuing years, Jason married a young woman and had several children, some of whom had died in infancy. I remembered that because Mother had been called on many times to pray for the health or officiate the burial of their infants. But we had long since lost contact with Jason Green.

Now, suddenly, our paths were crossing again. It was fate.

Jason stood in the doorway looking at me and talking to B. J. Unlike her siblings, B. J. was short, black, and heavy. Everybody else in the family was light-skinned or high yellow, like Jason. He was wearing crushed velvet, maroon bell bell-bottoms and a matching floor-length vest. Five foot nine in his stocking feet, he rarely went anywhere without wearing his platform shoes.

We were about the same height these days, when he was shoe-less. At one hundred nineteen pounds and five foot eight, I had finally come into my own.

Back in those days, a black man was judged by two things: the size of his hands and the size of his Afro. He had large hands and a huge Afro. He also had an incredible smile, his lips spreading slowly to reveal his trademark—a gold front tooth.

"Hi," he finally said, moving toward me.

My heart leaped into my throat. Here was the ideal person to teach me about "the world." I had been looking for someone to do just that ever since I had decided to backslide. I needed someone to show me the life that had been glamorized so many times in church whenever ex-prostitutes, drug dealers, pimps, criminals, and alcoholics got saved and then described every sordid detail of their wayward lives in their testimonials. Whenever I heard one of those stories, I couldn't wait until I was old enough to experience for myself. Then after stocking up on life's experiences and getting a few sins under my belt, I would return to the Lord, just as they had (if it wasn't too late). I'd be taking a huge chance, but it all sounded too good to pass up.

Now, I had my chance. And who better than Jason to teach me the ropes? Jason epitomized "the world." He was everything the church and Mother had always told me to stay away from.

Later that night, Sally Mae and Jason and I were back in B. J.'s kitchen, when Jason asked, "Would you like some tequila?"

"What's that?"

"You don't know what tequila is?"

"No."

He smiled sweetly and shook his head. Then he grabbed a lemon, sliced it, and placed it in front of me. "I'm going to show you how to drink tequila. Okay?"

Jason poured the aromatic, golden liquid into two shot glasses. He licked the back of my hand. His hot breath and moist tongue sent chills up my spine. Then he sprinkled salt in the wet area.

"Lick the salt off the back of your hand, then drink the tequila without stopping. Bite the lemon. What do you want as a chaser?"

"A chaser? What's a chaser?" I asked.

"Oh, brother, you don't know anything, do you?" He chuckled.

"No," I said. "That's why I'm here with you. I want you to teach me."

I smiled as sweetly as I could at Jason, shrugged my shoulders, and then followed his drinking instructions. While he stood there watching me, I gagged on the tequila and began to choke. Jason patted me on the back and gave me a glass of water.

In no time, I felt a buzz. Jason watched me and smiled. Sally Mae stomped off to her bedroom and slammed the door, apparently jealous of the attention Jason was paying me. We both ignored her. I was in seventh heaven. A man, a good-looking man, was paying a lot of attention to little ol' me.

"Aren't you going to have some?" I asked.

Jason smiled at me again. It made me moist all over. His voice was soft and sweet, and he smelled good.

"Yes. But can I have whatever chaser I want?" he asked. I had no idea what he was talking about, but nodded anyway.

Jason licked the salt off his hand, tossed the tequila down his throat, and pulled me gently toward him. He planted his full, soft lips on mine and glided his sweet tongue into my mouth. I had never, ever been kissed before, not counting what Junior had done to me on a dare on the bus ride back from Omaha. When Jason finally released me, he left me breathless and dizzy. The combination of his cologne, his soft, honey-filled, sexy voice, and the sweet tequila knocked me off my feet. I was in *love*.

Later, Jason drove me home. After we pulled up to the curb, he leaned over and kissed me lightly on the forehead, and then he got out, walked around the car, and opened the door for me. I did not want to get out. I did not want to leave him.

When I finally got out of the car, he winked at me. I blushed.

"See you later," he said. And then he drove off.

Jason lived in an apartment above B. J.'s with two prostitutes, who were also exotic dancers. Unemployed, Jason said he was their manager. He also fancied himself a drug dealer. But he used up his own inventory and never had any to sell to his customers.

I neither saw nor heard Jason book any of his girlfriends' shows. Instead, after the two women were away for a week or two, they would return home with a lot of money, which they had to turn over to Jason. While they were away dancing, Jason spent his free time with me.

I was flattered, to say the least, that Jason, ten years my senior, found me attractive. Worldly, sexy, and wise, Jason was going to be my dress rehearsal for the real men who were to come.

I had been seeing Jason for over two months, on my days off. When his two women—Jennifer and Cat—were away dancing, he would take me upstairs to his apartment and we would cuddle with our clothes on. I'd fall asleep in his arms.

He reminded me of my Daddy—soft, gentle, and affectionate. But tonight, he was in a bad mood. It was three o'clock in the morning and he had grown impatient with me.

"But Jason, I'm not ready for sex," I said again. "You told me you wouldn't pressure me and that you'd be patient. I want to be married before I give myself to any man."

Finally, I tried to leave, but he begged me to stay. I fell asleep again only to be awakened by him an hour later, with the same prompting.

"Jason! No! I can't," I said. I was so tired, I was delirious.

"But I need you. I want to be close to you," he said.

"You *are* close to me. See, look!" I snuggled closer to him and dozed off.

It must have been six o'clock when I awoke. Jason hadn't fallen asleep. He had been staring at me all night long.

I couldn't understand why Jason wanted to have sex with me so much. I didn't know anything about sex, and after all, he had the other two women for that. I had always thought that a man had to have sex like a person had to have food and water, and I'd figured that Jennifer and Cat had already satisfied that necessity for him.

"If you say no again," he said, "I'm going to slap you."

I was scared, but I called his bluff. I didn't want him to know he had frightened me. I knew Jason was a violent man and beat his other two women unmercifully. Sally Mae told me horror stories about how he punched and kicked Jennifer, and how, just last week, after beating Cat to a pulp, he'd tried to throw her out the second-story window. I lay there, planning my escape.

"If I have sex with every man who threatens to beat me up, what kind of woman would I be?" I said adamantly. "*No!* I am not ready." The next moment, I heard thunder crashing and saw stars. My face was burning and there was ringing in my ears. Jason's hand had come crashing down on my face. I lost my breath and couldn't see. Instinctively, I tried to jump up to run, but he held me on the bed and climbed on top of me.

Oh, God! Please don't let him rape me or beat me. I didn't know what would be worse.

While Jason held me down, a stream of incomprehensible words spewed from his mouth. He wasn't yelling. He was calmly lecturing me. But I had no idea what he was saying. My mind was racing ahead to the awful stories that might be told about what Jason had done to me. I had visions of being beaten, kicked, and shoved out of the second-story window.

I was also praying that he remembered who I was. *Remember the woman who counseled you and your wife when your children were sick and dying? I'm her daughter.*

Finally, Jason finished lecturing and released me. I grabbed the shoe that he'd managed to get off of me the night before, but only after a struggle. The other one remained glued to my foot, because I had put up such a protest that he'd given up in disgust.

Then, with one shoe on and the other in my hand, I darted out of his apartment, down the flight of stairs, and out the front door. And I hobbled that way all the way to the safety of my home. While running, I'd kept looking over my shoulder, expecting to find him right behind me, ready to finish me off. But I never did.

When I reached sanctuary, Mother, Sister Diana, and Gloria were sitting in the living room. I must have looked like a frightened alley cat. I had been out all night, but they didn't say anything to me, and I dare not utter a word.

I wanted to confide in Mother, but I knew if I did that eventually everybody would know my business. I was already embarrassed enough. So instead, I raced upstairs to my bedroom and threw myself on my bed.

That afternoon, Mother pulled me out of a deep sleep to remind me that I had a graduation ceremony and a prom that I did not want to miss.

I went to my prom in style with Jeff Sellers. Linda and Becky were green with envy. I found the whole prom thing boring as heck, but worth every penny of my salvation; I was on my way to hell anyway, so I might as well make the best of it. I was thankful that my big brother in Christ escorted me to my prom. Unfortunately, Jeff Sellers did not dance.

The next day, I boarded a Greyhound to Los Angeles to visit Linda and Disneyland. Linda had completed boot camp and was now stationed at Twenty-nine Palms, California. I stayed in Los Angeles with friends of Linda who were religious fanatics—more fanatical than my own church. I didn't know that was possible. Another Pentecostal Church filled with condemnation and fear.

Eventually I was able to join Linda at Twenty-nine Palms Marine Corps base. Her gunnery sergeant allowed me to stay in base housing with his family. Men! Men! And more men! I was in my glory. And the young marines were excited to see a woman dressed in real clothes.

I would dress up my long legs and small, perky breasts—which by now, I saw no reason to confine to a bra—in anything I could find that was revealing: halter tops, short shorts, tight jeans, and bikini tops. If Mt. Sinai and Mother could see me now. I had the male marines eating out of my hand.

It was then that I realized I didn't have to settle for Jason. And from that point on, I was on a mission. Like the United States Marine Corps, I was looking for one good man. My mission: losing my virginity. Unfortunately, it was mission impossible, because I'd have to be sexually AWOL (Active without Linda). If she found out about my intentions, she'd tell Mother on me.

Three months later, I left the base still a virgin, and reluctantly returned to Iowa. By the time I got back, it seemed that in an odd twist of fate, my escape route had already been mapped out—by none other than Mother herself.

After years of never showing the least bit of interest in my education, Mother had taken it upon herself to send in college applications for Gloria and me. Neither Gloria nor I had ever expressed the desire to become registered nurses; however, Mother wanted us to follow in her footsteps. And so she had planned our destiny.

We were to attend her Alma mater, the Harlem School of Nursing, if they accepted us. My eldest sister and I obediently sat for the college-entrance aptitude tests in March. We both passed.

At this point, I did not care where I went or what I did. Just as long as it was away from Mother and Mt. Sinai.

Life is what happens when you're making plans, and in this case, Mother's plans were going to hell in a hand basket. It seemed that Harlem School of Nursing did not have its act together and couldn't even manage to get the appropriate correspondence out on time for Gloria and I to attend school less than a month later. So I had no choice but to wait it out in Sioux City.

As a result, Jason would eventually take what he wanted from me, as I became one of the three women he loved—like Mother, like daughter. I probably would have become a prostitute for him had I not been so difficult. I was hardheaded and stubborn. I was used to being beaten and humiliated. When he beat me, I beat him right back. Moreover, I hid my money, refusing to give it to him like the other two women did, since all he'd use it for was drugs. Though, ultimately, he would find it, and I would reluctantly have to "lend" it to him, knowing full well that he had no intention of paying me back.

In August, the Swift Premium Turkey factory was hiring. I went and was hired immediately. I worked five days a week from nine to six assembling Butterball boxes to ship the turkeys in.

I lived for the weekends, when I could attend my kind of church–the Swinging Inn. There, I was surrounded by former Pentecostal children who were now hookers, drug dealers, or unwed mothers. We were the first to arrive at the Swinging Inn and the last to leave when it closed at night.

Once, I tried to take a white boy I worked with to the Swinging Inn. The black men beat him up before he could get into the club. After that, I was too embarrassed to return to Swift's. So I went to work for Iowa Beef Processing (IBP).

After a while at IBP, I learned that you can't work a backbreaking job and party all night. Something has to give. And one night, it finally did.

Addie, a high school friend of Gloria's, and Ann, a childhood friend and ex-member of Mt. Sinai, were on their way to Joe's Cocktail Lounge, where Addie worked. And Addie invited Sally Mae and me to come along for the ride. During the school year, Addie attended college out of state. So she only danced at Joe's when she was back home on break to earn extra income. Sally Mae and I only agreed to go with them because we thought our men (Jason and whoever Sally's man was at the time) were messing around on us with these two women.

When we got there, however, Addie introduced us to Joe, the owner, and said, to my surprise, "They're thinking about dancing for you, Joe."

Sally and I lied about our names and ages. Then Joe laid down the rules about drugs and prostitution, and told us he would let us try it out, to see if we wanted to work for him. Then he gave us free drinks to help loosen us up.

Addie was petite and sexy. She had small breasts, a six-pack stomach, and lean but muscular legs. When she got on stage, she was wearing black go-go boots and black lingerie.

The music began, and I soon learned Addie was a contortionist. She lifted her left leg slowly over her head and held it up. Then she danced on her right leg to the beat, before twirling on the floor like a ballerina and then doing splits like a gymnast.

The whole place stopped what they were doing to watch Addie—except Sally Mae, who suddenly got louder and louder while shooting pool with one of the patrons. Addie had the crowd spellbound. I was glad a white woman who had absolutely no rhythm followed Addie instead of me.

As the white woman took the stage, Addie took me to the back and lit a joint. She passed the joint to me, but I turned it down. I did not like the effect it had on me and I remembered Gloria's horror story. Instead, I had two shots of tequila and a couple of drinks, compliments of one of the patrons at the bar. And then it was my turn.

I borrowed Addie's tall black boots and stripped down to the underwear I was wearing—pink bra and pink bikini underwear. I was nervous and shaking as I stepped onto the stage. The music was loud and I could feel the beat pulsating through my body. All around the stage sat drunken white men, looking at me and fantasizing about me. I loved it. It turned me on even more than Jason did.

Addie and Anne began cheering me on. "Go girl! Shake that money maker!" Then Sally Mae joined them, as did the other dancers. Men held up money for me and I went for it. I was turning myself on. I had completely forgotten why I was there in the first place.

After my dance, Sally Mae went. She borrowed an outfit from one of the dancers as well as her boots. She was good too. Then Addie took me to the back and showed me the ropes. She showed me how to take money from the men while avoiding contact with them. By the end of the night, I had over one hundred dollars.

After we finished our second set, Sally Mae and I dressed in our street clothes and sat down at the bar to talk to Joe, the owner.

Joe told Sally Mae and me that we could have the job if we wanted it. He said he'd pay minimum wage plus tips. We told him we would think about it; after all, I already had a job at IBP.

The decision wasn't difficult. Would I rather make two hundred dollars a week standing in a cold refrigerator every day, scraping the blemishes off of cow carcasses? Or would I prefer to make well over that amount drinking and dancing only a couple nights a week. Hmm!

As we sat at the bar pondering our decision, I watched as the sole black man in the joint got up from his stool and approached us. We stared blankly at him, wondering what he wanted.

He was drunk and spraying his words. "Say, ain't you that preacher's daughter, uhhh wha's her name, Sistah Roberts?"

I was dumbfounded. "Ahhh, no!"

"Yesh you is," he said in a deep slur. "And you," he looked at Sally Mae, "your Daddy is a preacher too, ain't he?"

"No!" Sally Mae laughed. "You talk like a crazy man."

"I may talk like a crazy man, but you look just like Reverend Baker. Crazy or no, I know his daughter when I see her," he said. And then he staggered away.

Preachers' kids live in a glass bowl. Everybody knows your business.

Little Sister

Sioux City
Fall 1972

*There were two women, the daughters of one mother. . . . [A]
nd the names of them were Aholah the elder, and Aholiabah
her sister. . . . Aholah played the harlot. . . . [W]hen her sister
Aholibah saw this, she was more corrupt . . . in her whoredoms.*
—Ezekiel 23:1–11

My new career at Joe's Cocktail Lounge proved to be a big disappointment to Jason. I didn't care. I let the men buy drinks for me, but would not let them put money in my bra or underwear. I enjoyed the attention. I enjoyed taking my clothes off and watching men salivate over me. But I didn't want them to touch me—not yet.

I also still had no intention of using my money to support Jason's drug addiction. I was doing this for fun and to pass the time until I left for college.

Jason and Joseph accompanied me to Joe's to get my first week's pay. Joseph went there to see Addie. Sally Mae's suspicions proved correct. Her man was dating Addie openly and seeing Sally Mae under secret cover. Joe handed me my money in cash. It wasn't much.

Jason sighed and shook his head as he took my three twenty dollar bills from me and stuffed them in his front pants' pocket. "Let me borrow this."

When we left, Addie was dancing, and I thought about how I was like her, just doing this for fun and to buy time. I did not have any aspirations of dancing for a living like Jennifer or Cat. I felt I was better than this bunch of losers.

Jason was in the driver's seat and Joseph was in the front passenger seat by the window. I snuggled up between the two of them. As we pulled out of Joe's parking lot, it began to snow.

Jennifer, who had been working for one month straight, must have hit the jackpot because Jason was driving around in style in a new used jalopy. It still had the dealer's sticker taped to the window.

He must have used the rest on drugs, which is why he needed money from me. I didn't dare tell him that I had my last two paychecks from IBP waiting for me.

Jason was driving like an old lady because the streets were slick with fresh fallen snow. At the stop sign, he turned on his right blinker and proceeded slowly down Market Street toward the Swinging Inn. As he pulled into park we saw flashing red and blue lights behind us.

"Oh, shit!" Jason said.

"Man, this is bullshit!" Joseph shouted.

"Man, just be cool," Jason cautioned him. "Let me handle this."

Joseph's eyes were bloodshot, so I was sure he was high. Plus, he had just returned from Vietnam, so he was still in an attack mode.

The white Sioux City police officer sauntered up to the car and shined his flashlight in.

"What seems to be the problem, officer?" Jason asked in his smooth voice.

"Ain't no problem!" Joseph responded.

"Joe, please! Just be quiet," I begged him. "Get out of the car and go in the bar."

"Is this your car?" the officer asked.

"Yes, sir," Jason said. "What seems to be the problem? Did I do something wrong?"

"License and registration," the officer barked.

As Jason handed him his license, he said, "I just bought the car today. It's not registered."

"Hey, man," Joseph shouted at the officer through the open window. "What's the problem? Just because a nigger is driving a new car, don't mean you have to—"

"You be quiet!" the cop ordered.

"No! You be quiet!" Joseph yelled back. The joist was on.

"If you don't shut up, I'm going to arrest you!"

"Do it! I dare your punk ass to do it!"

"Joe! Be cool, man!" Jason begged him.

The officer was hot. He leaned into the car, past Jason and me, trying to reach for Joseph.

"Listen, you! I'll arrest you for obstruction of—"

"Do it, you white motherfucker. I dare you to." Joseph began to exit the car.

Jason and I were getting scared.

"Get back into the car!" the cop ordered.

"No!" Joseph screamed back. "Make me, you motherfucking pig!"

The officer began walking around the car. Before he got to the other side, five police cars showed up out of nowhere.

The officer grabbed Joseph by the neck and threw him to the ground. Instinctively, Jason and I exited the car. Holding steadfast to the vehicle to keep from slipping on the ice, Jason cautiously made his way around the car to the aid of his fallen comrade. As he did, the white police officers jumped him.

Swinging Inn patrons had begun arriving to enjoy an evening of music, but the sirens of Sioux City's riot police were the only tunes that could be heard.

Decked in a large bearskin coat, blue jeans, high-heeled boots, a long, flowing Tina Turner wig, and heavy makeup, I stood near the hood of the car, watching as two white cops sprayed mace in Joseph's eyes and the face of my fallen lover. Another cop was pinning Jason's and Joseph's arms behind their backs as the first two sprayed away. They were completely helpless.

Protected from the cold by the coat Jason had stolen for me from the Goodwill by daringly taking it in front of a white store clerk, I reflected on how he was now boldly attempting to protect his friend from the stone-cold white cops. Now someone needed to protect Jason. The only way I could do that was to seek help from his baby sister, B. J.

I dashed into the Swinging Inn and found B. J. at a table, sipping a drink. She was also wearing her long, flowing Tina Turner wig.

"B. J.!" I screamed. "The police are outside beating up Joseph and Jason."

B. J. jumped up from her chair as fast as her short, heavy body could manage and headed out the door. She raced to the assistance of her brother.

"Wha's goin' on here?" B. J. asked with authority as she stepped onto the sidewalk. The white cops on a black beat must have mistaken her for me, what with her identical wig, because then a white policeman took out his billy club and brought it crashing down on her head. B. J. hit the ground before the count of three. She already had a back problem and had just recently recovered from surgery.

"Oooooh," she groaned from the ground, looking up at me.

I ducked back into the Swinging Inn and took a seat at the bar. "Rum and Coke, please." I took a Kool's out of the pack, lit it, and took a deep drag.

When I noticed many of the spectators wandering back into the bar, I figured the coast was clear and went out to look. Several policemen were still hanging around, writing reports and taking measurements.

"What happened?" I asked the white cop who had stopped us. He was tagging Jason's car, which still had the headlights on. He pretended not to hear me.

"Sir, what did they do?" I asked sweetly.

The officer shot me a glance and did a double-take. Then he resumed writing on his little pad.

"They ran down the damn stop sign," he responded.

I looked up and toward the end of the block at the stop sign.

"Looks like its still standing to me," I said. Then I walked down the block to the safety of my own home.

When I got there, I called Mother at work. I had been staying at B. J.'s house, but I did not want to go there that night.

"He's been arrested," I wailed into the receiver.

"Calm down," Mother said. "What happened?"

I was crying hysterically while Mother listened calmly on the other end.

"Okay. I want you to stay home tonight," she said after I had told her my story. "The Lord is telling you it is time for you to come home. Next month, you will be leaving for college. It is time to let your friends go, before they drag you down with them."

I knew she was right. Harlem School of Nursing had finally contacted Gloria and me, and we were to start classes in the early part of January. If I could just behave myself and stay out of trouble until the end of December, I could indefinitely be out of harm's way.

I felt my mother's love for me coming through the receiver. Then she said a prayer over me, Jason, B. J., and Joseph. That night, I lay in bed, sleeping peacefully, while Jason and Joseph slept on hard cots behind the bars of the Sioux City Jail, and B. J. lay in traction at St. Vincent's Hospital.

The next day I gathered my belongings from B. J.'s and went home. Mother had a job for me to do there anyway. She had taken in a blind couple, Earl and Marcia, who had a newborn they couldn't take care of because they could not see him. Mother opened her home to them after the state of Iowa had found their house infested with mice and roaches and threatened to take the baby away.

"You need to get yourself mentally prepared for college," Mother said when she returned from work the next morning. "Leave Jason alone. Like I told you before, books and boys don't mix."

I stayed in my bed for most of the morning, thinking about what Mother had asked me to do for Earl and Marcia. They were nice, but I was eighteen years old, and a month of babysitting the three blind mice seemed like an eternity.

Plus, I agreed with Mother about Jason. I wanted to get away from him, but as long as I lived in Sioux City, he would always be there. And I would never get to date anyone else. I knew because I had tried that once and Jason beat me and the guy up. I needed to get away fast. I was afraid something might go wrong.

Finally, I got out of bed and went downstairs to find Mother in the kitchen. "Why can't you just send me to Daddy's now?" I asked her.

"Because I need you. Even before all this happened, I was going to call you and ask you to come home to help out."

Mother said that if I promised to watch the three of them, and stay away from Jason and the Swinging Inn, she would help send me to college. Even as I agreed to her list of demands, I knew I had no intention of following through.

Still, I gave it my best shot. For two weeks, I took care of the three of them. I took Earl and Marcia to the movies to see *Lady Sings the Blues*, which meant sitting in the theater with them and explaining everything that was happening on the screen. I washed, clothed, and fed their baby. I also helped prepare our Thanksgiving meal. The only places I was allowed to go the entire time were church and anywhere related to Marcia and Earl.

I could not stand looking at Earl and Marcia. Both of them had been in terrible car accidents that had messed up their faces. Marcia had been the only one in her car to survive, after she and a group of her Indian friends had been out partying all night. She had been left maimed for life, her face smashed in and her eyes perched in two different directions.

Earl was just as bad. His black face was hideous and so were his eyes. But he was stubborn and refused to cover his wandering eyes with dark glasses. It made me sick to look at them.

I was going plain crazy when Sally Mae called and pushed all the right buttons. She said Jason was asking for me and that he was out of jail, because Jennifer had sent him money to make bail. B. J. was still in the hospital. Her back was really messed up.

Then nonchalantly, out of the blue, she said, "Oh, girl! Ginny Jones is trying to take your man." Then before I could even respond, she said, "See you, girl. I'm on my way to the club to have a cold one and a Kool's."

Sally Mae always knew how to get my goat. She'd either make allegations that someone was trying to make a play for Jason (with Jennifer being number one in his life, Cat number two, and me number three, there was no room for any other women; I had to put my foot down somewhere), give me the latest gossip from the Swinging Inn, or tempt me with drinking and smoking cigarettes, and playing Motown tunes on the stereo.

I felt like a wild, caged lion. I stepped outside and looked up the street toward the Swinging Inn. Judging from the number of cars in the parking lot, it was crowded. And with that, I planned my escape: I would wait until Mother left for work and the three blind mice were asleep, then I'd head over.

The baby didn't go to sleep right away, but when he finally nodded off, I slipped out of the house and raced down the snow-packed street toward the Swinging Inn.

Inside, Jason was standing at the bar, his back to me, whispering something in Ginny's ear. I watched as she laughed gingerly, tossing her long, auburn hair over her shoulder. I walked up to him. As he turned, I watched as his face light up when he saw me. Ginny dropped her eyes sheepishly, as if caught in the act. I gave her the "I know you are trying to take my man" stare.

The last time I'd seen Ginny, she'd been dating my cousin Albert, even though Becky had been Albert's main squeeze. In fact, Becky had given birth to his son.

Now that I thought about it, though, Albert was no longer known as such. He had changed his name to J. C. after he'd become a pimp and a drug dealer and too many people had teased him about his name. Who had ever heard of a drug dealer named Albert? People laughed and teased and called him "Albert and the Chipmunks." A drug-dealing pimp needed a proper name to get his "propers."

Anyway, J. C., as he was known now, always beat Becky the way his father beat his mother. He did not allow her to go out. Becky was in a self-made prison, while he ran the street with his whores and with Ginny, when she would have him.

Jason pulled me close and kissed me. I was in seventh heaven.

"I missed you," he said.

"I missed you, too."

He smelled good. I loved the way he looked at me.

"They dropped the charges against Joseph."

"How's B. J.?"

"She'll be fine. They set the court date for the first week in January."

"What court date?" I pulled away from him.

"My trial. We are taking this to trial."

"Umm. . . ." I did not want any part of a trial. "I'm leaving at the end of December. I won't be here."

"Well, I need you to testify. But we'll worry about it when the time comes."

I prayed that I would be long gone by that time. But I couldn't worry long, because before I knew it, Jason was leading me off the dance floor and out the door.

"Jason, I can't go with you tonight," I said, pulling away from him as soon as we were outside. "My mother will get mad at me."

But he would not listen. He pulled me up next to him and then continued walking toward his apartment.

That night, I fell asleep on Jason's chest. When I woke up, it was after five A.M. I was panicked. I had to get home before Mother returned from work and before Marcie and Earl realized I was missing in action.

I raced home and gingerly opened the front door. I stepped quietly inside and listened. The house was dark and quiet.

Good. Everyone is still sleeping, I thought. I stole up the stairs and slipped into my room. Just as I was about to lay my head on my pillow, I heard a light tapping at my door.

"Debra, your mother is on the phone," called Earl.

I had been set up. Mother had told Earl to call her when I got home, and the little blind rats had ratted me out.

Mother was livid. "Get out! Pack your things and get out!"

"But . . ."

"No buts! You're going to have to find your own way to college."

I called Daddy immediately.

"I'll send for you, Mosquito," Daddy promised.

"What about college? I want to go to college."

"Don't worry; I'll take care of everything."

"But when?" I cried. "I need to get away from here now."

"I'll wire the money at the end of the week," he said.

Daddy had never kept any of his promises to wire money, so I knew not to hold my breath—but you can't blame a girl for trying.

After that, I had no idea where I would go. B. J.'s three-bedroom house was crowded. Besides I had seen the handwriting on the wall. I knew the white cop had mistaken B. J. for me. Next time, I might not be so lucky.

I was sitting on the bed praying when the telephone rang. It was my cousin Samuel. He had found a place for me to stay. I was astounded to find out he already knew Mother had evicted me. But it was like this when I started dancing at Joe's; Mother found out the next day and threatened to come watch me dance. The news had spread around town within an hour of Mother calling me from work. Samuel offered me sanctuary at his girlfriend's house.

Carol was a white girl who had graduated with honors from Central High. She'd been in my graduating class. Carol had been around the block a couple of times. Most of the black men in Sioux City had had her at one time or another. After Albert, or J. C., had finished with her, he'd given her to his brother Samuel.

A foreman on the night shift at IBP, Carol was a smart, pretty, big-breasted, leggy, blue-eyed blonde. I wondered why she was so insecure that she felt compelled to give herself to a bunch of men who neither cared for nor respected her.

The only exception to that rule was Rickie Jr., who had befriended Carol and did not use her or sleep with her. I think he secretly loved and admired Carol and was just waiting for her to notice him.

Anyway, because she had so much going for her, all of the black girls, including me, were intimidated by Carol. In fact, we downright hated her.

Just two weeks before, I had helped raid her house with two other PKs (Pentecostal Kids). One of the PKs had gotten the impression that

Carol had slept with her boyfriend or was at least thinking about it. The PC wanted to raid Carol's house as a warning. Rickie Jr. sat in the front room, telling us to leave Carol's stuff alone, while we ransacked her house and took what we wanted. I took a couple of Carol's dresses and a pair of her shoes.

"I'll be at work, but I'll leave the key under the mat," Carol now said to me in a sweet voice. "Make yourself at home."

I felt like a heel.

That afternoon, I moved into her house while she was at work. I slipped the dresses and shoes I'd stolen from her back into her closet. Hopefully she hadn't missed them.

Later that evening, I sat on the couch with Rickie Jr., smoking a joint while Bob Dylan crooned in the background:

Tell me, how does it feel to be left alone
With no direction known, like a rolling stone.

In My Father's House

Newark, New Jersey
January 1973

In my father's house are many mansions; if it
were not so I would have told you.
—John 14:2

Gloria left for Newark a month before me. By the time I got there she was already unpacked and enrolled in the Harlem School of Nursing.

Daddy's house was in complete shambles. Everything inside was covered in a fine layer of black soot. Apparently, there was something wrong with the furnace, but when Sister Davis (or, rather, Sister Roberts, as she now called herself) tried to get it fixed, Daddy erupted like a volcano, spewing words mixed with spit. He was a ranting, raving lunatic.

"I said I was going to take care of it! Now, get off my back, woman!" he shouted.

Sister Davis rolled her eyes and shook her head. It seemed he had been saying that for years. Everything in the house—clothes, canned goods, silverware, even people—looked as if it had been used to clean the chimney. Daddy's hands always looked dingy.

And if that weren't bad enough, he was missing a few front teeth, his clothes were tattered and torn and old, and he was flat broke. I couldn't believe this man used to be my handsome father.

Sister Davis, I mean the new Sister Roberts (old habits are hard to break), was a nervous wreck and a chain smoker. I continued to address her as Sister Davis; she was polite and never tried to correct me. I always stole into her bedroom when she was gone and smoked up her cigarettes. She pretended not to notice.

She worked for the telephone company full time and was a full-time mother of her and Daddy's two youngest children. She loved her babies. She and Daddy spoiled them rotten, especially my little half sister. Although I knew the babies were my half siblings, I could not bring myself to admit it out loud. Neither could Daddy or Sister Davis. We skirted around the issue, pretending that Daddy and Sister Davis were not adulterers and on their way to hell.

Daddy even continued to pretend that he was simply renting space from Sister Davis and sleeping in the little side bedroom. I found his pretense ridiculous in light of the fact that Sister Davis was calling herself Sister Roberts.

Regardless, my little brother and sister and I favored one another. Whenever I went anywhere with them, I'd hear, "Your little brother and sister are so cute," and "They look just like you." There was no way to deny either of those things.

I had mixed emotions about both of them. On one hand, I loved them to death, except when my little sister was having a temper tantrum, which was most of the time. On the other hand, I blamed them for taking my Daddy away from me. There was no question in my mind that I had been replaced.

Mostly, though, I blamed Sister Davis. She should have left my Daddy alone and told him to go home to his wife and children.

As for my other two half siblings by Sister Scott, I did not get a chance to bond with them. Nor did I want to. I did not see them unless Sister Scott brought them to a church function or over to Sister Davis' house to spend time with me. Even then, I resented her for trying to force them on me.

Daddy, of course, never formally introduced any one of them as my siblings. I don't know what was going through their heads, but I know what was going through mine: they were all in denial!

Once, an inquisitive man from one of the other COGIC churches was visiting Daddy's church. After the service, he approached Daddy and me. We were standing outside with my two brothers, two sisters, and a group of other children.

"Let's see," the man said to Daddy. "Which ones are yours? I know this one is," he said pointing to me. "And, this one." He paused as he looked around at the group.

I could tell Daddy was getting nervous. He began to grin and laugh, which was his typical reaction in messy situations. Then he said, "They are all my children in the Lord."

I was hurt. I had wanted Daddy to single me out as someone special. But then that would have brought him shame. And I was used to this kind of parental attitude anyway. It was the same with Mother and had always been. She was everybody's mother.

My parents never made any attempt to make my sisters and I feel unique. We were each just one in a group of many.

The only difference between my parents, other children, and me was that those people also had their own parents—parents that they did not have to share with me.

———————

Lazy bones, sleeping in the sun.
What you gonna' do, when your work ain't done?

Daddy sang to me as he climbed the stairs to deliver the bad news. I had been stuck in the house for days and I was bored, but I dared not go out on the streets of Newark. There were too many black people out there. It was sad but true: I had become afraid of my own people. Growing up in Sioux City had cost me my identity with my culture.

"Daddy, do you have the money?" I asked as he entered the room.

"No, baby. Daddy can't get it now. Why don't you wait until September? I can get it for you then."

This news did not come as a surprise. Long ago, I had arrived at the conclusion that I couldn't trust my Daddy to follow up on his promises. So I'd had the sneaking suspicion when I'd left Iowa that he would not have the money to send me to college. But you can't squeeze blood out of a turnip.

I began to cry. School had started over two weeks ago, and Gloria had already settled in. If he did not come up with the money soon, I would have to sit out the semester.

"Don't cry, baby. You know Daddy would give you the money if he had it, but you see, I've got to pay for—"

"Help me get a job then. I'm a good worker."

"You don't need to work. Just stay here and rest," he said.

But I was desperate. I didn't want to return to Iowa, and I couldn't be stuck in Daddy's dingy, raggedy house like this until September.

I determined to find gainful employment. If Gloria and Cynthia could do it, then so could I. I wished Denise, Sister Davis' daughter, hadn't gotten married; at least then I would have had someone to hang out with.

Denise had gotten married just a few weeks after I'd arrived in Newark. In those few weeks before the wedding, we'd spent time together, getting reacquainted. I'd helped her plan for her wedding, and she'd taught me about birth control and protection—something no one had ever mentioned to me before. She'd made me promise go on birth control before I had sex again. I'd promised I would as soon as I got a job.

The day of Denise's wedding, Daddy was nowhere to be found. Sister Davis paced the living room, ducking into her bedroom every now and then before emerging a few minutes later smelling like cigarette smoke.

Smoking and adultery; Sister Davis was guilty of both. I knew her name was not written in the Lamb's Book of Life, not to mention Daddy's. Yet this knowledge somehow gave me comfort. It made me realize that they were not perfect. We were birds of a feather in that way: we all loved God, prayed to God, read our Bibles, and went to church—but we had imperfections.

Finally Daddy showed up. He was wearing a dingy white shirt and black pants that were about two sizes too tight for him. His pockets were buckling and his butt was bursting at the seams. He had been out picking up fares in his taxicab.

Sister Davis immediately began to fuss at him, tears welling in her eyes. "Rob, I don't want to be late for my daughter's wedding. You know it starts at two o'clock! Where were you?"

Everyone called Daddy Rob. This was because his children were not permitted to call him Daddy. They had to call him Elder Roberts. But this had been a mouthful for the babies, so instead, everyone started calling him Rob.

"Woman, don't start nagging me," Daddy snapped, now in the kitchen wearing nothing but his under shorts. He moved all of the dishes in the sink to one side and started running the water. "We will get there on time. I just need to wash up."

"Oh, no!" Sister David moaned. "You have to wash up?"

Daddy just looked at her and flashed a toothless grin. Sister Davis stormed past him to her bedroom and slammed the door. Daddy began to wash his body in the sink. The pooling water was black and dingy, compliments of the soot.

Once dressed, we stepped over the spare car parts scattered over Daddy's front yard and piled into his taxicab. Daddy had a bunch of cars, all parked out in front of his house, but none of them worked, save the taxicab. It was the family's only mode of transportation. Having only one working car didn't bother Sister Davis, however, since she had never learned to drive.

"You may now kiss the bride," the minister said as we walked in.

Sister Davis began to cry. Daddy played it off as though it were nothing. Later, Denise told us that they had tried to wait for us, but after an hour, the guests and the groom had gotten anxious. She said it had been a beautiful wedding.

The reception followed at Sister Davis' ex-husband's house. Denise, sensing her Mother's plight, got her a glass of something that looked like orange juice, and then another, and another. Within an hour, Sister Davis loosened up like I had never seen her do before. She kept hugging me and kissing me.

Later Sister Davis and her sisters gathered around the piano and sang gospel. Tears flowed down their flushed faces as they howled.

Daddy couldn't stay because he had to get back to work.

"See if Brother Simpson can give you all a ride home," Daddy told Sister Davis as he kissed the bride and left.

I guessed I shouldn't have felt so bad. Daddy did not seem to have time for his new family either.

The alcohol and music flowed as we danced and drank ourselves into happiness.

"What did you put in that orange juice?" I later whispered to Denise.

Denise, using her fingers as a measure, said, "About this much orange juice, and about thaaaaat much vodka."

Sister Davis was drunk. Oh, yes! Another imperfect person. Lawds, yes. I knew I was in the right place now.

That evening, back in my upstairs bedroom at Daddy's house, I sat in the window blowing smoke through the screen. I missed home and I missed Jason. At least when he was with me, he was with me. My parents simply did not have time for me.

Just then I heard a creak on the top step.

"Mosquito?" Daddy called. "You in here?"

Oh, God! What would Daddy do if he saw me smoking? I extinguished my cigarette and rushed to hide my ashtray under the bed, while waving the smoke away. Too late. He walked in and caught me.

"What are you doing?" he said, looking puzzled. "I didn't know you smoked."

I stared at him like a doe caught in highlights.

"Are you trying to hide it?" he asked. "I love you. Be yourself. You don't have to hide yourself from me."

I know coming from him it shouldn't have mattered. After all, look at the mess he had made of his own life. But at least it showed he knew he was not perfect and couldn't hold a double standard.

"Your mother called me," he said. "She said you were a prostitute and on drugs. But I told her no, that I know you better than that. Not my mosquito."

"I am not on drugs, Daddy. And I am not a prostitute."

"Well, you have to find yourself. You're a smart girl. You'll be okay."

Daddy kissed me on the forehead, and then I watched as he walked out the door.

"Thank you, Jesus," I whispered.

Maybe I was going to be all right. I only wished he had been there when I was growing up. Maybe things would have turned out better. Maybe I would have turned out better.

I was in New Jersey for four months after that and had every intention of staying put. I tried to find a job, but no such luck. I even tried to contact my Uncle Percy to see if he could help me find a job. I went to his office and left a note on his door. But he was a phantom.

Newark was also filthy and crowded, and had too many Negroes. I had no sense of who I was or how I fit in around my own people, so I was afraid of them; I found them rude and intimidating.

So when my income tax return arrived in the mail, I booked a one-way ticket back to Sioux City and to Jason.

Drinking from My Sister's Cup

Sioux City, Iowa
Summer 1973

*Thou hast walked in the way of thy sister; therefore I will
give her cup into thine hand. . . . [T]hou shalt drink of thy
sister's cup, deep and large; thou shalt be laughed to scorn.*
—Ezekiel 23:31–33

Your test results are positive. You are pregnant," said the dour-faced Iowa doctor. "You said your last period was in April. That would put you at about sixteen weeks along."

My initial reaction was one of exhilaration. *I'm going to have a baby!* I thought. But I tried to suppress my excitement.

"Abortions are legal," the doctor told me. "But the state will not pay for it. Here is some information on the agencies who might be able to help you get an abortion, if that is what you decide."

Kill my baby? I thought. *I don't think so.* But I took the paperwork from him and placed it in my purse—just in case.

"As far as syphilis or gonorrhea is concerned, you're negative for both. Your condition is called pita roseate. It is a skin rash experienced mostly by Negroes and teenagers. We think it is caused by nerves. If you could see your back, you'd see the rash has formed a Christmas tree shape. Your tree is almost complete, so I'd say you are at the end of your rash."

My face and extremities were covered with ashy little bumps and white blotches. My face looked like that of a leper, and my whole body itched incessantly.

"Why did you think you have syphilis?" he asked. "Are you having sex with more than one person?"

I shook my head. I did not have more than one partner, but the same could not be said about the father of my unborn baby.

"My mother is a nurse, and she said it looked like a really bad case of syphilis."

"Hmmm." He examined my skin again. "I've never seen a rash like this caused by a communicative disease. Anyway, there is no cure. Only thing I can recommend is oatmeal baths. Use cocoa butter so your skin will not scar." I had tried to use cocoa butter, but its smell made me nauseous.

"If you decide you want to have an abortion," he said, "you need to take care of it right away. You have to do it before the end of the first trimester."

I thanked the doctor as he left. Then I sat there for a moment, wondering what my next move should be and how I would tell Mother.

"Mother," I practiced, while getting dressed. "I have good news and bad news. The good news is I do not have syphilis. The bad news is I am pregnant."

I shuddered at the reaction I imagined she would have, the reaction I knew she would have. I could not tell Mother.

I pulled the information about abortions out of my purse. I didn't want to have an abortion and I didn't have any money, but still . . . going into my second trimester, any decision I made would have to be made real soon.

Perhaps I could get the money from Linda. She was still in the marines and bringing in a decent, steady paycheck. But if she found out what I planned to do with the money, she wouldn't give it to me. I'd have to make up a credible story to get something from her. And even then, she would call Mother to get her permission—and of course, Mother would nip that in the bud.

It was exactly one year from the day I had walked away from the Lord. The wonderful, carefree life of a backslider I had expected to live hadn't quite materialized. But at least I had fared better than Gloria—so far.

By the time I had returned to Sioux City from Newark, it was April. Mother had moved, and Sister Diana was gone. Mother didn't talk about her and seemed evasive when I questioned her about what happened. Marcia and Earl had also gotten their own apartment again, one floor below where Cynthia lived with her one-year-old daughter Doresa. (As soon as Cynthia had gotten pregnant, she'd lost interest in her husband, returned from Minneapolis, and promptly filed for divorce.)

When I first got to town, I stayed with Mother in her small two-bedroom house, along with her mutt, Shag. She had passed the reins of her church to Pastor Baker, Sally Mae's father. Still, Pastor Baker did not make a move without Mother's approval.

What a coincidence, I thought. *As soon as her daughters are all grown and out of the house, she decides to be a stay-out-of-the-pulpit mom.*

I had learned right away that Zenith was hiring. I applied the next day and was hired immediately. My job was to weld thingamagigs as they traveled down the conveyor belt. Later, the thingamagigs would be put into a Zenith color television. When Sally Mae found out, she came down and got hired right alongside me.

Neither of us could keep up. Together, we formed the team of Lucy and Ethel as we chased our thingamagigs down the conveyor belt, yelling, "Break! Break!" Eventually, someone would turn off the conveyor belt, and Sally and I would weld together the pieces we had missed. And then the process would begin all over again.

Outside of work, I did a good job fighting the urge to see Jason by hanging out with Jim. We just picked up where we had left off.

By then, Jennifer was seven or eight months' pregnant and had to hang up her dancing shoes for a while.

Jason, on the other hand, had started working. Found guilty by a Sioux City Superior Court judge, he was forced out of "retirement," as part of his sentence was to find gainful employment.

Jason went to work as a dog catcher. He even had to wear a uniform. But though you can give a man a job, you can't make him work. Jason drove around in a Humane Society truck, smoking cigarettes, while strays roamed the streets with arrogant indifference, as if they knew they were safe as long as Jason was on the job.

I was surprised I didn't run into Jason more often, since I'd eventually moved out of Mother's place back into B. J.'s house, where I lived with B. J. and Sally Mae. There, I had the freedom to come and go as I pleased, whereas Mother, as usual, had been too judgmental and too restrictive. I wished Mother could have been a little more like Daddy, and accepted me for me. I might've stayed if she had.

As it turned out, however, my run-in with Jason had been waiting for me right around the corner. It happened the day Jim had taken me out on his Harley. At some point, we'd stopped for a bite to eat and then, afterward, continued our joyride. It had been a beautiful day, and, as always, he had been the perfect gentleman and treated me like a lady. But gentlemen don't get very far in this world, do they?

Jim and I pulled up to the curb in front of B. J.'s house. I slid off the Harley behind Jim. He pulled me toward him and planted a big, wet kiss on my lips. I grew moist between my legs. I wanted Jim, and I was sure it would just be a matter of time before I had him.

Then, abruptly, Jim pushed me away and glanced toward the house. B. J.'s front door was open, so that only a screen door covered the entrance.

Jim's eyes expressed concern. "He's in there."

"Who?" I said.

"Jason."

My heart began to race. I wondered how much Jason had seen. Good! I wanted him to see. I wanted Jason to get the picture: get lost. It is over. I want to get on with my life, with Jim or anyone else I wanted to.

Of course, I didn't tell Jim that I was glad Jason was watching. Instead, I just said, "Really?"

"Maybe you shouldn't go in there."

"I'm not afraid of him. He can't control my life."

"Well, I'm worried about you," Jim said. He patted his Harley. "Get on. Come home with me tonight or let me take you to your Mother's."

"I refuse to run away," I said. "I've got to face the music sometime."

Jim was hesitant to leave me, but after seeing how determined I was to stay, he eventually gave up trying to persuade me otherwise and rode off.

I danced into the house, full of myself.

B. J. and Sally were sitting on the couch, and they looked worried. Jason stood beside them, dead silent.

"What's going on?" I asked.

The three of them just looked at me. So I shrugged and sashayed into the kitchen for a drink. As soon as I got through the doorway, Jason grabbed me from behind and threw me into the wall. As I turned to look at him, his backhand caught my right check. I tried to run, but to no avail. Then I tried to find something, anything, to defend myself with. I grabbed a pot out of the sink and threw it at him. He brushed it off as though it had been a flea and laid into my face again. Then, with the full force of his body, he pushed me out of the kitchen into the living room, where B. J. and Sally sat acting as though nothing was happening.

"Jason, what the fuck are you doing?" I shouted. Then I guessed nobody was supposed to curse at Jason, because that made him even angrier. He grabbed me and hurled me into the bedroom, slamming the door behind us.

"Goddamn it!" I yelled. "Leave me alone!" I began throwing my fists into his face, but Jason was a skilled fighter, and I was no match for him. The harder I fought, the more he punched. Finally, I just gave in to the beating.

"Jason! What are you doing?"

"What the fuck is that shit? What are you doing with him?" Those had been his first words to me since I'd walked in the door.

"Who?" I said.

He must not have liked my innocent act, because he responded by letting me have it across the face again.

"He is just a friend," I lied. "When you didn't write to me or call me in New Jersey, he did. He is just my friend. But I told him I was in love with you."

Jason looked at me. I could tell he was unsure whether I was telling the truth, so I continued the lie. "I told him I could never be with him because I am in love with you. I just didn't know you still cared about me. I promise I won't see him again."

Jason bought it. Sort of. At least enough to stop pummeling me.

I couldn't believe this was happening. Here he had a pregnant woman at home, and I wasn't allowed see anyone else. And then to add insult to injury, he wanted to have sex with me, right then and there. He tugged at my pants as I struggled to keep them on.

"Jason, I don't have any protection," I pleaded. "I plan to go to Planned Parenthood on Monday and then we can do it." I was trying to stall as we played tug of war with my clothes.

"Don't worry," he said, pushing harder. "I won't get you pregnant."

He lied too.

When I came out of the room a little later, Sally, who had fallen asleep on the couch, woke up and looked at me with a big grin on her face. Then she covered her mouth to stifle a giggle.

"What the fuck are you laughing at?" I glared at her.

"Debbie, I'm sorry," she said, though she continued to laugh. "I can't help it. You just looked so funny. You kept saying, 'Jason! Jason!' in this high, squeaky voice. I'm sorry, but it just seemed so funny to me."

I couldn't believe it. As if it weren't bad enough that my two "friends" just sat there while I got the crap beat out of me, now one of them was laughing about it.

I wanted to run home to Mother, but I didn't want to hear her say "I told you so." I'd rather stay and get beat up by Jason. After that, I avoided Jim like the plague.

The next day, I retook the navy entrance exam and flunked it again. Not long after that, I began to throw up all the time and developed a terrible skin rash. And then not long after that, I went to the doctor because Mother had said she heard I was pregnant and had syphilis—at which point, the doctor, as you well know by now, confirmed my worse nightmare.

I was nineteen years old and pregnant by a Kmart-blue-light-special, drug-dealing, no-dog-catching-dogcatcher pimp. What a fine mess I had made of my life, and all within just one year of walking away from God, Mt. Sinai, and Mother. God's wrath had finally caught up with me.

Woe, Is Me!

Sioux City
January 1974

[I]n all thine abominations and thy whoredoms,
thou has not remembered the days of thy youth.
Wo, wo, unto thee, saith the Lord God.
—Ezekiel 16:22–23

Jennifer's baby died last night," B. J. said on the other end of the receiver. Her cracking voice told me she'd been crying.

"Get out of here!" I was in shock. "You've got to be kidding." As though someone would kid about the death of a baby. "I didn't know her baby was even sick. What happened?"

I was in a bed at St. Vincent's Hospital in Sioux City, recuperating from having spent the entire day before in labor. I looked down at my own baby, who'd finally made her appearance at nine o'clock last night. As pale as could be, my daughter looked like a white bunny rabbit with a full head of jet-black hair.

While B. J. rambled on about Jennifer's baby, I tuned her out and thought about what my own baby's Daddy had said to me right after I delivered her.

"I am not going to marry you," Jason had said adamantly.

So? I thought. *Who asked you? I don't want to marry you anyway.* But I said nothing.

"What did you name her?"

"Ebony Sheryl," I said.

"Why did you name her that?" he snapped.

I reflected on that. In 1972, just before my descent began, I'd won the Miss Ebony Contest in Sioux City. I couldn't believe it, and neither could my competitors: the little, ugly, holy-roller girl was voted Miss Ebony. Apparently, without my knowledge, I had actually turned out to be something of a looker.

When Mother was asked whether she was proud of me for winning, she said no. She said she did not want me to know I was pretty, which was probably why she always told me how ugly and bucktoothed I was. I guess, in some way, she was trying to protect me. It didn't work. I grew up with such low self-esteem that I eventually became easy prey for Jason Green.

Winning that contest had given me such a burst of pride.

But "pride goes before a downfall," Mother always said. And so I named the product of my downfall—my daughter—after my pride: Ebony.

As for her middle name, I was trying to name her after the music group the Sherells, but I didn't know how to spell it.

"You should have waited and asked me what I wanted to name her," Jason said. "I guess it doesn't matter anyway, 'cause how do I know she's mine? She looks white."

He was right. She was pale. But mostly, Jason was referring to the fact that his family had denied Jennifer's daughter as blood, because her skin was pale and her hair was straight. She almost looked like she was mixed. It was improbable that Jennifer, who was as black as a skillet, and Jason could have made a baby who looked like that.

"All of the babies in my family look white when they're born," I told him. "Even Linda. We darken with age."

Jennifer's baby, on the other hand, had shown no signs of darkening, even after nine months.

"For all I know, Ebony could be the truck's baby," Jason said.

That stung. If I'd had any spine left in me, I would have slapped him. I had wanted to have sex with other men, but Jason would have killed me had I tried. He knew I hadn't slept with anyone else. He knew Ebony was his, all right.

"I'm not going to give her my last name, either," he said. "After all, when she gets married she will just change it anyway."

That was the sorriest excuse I'd ever heard. But it also made me wonder if he had given his last name to Jennifer's baby.

I dropped my head. I'd been hoping he'd agree to give her his name, because the resulting moniker would have had a nice ring to it: Ebony Green. But, when it rains it pours.

When I tuned B. J. back in, she was going on about how she believed Jennifer somehow caused the death of her baby. It was too bad; now Ebony wouldn't have an older sister.

"Something told me to go look under the bed and I would find a box," B. J. continued.

"So did you look under the bed?"

"Well, no."

B. J. was always talking about her intuition and sixth sense. It never panned out, though, except for the time she was upset with Sally for sweeping her foot with a broom.

"Don't do that," she'd yelled. "If you sweep somebody's foot with a broom, that means they're going to jail."

Sally Mae and I had laughed at her. But, sure enough, a week or so later, B. J. was on her way to jail, via the hospital bed, after the police had mistook her for me. I was glad Sally hadn't swept my foot with the broom.

"See, I think Jennifer gave that baby—"

I stopped listening. I had enough problems of my own to deal with. I was nineteen years old, the single mom of a newborn, and, as I'd just learned earlier that day, homeless.

You see, when I'd found out I was pregnant, I had moved back into Mother's house. The smells at B. J.'s—frying foods, cigarettes, alcohol—had made me sick to my stomach, since I'd had morning, noon, and evening sickness until my eighth month. I also did not want to be where Jason had *carte blanche* access to me.

That's not to mention that nearly the entire pregnancy, I'd been covered from head to toe in such a severe rash that I was too embarrassed to go to the Swinging Inn. It was rumored on the streets that I had syphilis, and that every time I went to the Swinging Inn, they threw the glasses I used away. It was all a part of my punishment from God.

The afternoon after that fateful doctor's appointment, I walked to Mother's house like a wounded dog. I wanted just to lie down and hide from the world.

When I told Mother that the rumor she'd heard about me was true, she showed no emotion. She wore her usual poker face— impossible for me to read.

I moved back in with her that week, after which point I went to work, paid rent, and fixed up my room for my baby and me. Sometimes I would catch Mother in my room going through my drawers, looking at the baby clothes I had purchased at the Goodwill. I had washed them, ironed and folded them neatly, and placed them in a dresser drawer reserved for the baby. I bought a little bassinet, which I set up in the corner of my bedroom.

I went back to work at Swifts until the turkey season was over and then got a job at Markmy Dale's Nursing Home. Cynthia worked at Markmy Dale's too, but then had to take time off for a hernia operation. I filled in her hours until she could return. I worked at Markmy Dale's until the day before Ebony was born. She wasn't due until the eighteenth of January, but she arrived on the fifth.

When my water broke, I was at Cynthia's apartment. Cynthia raced downstairs to Earl and Marcia's apartment to use their phone to call Mother.

According to Cynthia, Mother had said, "Don't call me; call the Greens," and hung up on her.

Cynthia did, and Jason's family came to my rescue. They took me to the hospital, and his mother sat with me the whole day, holding my hands. Cynthia showed up for a while, as did Jason and his sister Cookie. But Mother was a no-show.

I lay there in labor all day, crying for my mother. I knew I had been a big disappointment to her. I was a disappointment to myself. But Mother never so much as called to check on my well-being.

The next day, I called Mother and asked if she was going to come see me and the baby. She said no. But she stayed on the phone with me long enough to let me know that neither my daughter nor I were welcome to come back to her house.

I thought about all the unwed mothers she'd brought into her home and required us, especially me, to take care of. I thought about all the alcoholics, prostitutes, drug dealers, and crazy people she let use our beds while we slept on the floor, because it was what the Lord required. Yet where was the Lord and Mother's love when one of her own children needed it?

And now I was supposed to be able to make other living arrangements from a hospital bed, and in this kind of weather.

"When's the funeral?" I asked B. J.

"I don't know yet," B. J. sighed.

I never did tell B. J. that Ebony and I were homeless. After I hung up with her, I lit another cigarette and looked down at Ebony, who was peacefully sucking on my breast.

"Why wasn't it you that died?" I asked her. It was cruel, but at that moment, I blamed her for my plight. *If God was going to take someone, why not you? At least Jennifer's baby had a home, a Daddy, and grandparents who loved her.*

The nurse came and took Ebony to the nursery, and then returned to my room with a vanilla milkshake. For about a half an hour, I just sat in my bed, crying, smoking, and drinking my milkshake, thinking about the mess I had made of my life.

And then he walked in.

He was young, good-looking, blonde, and Catholic.

"Hi," the priest said. "How are you doing tonight?"

"Fine," I lied.

"Would you like me to pray with you?"

Tears filled my eyes. "Yes, please."

I don't even remember what he prayed. I just know that for a moment, I felt a sense of peace.

The next night he came by again, and then the next night, as well. Each time he came, he took his soft, firm hands and held mine, as he said a prayer over me and my baby.

As far as I knew, the Catholics were on their way to hell same as I. But at this juncture, I couldn't be too choosey. I was desperate. And a Catholic priest was better than nothing.

None of the folks from either Holiness church came to see me. None of them had called me or offered any prayer on my behalf. Only the Catholic. God was trying to tell me something. I just wasn't listening.

Cynthia called me the next day, livid. She told me that Mother had stood up in church that morning and denounced me to the congregation, proclaiming she had kicked me and the baby out. Apparently, Jason's mother had been there, and she walked right out.

"Mother is sooo wrong," Cynthia said. "I am so mad at her. That is not right."

Then she told me we could come stay in her apartment, that she didn't care what Mother said. She said she had wanted to come visit me at the hospital, but no one would give her a ride, and she could not find a babysitter for Doresa. I told her it was okay and thanked her for the offer.

A little later, B. J. called. She had heard the gossip. "Why didn't you tell me you and Ebony don't have anywhere to go? I can't believe what your mother said at the fellowship service! Come to my house. You are welcome here."

"I don't have any money and I don't have a ride," I responded. I had left my wallet at Mother's house—not that it had much in it anyway, since I had been giving almost all of my paycheck money to Mother to save for me.

"Don't worry," B. J. said. "We'll pick you and the baby up around noon, okay?" I was relieved.

B. J. arrived with a boyfriend I did not know. I bundled up my little package and we left the hospital. B. J.'s large house was now expensively decorated, compliments of the drug proceeds from her new boyfriend. Two men sat on the couch smoking marijuana, and the house reeked of alcohol, marijuana, and cigarette smoke.

She hadn't had a chance to fix up a room for Ebony and me, since it was such late notice, so I laid Ebony on B. J.'s bed and lay down beside her.

"Oh, Lord," I pleaded. "Please touch my Mother's heart so that she will let me and my baby go home." I was weak and tired and did not want my baby in this environment. It made me wonder even more about the sudden death of Ebony older sister.

Ebony and I fell asleep for an hour, until some loud music woke us up. She began to fuss. I did not have any of her bottles, and no diapers, and I wasn't going to breast-feed her here, in a household of strangers.

I called Mother and asked if I could drop by to pick up a few things, including the money I had asked her to save for me. She said that was fine. I called a cab and started wrapping up Ebony.

"Leave the baby here," B. J. said from within a swirl of cigarette smoke.

"No. I'm going to take her with me," I said, and then I grabbed my baby and jumped into the waiting cab.

When Ebony and I arrived at Mother's house, Mother and Brother Richardson were standing in the dining room talking. Brother Richardson's wife, Sister Cee-Cee, was one of the women Mother had sat up with and comforted when she'd been in labor. But of course, Sister Cee-Cee was not a sinner, and I was—and by association, I guess, so was my baby.

"Hi," I said, heading straight for the stairs. I didn't want to see Mother, and I was sure she didn't want to see my baby.

"Let me see the baby," she said, rushing up to us, almost cooing.

I stopped and did a double take.

"What did you name her?" Mother asked.

"Ebony."

"Ebony?" Mother laughed. "She is going to hate you for that."

I handed Ebony to her grandmother and raced up the stairs before she could see me crying. I found my room as I had left it: neat, clean, and organized. I fell on my knees and asked God once more to change my Mother's heart. Then I heard her coming upstairs, so I wiped my eyes and pretended to be looking for something.

"Oh, she is so beautiful," Mother said. "She looks just like you did when you were born."

"Did you hear?" I asked. "Jennifer's and Jason' baby died."

"Oh, no, girl." Mother was shocked. "When? What happened?"

"Nobody knows."

I began to pack, and Mother laid Ebony in the bassinet.

"Well, I've got to go to church," she said. "Why don't you stay until I get back? I'll give you a ride to B. J.'s."

So as soon as she left, I gathered Ebony from the bassinet and laid her on the bed with me. Together, we fell into a deep sleep.

After the evening service, Mother brought Cynthia and Doresa over to see us. They walked into my bedroom, trailing Shag, the dog, who fell in love with Ebony right away. Doresa, barely two at the time, was fascinated with her new cousin.

While Mother dressed for work, we all sat around, talking. At some point in the conversation, Mother said, "Debra, I think you and the baby should stay here for awhile. Why don't you think about it and give me your answer in the morning."

Praise God, I thought. *And you guys say God doesn't hear a sinner's prayer.*

Two weeks later, Jason arrived at Mother's front door asking to see his daughter. Until that point, he'd pretty much been in seclusion with Jennifer ever since the burial of their baby.

Jason was sitting on the couch next to me, holding Ebony, when Mother came downstairs.

"Hello," she said sweetly. "How are you doing, Brother Jason?"

"Fine," Jason said, sounding a little guarded.

My stomach began to churn. I felt light-headed and dizzy. It must have infuriated Mother that we looked like one big, happy family.

"Listen," she said, looking right at Jason. "You are not welcome here. If you want to see Debra and the baby, then you will need to get them a place. You need to leave."

Get us a place? I thought. *Is she crazy? There's no way I'd live with Jason. That would be like throwing Ebony and myself to the big, bad wolf.*

Jason was visibly shaken. "She is my baby! I have a right to see her!"

"Not in my house, you don't," Mother said. She was calm but forceful.

Jason stormed out. A couple minutes later, he called Mother from his mom's house two blocks up the street. Hearing the two of them argue made me a nervous wreck. I was afraid Mother would get mad and kick me out of the house again.

Mother had never told me that Jason was not welcome to come visit Ebony. I'd had no idea. But now all I wanted was to keep the peace and keep them both happy, so I wouldn't lose my home again.

After that incident, I began to become fearful at night again. Memories of the demons from my childhood haunted me. I'd wake up in the middle of the night, with my palms wet and my body flushed in sweat. My heart would be racing and my head pounding. I'd think I was having a heart attack or maybe even going crazy like Len Sellers had.

At first, it happened only at night, but then it began to happen during the day. I didn't know what was happening. Were my sins finally catching up with me?

The Pale Horse

Des Moines, Iowa
February 1974

*[B]ehold a pale horse—and his name that sat on
him was death, and hell followed him.*
—Revelation 6:8

Mother insisted that I accompany her and some of the Mt. Sinai members to Des Moines, Iowa. She was to be the guest speaker for a two-day women's retreat at a COGIC church there. (Although still not accepted as a preacher by the COGIC, some of the churches allowed her to speak from their pulpits—as long as it was to other women.)

On the four-hour drive to Des Moines, as I sat in the backseat holding Ebony, I felt the anxiety that had been my constant companion since I'd given birth to her growing more intense by the minute. It felt as though the interior of the car was closing in on me, and I was trapped inside. *We are going to get into a serious car accident, like Mother Goodlow's son. They will have to scrape me off the highway.*

I shut my eyes, trying hard to ignore the sound of my pounding heart inside my head, and began to pray. It was all I could do just to wait until we reached our destination, so I could get out of the car. We finally arrived safe and sound, but the anxiousness did not let up. I fought to ignore it. I tried to mingle with the others from our church to keep my mind off of it. But I couldn't shake it. It felt as though I was standing outside myself and observing my every movement. I was aware of my every action.

Most of us stayed at the pastor's home. When we got there, I was afraid to be left alone with my baby. What if I went crazy and tried to harm her? I followed Cynthia from room to room just to be safe.

On the first night of Mother's speaking engagement, she stood in the pulpit dressed in her black robe. Behind her stood several members of our church dressed in various colored robes; about fourteen of us had accompanied Mother on her trip.

Mother was preaching from the book of Revelations, her favorite. She was talking about the seven seals. I was sitting in the back pew, just in case Ebony woke up and began to fuss. I wanted to be able to take her out of the service without causing disruption.

As I sat there, listening to Mother, a feeling of foreboding engulfed me. Mother asked someone from the congregation to stand and read Revelation 6:8. A heavy, colorfully dressed, dark-skinned woman with a mustache opened her Bible and bellowed with her deep, manly voice, "And I looked up, and behold a pale horse; and his name that sat on him was DEATH, and hell followed him."

Of all the people standing on stage, the one my eyes immediately focused on was the one dressed in black. Something told me right then that she represented the pale horse. The name of the rider of the pale horse was DEATH! I zoomed in on her, as if my eyes were a camera lens. It was an omen. I wasn't going crazy; I was going to die.

I shook Ebony awake; I needed an excuse to get out of there. When she began to fuss, I excused myself and went down to the church basement. When I got there, the ceiling began to close in on me. I bolted back upstairs, my hands wet and my legs like jelly, and ran outside. There I stood in the cold, my daughter in my arms, and tried just to breathe.

The next night, as Mother continued her seven seals sermon, I sat in the back again, panicky and jittery. I was glad when Ebony began to fuss. I left the sanctuary for the entire sermon and returned when I thought it would be time for the offering. After that, we could leave.

As I took my seat at the back, however, Mother stood there asking the backslider among them to return to the Lord. I wanted to return to the Lord, but I did not want to live a life dominated by my Mother.

I thought about Gloria, losing her zeal for life, looking like a bag lady. I thought about all the other saints just like her and all the dos and don'ts required of you when you were saved, sanctified, and filled with the Holy Ghost. What kind of life was that?

Besides, I knew I couldn't live the life that Holiness and Mother required. Neither could they, for that matter. The saints at our church were constantly on the altar crying and repenting for the all the sins they had committed. Everything was a sin, and it made me feel guilty about just being me. I couldn't take the pressure.

That is what it was—there was too much pressure in being holy. But as a sinner, I could do anything and everything I wanted and not feel guilty. In fact, the saints even encouraged it: "If you are going to die and go to hell, you might as well go first class, and do it all," they would say. And so that had become my goal: to become a first-class sinner. Either way, I lost. Perhaps I would be better off dead.

"The Lord showed me that somebody is going to *lose his mind* if he does not give his heart tonight," Mother continued.

Lose my mind? Now that was different. I mean, I couldn't be a first-class sinner if I was stuck in Cherokee, Iowa, at the mental hospital. I was sure that it was me to whom Mother was referring. After all, she was looking right at me, wasn't she? I was sure she knew everything going on inside my head.

Panic struck. Was it really possible that God was revealing to Mother that I would lose my mind? Like Len Sellers had? Len had really never fully recovered from his nervous breakdown. For the past three years, he'd been in and out of the mental ward, and even when he was out, he was not the same person. His medications made him appear bloated and zombie-like all the time.

It was the same with Sister Barbara after her nervous breakdown. Even once her days as a catatonic were over, she was never fully herself again.

I did not want that to be me. Still, I could not bring myself to walk up to that altar to give my heart to Jesus. He simply expected too much. I knew I'd never be able to keep his commands and follow his ways, so what was the point? There wasn't one. It was hopeless. And I was hopeless.

I remained glued to my seat until the service was over.

I was nervous about the ride back to Sioux City. I did not want to experience the same feelings I'd had on the drive here.

At the beginning of the trip—Cynthia and Doresa and the baby and I in the backseat, Mother at the steering wheel, and Sister Pat Brown in the front passenger seat—Mother was playing a taped church service on a portable cassette player that sat between her and Sister Pat. Everything was going smoothly. Tired from my lack of sleep, I quickly dozed off with Ebony.

"Motherrrr?" Cynthia whined from the backseat. My baby stirred and began to cry.

"Yes," Mother replied.

"Remember when you were preaching about Revelations last night?" I knew Cynthia was just trying to think of something to talk about; the silence in the car was probably killing her. But her chosen topic made me nervous. I felt the lump return to my throat, and I began to swallow hard.

"Now the pale horse represents death, right?" she asked.

I wiggled in my seat, trying not to listen. It was getting harder by the second to swallow over the ever-growing lump in my throat.

"Yes," Mother said.

"And remember when you said somebody was going to lose their mind?"

Oh, sweet Jesus, please shut up! I readjusted my daughter's position on my breast, trying to distract myself. I could feel something weird happening to my legs. They were numb and tingly. And the sensation, or lack thereof, was gaining ground as Cynthia continued to talk.

"What did you mean by that?" Cynthia asked.

"I don't know because I didn't say it. The Lord told me to say it," Mother said.

I readjusted myself in the seat again. I was now swallowing buckets of air.

If I go crazy, what will happen to my baby? I wondered. *Will I just open the door and toss her out, and then be like Len Sellers and go run stark naked down the highway, masturbating?*

My heart beat faster. I could not breathe. I rolled down the window and tried to get a breath of fresh air. The cold wind rushed in and everyone in the car turned to look at me.

They know it, I thought. *They see it. They can tell I am about to lose my mind. Oh, God! And what if my craziness is hereditary? What if the milk my baby is drinking from my body right now is contaminated with the craziness gene?*

"Now when you said that," Cynthia continued, "does that mean the person is going to have a *nervous breakdown?*"

Oh, God! She said the words.

Just like that, the tingling sensation shot up my legs, raced past my stomach, and landed in my head, leaving me light-headed and dizzy and even more breathless. My arms started trembling, then, and I felt I couldn't hold Ebony tight enough. I was sure my sanity was evaporating out of the top of my head.

"Oh, God!" I screamed in terror at the top of my lungs. "Save me! Please forgive me! I'm a terrible person! I'm so bad and wicked! Please forgive me! Please save me!" Tears flowed down my face. My sudden outburst frightened Ebony, and she began to cry too.

My eyes were closed, but I knew everyone in the car was looking at me, except for Mother because she was driving. Instead, Mother hit the record button on her portable tape player as, for at least ten minutes, I begged and pleaded with God to save and forgive me for all the terrible things I had done. If this is what it took not to go crazy, then so be it.

When we got back to Sioux City, Mother raced me over to the Richardson's house, where Brother Richardson and Sister Cee-Cee tarried further with me.

It felt as though I was being forced into the kingdom of heaven, kicking and screaming. I did not really want to be saved; I just didn't want to go crazy.

The entire night, I was in a daze. I did not know what was happening to me, but only that I didn't want to feel like this. I tarried and tarried, but still the feeling did not leave. Not only that, but the feeling would remain with me for the next thirty years of my life.

Serve the Lord with Fear

Sioux City, Iowa
Spring 1974

Make a joyful noise unto the Lord, all ye
lands. Serve the Lord with gladness.
—Psalms 100:1–2

O kay, Lord, here's my situation. I am nineteen years old. I'm a single mother. I'm living in a mouse- and roach-infested house with my sister, Cynthia, who, by the way, is driving me crazy. I receive two hundred and twenty-five dollars a month to sustain my daughter and myself. And I have no marketable skills," I complained to God.

It was all true, even the infested-house part. Cynthia's daughter Doresa was now three, and a family of mice had taken up residence in her bedroom closet. The apartment we lived in should have been condemned.

"And then Jason and Jennifer went and got married!" I continued what had become almost a daily prayer. "Just a month after I was forced—and I do mean forced—back into the church. Now, every time I even think about seeing Jason, or about having a cigarette or a Tom Collins, or about going out on a date—the sensation returns: the tingling, numbing heart palpitations, the shortness of breath, the cold sweaty palms, the swallowing of air. So what do I do? This can't be all there is to my life. I have to get away from Mt. Sinai, from Sioux City, and from my mother. Please. Help me!"

I tried to talk to Mother about my now ever-present panic, but every time I did, she just said it was the Lord calling me higher. But what else could I possibly do for God? As it was, I didn't do anything or go anywhere sinful. I didn't wear makeup or skimpy clothes. I wore long granny dresses and went to church two nights a week, plus all day Sunday. I prayed, I read the Bible, and I fasted.

"What more do you want from me, God?" I would pray. "It seems there is just no pleasing you. And I do not have peace. I do not have the joy unspeakable and full of glory that we sing about in church. Instead, I have fear."

Fear and the sweet by and by was the only thing my Pentecostal colleagues and I had in common. So what was the point of living? Why not just bypass the here and now and go home to be with the Lord?

"God kill me or get me out of here," I prayed, "before some wino comes around the corner and tells the church I'm supposed to be his wife."

And God sent me a message in the form of a fallen angel.

"What are you going to do once you have the baby?" I asked Linda's friend Tisha. Tisha was a short, dark, pretty girl, large with child and recently discharged from the Marine Corps. Linda had witnessed to Tisha about getting saved and then sent her home to Mother hoping that Mother could help her.

Tisha and Mother clashed immediately. Mother wanted to boss Tisha around and Tisha was having none of it.

The father of the child she was carrying, a white guy she'd met in the marines, was married to someone else. He'd promised to marry her, but then later changed his mind and went back to his wife.

"I'm going into the navy," she said. Tisha had only been living with Mother for a week and had already made plans to escape.

"I thought you couldn't go into the military if you had a child," I said.

"The navy changed its rule this year. If you give a family member guardianship over your child, they'll accept you."

It was the answer to my prayer if, and that was a big if, I could pass the test—which I had already taken and failed at least four times. That night, I prayed and asked for God's help.

"Congratulations," the navy recruiter said to me the following week. "You've passed the test. The hospital corpsmen billet is closed, but with your score you can be a dental technician. It's the same thing.

"I'll take it," I said.

When Jason found out I was leaving for the military, he came over to try to talk me out of it. I actually listened to his rap long enough to hear his promise to divorce Jennifer and marry me. I did not want to be married to Jason. I wanted something better for my baby and me.

Jason was lucky I had even stuck around to hear him out. He had tried to visit me at Cynthia's apartment several other times that year. He would either show up unannounced while I was sitting on the front porch or in the apartment. He would come to see Ebony or take her with him; but seeing her had nothing to do with me. When he showed up I would scurry back to the apartment or give Ebony to Cynthia to give to him. If he tried to talk to me, I would cut the conversation short and run back to the safety of my apartment. I did so because each time he came around, the anxiety overwhelmed me, and I'd get that nervous jittery feeling like I was about to lose my mind or God would punish me if I spoke to him.

I was afraid of everything. I couldn't be in a room by myself. I always had to have a seat on the outside, where there was an escape; otherwise, I would feel trapped and begin to panic. There were certain places I couldn't go because I would become anxious and panicky. Despite the "I'm losing my mind" cloud looming over my head, I had to take a chance and get out of Sioux City. On January 4, 1975, at three in the morning I bathed and dressed in the dark, so as not to disturb the rest of the household. The navy recruiter would be there at five to pick me up. I was already packed and ready to leave.

My almost one-year-old girl lay in her crib, snoring lightly. She was on her stomach, her beautiful, cherubic face on its side.

Mother's words rang in my ears. "Don't worry about the baby," she'd reassured me. Mother was all for my joining the navy.

"Leave her here in God's hands," she'd said. "When you get settled, send for her."

I rubbed Ebony's back gently. It was the day before her first birthday, and I wouldn't be there to celebrate it with her. She stirred a little.

"Mommy's sorry she has to leave you," I whispered, "but Aunt Cynthia and Dorie-do-dah-day will take care of you until I come back and get you. Mommy's got to go and make us some money to make a better life for us."

I could hear the recruiter coming up the stairs, so I kissed my baby girl on her forehead. Then I wiped my face, picked up my suitcase, and closed the door gently behind me.

I completed boot camp in Orlando, Florida, and made Honor Recruit around the same time Gloria graduated from nurses' college. I was then sent to San Diego, California, for "A" School training. While there, I ran into a handsome black man I had met in boot camp. He was sweet and a gentleman. We got along great, except he was Baptist. I had to cross him off the list.

Then I was sent to Washington, D.C., where I joined a large, black, Jesus Only church. The first night I went, someone stole my wallet when I was at the altar for prayer.

When I tried to join, they asked me how I had been baptized. I couldn't remember; I had been baptized so many times.

"I think it was, 'In the name of the Father, the Son, and the Holy Ghost,'" I replied.

Beeeep! Sorry, you lose. You have to be baptized in Jesus' name only! In addition to that, they also believed that "God hadn't called women to preach."

I found myself in the same position in which my church had placed so many others: I wasn't going to heaven unless I followed their rules. This opened up all sorts of possibilities in my mind, the main one of which was that the saints back in Sioux City, who had pretty much given up on life, would also be in for a rude awakening in the afterlife. In other words, when the rapture took place and they appeared before our maker, guess what? The saints from Mt. Sinai weren't going to be in the number either. They were going to be left on earth with the beast along with the Catholics, the Protestants, the Jews, the Muslims, and all the other unrepentant people. Get the picture?

It was at this point that I began to see the ridiculousness of religion.

The church had a large group of young, unmarried people. They also had a huge choir, good music, educated people, and a dynamic leader. I joined the choir and met a handsome saved, sanctified, and filled-with-the-Holy-Ghost young man.

He invited me home for dinner one Sunday after church. We ate and then returned together for the evening service. After church, the youth choir director—who had been shouting, dancing in the Spirit, and speaking in tongues during the service—threatened to beat me up if I didn't leave her man alone.

Hmmm! I wondered. Was the Universe trying to tell me something?

After that, I left the church.

Book III

Revelations San Diego, California 1992–2005

And God shall wipe away all tears from their eyes, for the former things are passed away. And he that sat upon the throne said, "Behold, I make all things new." And he said unto me, "Write . . ."
—Revelation 21:4–5

The Land of Milk and Honey

San Diego, California
August 31, 1992

And I have said, I will bring you up out of the affliction
of Egypt unto a land flowing with milk
and honey.
—Exodus 3:17

D addy stood in front of the mirror, all decked out in a French-cut tuxedo designed by Jean Yves or something like that; neither of us could pronounce the name. No matter. He looked great at seventy-something. (Nobody, including Daddy, knew his true age, because he had never been honest about it and then lost count.)

Daddy said the Niggahs at the Newark Board of Education kept trying to force him to retire from his job in the Security Services and Drug Enforcement departments. Daddy's job required him to carry a loaded gun, and both we and the "Niggahs" at the Board of Education worried about him, because he kept falling asleep on the job. We were afraid that one day someone would grab Daddy's gun while he was taking his catnap and shoot him with it. But Daddy denied ever sleeping on the job and said he felt too good to retire. Besides, Daddy said that if he retired, he'd be forced to eat dog food. We assured him we would never let him eat dog food, but for the time being, Daddy kept fudging his age and continuing to work his three jobs in Newark.

Daddy was still in good shape. His hair was still black and wavy. His cummerbund sat snugly on his firm stomach and lifted and strained over his butt. I straightened Daddy's cummerbund as best I could, all things considered, and adjusted his black bow tie. Daddy kissed and squeezed me, and said proudly, "My Dept-bra." (He never pronounced my name correctly.)

We stood back and looked at our images in the full-length mirror in the Bridal Suite at a hotel in San Diego. This was the second time Daddy had done me the honor of escorting me down the aisle to give me away. The first time, I'd had to threaten him.

"If you do not show up for my wedding, I will never speak to you again," I'd said. After all, Daddy had never been there for me, or for any of us girls. He hadn't been there to see any of us graduate from high school or the military; he hadn't been there when Linda had been sick and dying in the hospital; no Christmases, no Thanksgivings, no birthdays, no nothing. He'd always tell us how much he loved us, how he would do anything for us. He'd always promise to come. And he'd always be a no-show. I was tired of letting him off the hook. It was time for him to put up or shut up.

"If you don't make it to my wedding and give me away," I'd threatened, "don't bother talking to me, ever!"

My sisters said I'd been too harsh and shouldn't talk to Daddy that way. But I was a Taurus the Bull, and I was not going to apologize.

Daddy had taken my threat seriously and shown up a day before my first wedding, on August 19, 1977. This did not give him much time to counsel me about the evils of wedded bliss or to thoroughly cross- examine my fiance. You see, Daddy had always had his own opinion about marriage; his motto was to avoid it at all costs for as long as you can.

But I had grown up under a different ideology. Mother's church had had its own opinions: one, saints don't date, and, two, definitely no sex before marriage—that was the ultimate sin.

I met my first husband six months before my enlistment in the navy was up. Before I met him, my only prospects had been to return home empty-handed and husbandless, and that was a fate worse than death; God forbid the church find me a husband. And then Jose showed up, just like that.

He'd been stationed in Washington, D.C., with the Marines. I'd been a dental assistant in the Navy, and he'd come to my chair to get his teeth examined for his re-enlistment checkup. I read his chart and noticed he did not list anyone in the box marked "Spouse." This was promising. He also listed his mother in the box labeled "Next of Kin." In the box marked "Religion," he wrote "Catholic."

Hmmm, we can change that, I thought.

I liked the fact that he was Puerto Rican, single, tall, and strikingly handsome. He liked the fact that I had a big butt. (I had become a true Pentecostal; the only thing I dared indulge in, for fear of backsliding, was food. I visited the chow hall four times a day: for breakfast, lunch, supper, and late-night breakfast.)

Jose and I hit it off immediately, because he did not smoke, drink, or have sex outside of marriage. Well, actually, he did have sex outside of marriage, but when I told him I did not, he respected me for it and didn't try to push the issue. The only problem with Jose was his Catholicism. He also meditated.

Meditation? Ummm, I think that fits in the sinning category! I thought. *Oh well, we can change that as well.*

Jose and I had been dating for over three months when I received a letter from Panama. Mother had written to tell me that she'd met my future husband.

"He loves THE LORD," she'd written. "And he is my son in Christ."

Apparently, though, my future husband was also in the hospital. He was waiting to be medically discharged from the army for his cirrhosis of the liver caused by alcoholism.

Her "future son-in-law," she'd said, had seen my navy recruit picture and fallen in love with me immediately. Well, anybody who could fall in love with me after looking at my navy recruit picture had to be an alcoholic, if not addicted to some serious drugs; I wasn't wearing any makeup in it, and my hair was standing up on end like porcupine quills.

I wondered why Mother wanted to marry her baby daughter off to an alcoholic. Flashbacks of Sister Barbara and her husband from skid row had me panicking.

"No, thanks," I wrote back to Mother. "I've already fallen in love with the man of my dreams. I'm going to ask him to help me drive my car back to Iowa when I get out of the service in May." (I had planned to go back to Sioux City in May and go to college there, if one would have me.)   Mother wrote back, "Don't do it. THE LORD said don't do it. I'm sending my son in Christ to you—your future husband—and he will drive you home."

There were those three little words again, the ones that caused so much fear and panic: *the Lord said.*

I tried to fight the fear, but it came anyway, taking hold of my thoughts. *What if I am sinning by not listening to Mother?* I thought. *Would the Lord allow me to have a nervous breakdown like Len Sellers?*

Why can't you make a normal suggestion, like normal mothers, and then just let your children decide for themselves? I asked Mother in my head. *Why can't you ever have an opinion of your own? Instead, it's always what "the Lord said."*

Jose was the answer to my prayers.

A few days later, before I even had a chance to ask Jose to help me drive my car back to Sioux City, he simply said, out of the blue and as if in passing, " . . . and when we get to Iowa—"

Shocked, I interrupted him. "Are you going with me to Iowa?"

"You don't think I'd let you drive cross-country alone, do you?"

Now what do I do, Lord?

I knew I did not want Mother controlling my life through her made up religion; neither did I want to marry a substance abuser. Heck, I could have married Jason had that been what I wanted. Still, I was so afraid of making the wrong choice about what to do that instead of trusting myself and my own relationship with God with in me, I went on a three-day fast, hoping it would earn me some insight or favor from the Lord.

When May finally arrived, Jose and I packed all my earthly belongings in my little brown Gremlin and headed for Sioux City.

The Gremlin had Jesus bumper stickers all over it, which had been plastered on by its prior owner. I was embarrassed by them but felt if I removed them, God would think I was ashamed of him and be angry with me. The stickers remained on the car until I sold it three years later.

When we got to Iowa, my mother's son in Christ was already there. She had sent him there all the way from Panama, after which point she had called the saints in Sioux City and told them to look after him until she returned.

My cousin Peaches did more than look after him, however. By the time Jose and I arrived, Peaches, who had divorced Junior, was claiming him as her husband sent by God. Mother was not too happy about that, but I was ecstatic.

Jose fell in love with Ebony immediately. I was relieved when neither Ebony, Jason, the church, nor my hometown scared him away. Unfortunately, he had to return to Washington, D.C., as he was still enlisted, but when he got there, he called me every other day to tell me how much he loved and missed me.

"Ditto," I always said.

And then one day he called and asked me to marry him. Well, actually, I proposed to him. When the church found out he planned a trip to visit me in August, they forbade him to come unless it was for the purpose of marrying me. I figured that if I had to get married to someone, I'd rather it be him; God forbid Mother return from Panama and find both me and her alcoholic son in Christ eligible. And so I proposed.

The saints did not have to worry about Jose. He was a perfect gentleman and wouldn't try anything unless I initiated it. But then I would, because he had a body to die for.

Jose said yes to my proposal, just like that. And although Daddy did not like Puerto Ricans—he said they were Niggahs, too—he fell in love with Jose as soon as he met him. Everybody did.

But today's wedding was different. I was getting married today because I wanted to get married. I wanted a husband, a family, and a baby, in that order.

We were in San Diego, the land of milk and honey, and two hundred and fifty people had come to witness my lover and I exchange vows. The way my lover put it, the audience looked like the United Nations: blacks, whites, Hispanics, Jews, gentiles, Catholics, Baptists, and, yes, even Jehovah's Witnesses. There were judges, lawyers, doctors, ministers, therapists (my husband-to-be's), authors, and aspiring actors. They were all here to see us.

My lover, my best friend, and my husband-to-be was waiting for me at the altar. He was tall, handsome, blonde, blue-eyed—and did I mention he was a lawyer?

All of my mothers were there as well as all of my brothers and sisters. Today nobody was pretending anything. We were all Daddy's children and we all had different mothers—and what a beautiful family we made.

Mom was dressed in a green chiffon gown with white beading and sparkles. It was long and flowing and had an attached cape. She was wearing makeup. Her hair, treated with henna, shown hints of red highlights and she wore it up in a French twist, which was secured by a diamond hairpin in the back. And Mother, who hadn't worn jewelry in the more than thirty years since the Lord had told her to stop wearing it, had faux diamonds dangling from her earlobes. Of all my mothers, she looked the youngest and the prettiest.

Gloria, who was wearing one of my black cocktail dresses, was also there. Her hair was cut short and in a neat Afro. She was also wearing makeup, jewelry, and high heels. Just for the occasion, it seemed, Gloria was allowing herself to be in her right mind and spirit. Today, she was not talking to trees.

Gloria, who had been angry at both Mother and God, hadn't spoken to either of them for the past four years. In summer 1988, she went on a vacation, first visiting Linda in San Diego, and then coming to Washington, D.C., to see me. After that, she never went back home to Len. Oddly enough, Len now wanted her back and said the Lord did put the two of them together.

I was happy to see Gloria sitting next to Mother, smiling and "clothed in her right mind," as the old saints used to say.

Cynthia was sitting on the other side of Mother, wearing a long, glittering black gown, which we'd found for her at a second-hand shop. She, too, had her hair colored and was wearing it in a short, fashionable style that complemented her eyes and her makeup.

For the past twelve years, Cynthia had been in and out of the mental institutions, following the deaths of her first and second husband. But for now, she, too, was clothed in her right mind.

Mother was sandwiched between Cynthia and Gloria, and the three of them were laughing and talking to one another when Linda showed up with an escort. Her husband was unable to come because there had been a mix-up at the tuxedo shop. None of us believed this story, however, except Linda, who has had to make up excuses for Nick ever since they exchanged vows in 1978.

Linda, who looked younger than ever in her white cocktail dress, was in seventh heaven. She was relieved that her husband was not there to spoil her fun. Linda wore her hair in a long, fashionable weave over her shoulders. When she smiled and waved to the family, her dimples were deep and rich, and her pearly white teeth glistened in the afternoon sun. She acted as if the whole occasion was thrown on her behalf. All eyes were on her. Who was she? Was she the bride? Was she the bride's teenage daughter, Ebony?

My baby brother escorted Momma Scott and Momma Davis to their seats. He was very handsome; he looked like Denzel Washington. With his bronze skin and wavy, jet black hair, he resembled both Daddy and Momma Scott. He also had a wonderful smile and an infectious laugh. A singer, artist, musician, and actor, his voice was rich and melodious. I wanted him to be one of our groomsmen, but my husband-to-be said, "You pick your side and I'll pick mine."

That's fair, I guess, but I was trying to prove a point: I wanted to acknowledge and recognize my family. All of them. I wanted to introduce them to the world. I was very proud of them all, even my half-sisters, who were my bridesmaids, as well as my Samoan "sistahs," who I partied with.

It was time. I looped my arm through Daddy's and he squeezed my hand. I was wearing a white satin and lace wedding gown with encrusted, detailed beading throughout. The train, extra long, was beaded, embroidered, and breathtaking. The back of the dress plunged down and ended at my waist. I looked stunning, if I had to say so myself—and I did—I made a gorgeous bride.

My hair was long, black, and shiny, compliments of some Japanese or Korean girl who sold it for whatever the market would bear. I paid an arm and a leg to purchase it and then have it sown on my head. My hair dresser did an excellent job, though, and it was worth every penny. My makeup was soft, yet sexy and seductive—no tears and no smudges.

"My Mosquito," Daddy said proudly, grinning from ear to ear, as the organist began playing the bridal march.

Everyone stood, and I heard oohs and ahs and even a "she's beautiful" as Daddy and I began the procession. We walked slowly and proudly down the aisle as the guests, my friends and family as well as those of my lover, stood watching us. This was the happiest day of my life.

"I'm just lending her to you," Daddy said in response to the question, "Who gives this woman away?" This time, Daddy had come a week early to meet his future son-in-law.

He was very impressed with my soon-to-be husband. And did I mention the husband-to-be is a Jew? Daddy liked him, even though Daddy did not like Jews, per se. Daddy always said Jews were Niggahs too—the worse kind. But husband-to-be was different.

My brother, Reverend Victor—the son of Momma Davis and Daddy—said the prayer and read from I Corinthians 13 about the meaning of love.

Then we exchanged rings, kissed, and it was over. Now it was time to party. We danced and drank. Even Mother danced. But best of all, I got to dance with Daddy while Louie Armstrong crooned "What a Wonderful World" in the background; all the while my husband danced with Mother. For two old holy-roller folks who had never danced before, they did a great job.

A black federal judge and his wife sat at the table with Daddy and his three wives. When someone let the cat out of the bag about Daddy's situation, the judge was very impressed.

"Let me get this straight," the judge said to Daddy. "How did you keep all three of these women happy? Please tell me the secret."

Daddy donned a wide grin. But the women were not smiling.

The sanctified Roberts clan danced the floor into the wee hours, stopping only long enough for a family picture.

"Say Jesus," the photographer said.

"JESUS!"

Click!

Lazarus, Come Forth

San Diego
January 1998

Jesus cried in a loud voice, Lazarus, come forth and he
that was dead came forth bound hand and foot . . . and
Jesus saith unto them, loose him and let him go.
—John 11:43–44

Okay! That's it! I have had enough! was all that was going through my mind at that moment. Or, as my Daddy used to say, "De Lawd ain't said nothin'. Niggahs always lying on de Lawd!" I no longer wanted anything to do with the Christian's version of God.

The revelation came to me while circling the exit that led to the Coronado Bridge, trying to work up enough courage to drive onto it, park my car at the top, and leap head first from its railing into the cold blue water. But the panic that had plagued me my entire adult life would not allow me to do it.

I had since come to understand that the sensations I had with the tingling, numbing heart palpitations, the shortness of breath, the cold, sweaty palms, and the swallowing of air were not borne from God calling me higher, but rather from a medical condition called panic disorder. When I'd found out, I'd wondered why Mother, a registered nurse, hadn't recognized my symptoms immediately.

Unfortunately, it took me having a panic attack during an economics exam at the University of South Carolina to help me learn that's what it was.

I had studied hard for the exam and knew the information backward and forward, but as soon as I started the test, the room closed in on me. I began to shake and my palms became sweaty and I couldn't breathe. I wanted to run out of the room, but felt trapped because I was in the middle of an examination.

It was the same way I had felt that time when I'd been in the car with Mother and Ebony on the way to Des Moines. Ever since that time, I'd had the symptoms regularly, and for a long time—even during the military. But not this bad. Not this bad for a long time. The more I tried not to focus on the nervousness, the more nervous I felt.

I went to my college professor in tears. He was a bit skeptical, but let me leave the room and reschedule the examination. In the end, my grade was marked down, so I don't think he really believed me.

"You are not having a nervous breakdown," he assured me. "And you are not dying. You are having a panic attack. You may be agoraphobic." He prescribed medication and told me to seek psychological counseling.

I returned for the prescribed counseling for a while, this time with a female counselor, until she started examining my religious upbringing for my problems. At that point, I decided just to take the medication on an as-needed basis and not deal with the source of the problem. What did she know about religion anyway? She was a nonbeliever on her way to the gates of hell.

That only got me so far, however. Even with the medication, there were situations and circumstances I had to avoid to keep from having panic attacks. On a good day, I could cross a bridge without any problem, as long as I'd medicated myself with Valium. On bad days, I avoided bridges altogether. Then there were days I couldn't drive on the freeway or sit in a movie theater or go to church. There were times I couldn't reach the top of a ski slope, fly in an airplane, sit in a restaurant, or even drive a car. Well, I began to avoid a lot of situations.

I knew it: there was something wrong with me. I was defective. The crazy demons had finally caught up with me. And I tried to fix it: I sought counseling off and on throughout the years. But each time the psychologist would want me to take a closer look at the root of the problem—to talk about my upbringing and my religious beliefs—I quit. I didn't want to think about it. I was afraid that would lead to me losing my religion. So I chose to remain in darkness and in the throes of panic.

"I am miserable, just plain miserable," I confided to Mother. "I have a beautiful house, a beautiful husband, a beautiful little girl, a beautiful job, and I am beautiful. So how come I am so miserable? What is wrong with me? I am living in all this beauty and just as miserable as I can be."

After four long, torturous years of being married to Mr. Wonderful, I was ready to throw in the towel. I realized now I had married him for the wrong reason: I wanted the beautiful things in life but something was missing.

"I am tired of keeping up the facade," I continued. "I am tired of pretending to be happy."

I thought seeking and obtaining these material things would bring me happiness. I thought blindly accepting Jesus Christ as my personal savior and waiting for his return would bring me comfort. It didn't. Something was missing.

I worked on the superficial part of me. I exercised, ran the San Diego marathon, and took lessons—music lessons, Spanish lessons, golf lessons, acting lessons, writing lessons, and lessons on how to take lessons. I lost weight, got breast implants, bought some hair (the good, expensive kind), and investment lots of money in self improvement, I even modeled and did some television work. But I was still miserable.

Then, four long years later, while vacationing in Cancun and watching the sun rise over the crystal clear blue ocean alone—my wonderful husband lay in bed snoring, because he'd said it was too early to get up to watch the sun rise with his lovely, sexy wife with the new big boobs—I realized I had to stop lying to myself. I had to start being honest.

Now back from Cancun, I was seeking the advice of Mother, since she'd been one of the people who had advised me not to marry Mr. Wonderful in the first place.

Mother just grabbed a frying pan and poured a glob of oil into it. Then she turned on the burner and began to hum to herself. I was sitting at the table, watching my daughter play with her dog, just waiting for Mother to say something. Except for the humming, the kitchen was silent.

Mother unwrapped some whiting fish and rinsed it in the sink. Then she seasoned it, placed it in a paper bag filled with cornmeal, and shook it violently. When the oil began to pop and sputter, she lay the fish pieces in the oil. Finally, she looked over at me and said, "Get the Bible."

Uh-oh. She had just switched roles on me. You see, throughout my adult life, I had tried to explain to Mother the separation of "church" and "motherhood." And I'd told her, "I don't need a minister; I need a mother." But Mother had now donned her ministerial persona, just like that. I went and got the Bible anyway.

"The Lord told me to tell you that he is delivering you from your marriage to Mr. Wonderful," she said. "God is angry with you for marrying a Jew. That is why you are so miserable and unhappy."

While the whiting fish popped and fizzled on the stove, the Right Reverend Mother and I opened the huge colorful Bible she'd given me as a Christmas present in 1974, which I had been using as a centerpiece on my coffee table, and opened it to Deuteronomy 28. The Right Reverend Mother read the passages that dealt with the blessings God promised if we obeyed and hearkened to his voice.

"God has blessed you, right?" she said.

But it wasn't really a question. It was obvious to both of us that God had truly exceedingly and abundantly blessed me. Then she continued to read the curses.

"If thou wilt not hearken unto the voice of the Lord thy God, all these curses shall come upon thee and overtake thee: cursed shalt thou be in the city, and cursed shalt thou be in the field. Cursed shall be thy basket and thy store."

As the list of curses went on and on and on, I felt certain that I was overqualified for this category. My heart began to race and my palms became sweaty. The old familiar lump in my throat appeared as well as the fear in the pit of my stomach. I believed her now.

So when my husband suggested we go to marriage counseling and then later asked me in front of the counselor whether I still wanted to be married to him, I remembered the Word of the Lord and the curses, and I said, "No!"

"I still love you," he'd said to me after filing for the divorce. "I want to try to work this out."

I did not want to split up my family and I really did love him, even though I did not like him. Still, I made the mistake of asking the Right Reverend Mother what I should do. The Right Reverend Mother told me to reread Deuteronomy 28 and reminded me that the Lord was delivering me from him.

"Who do you think is speaking through him?" she asked. And before I could respond, she said, "Don't be fooled by the trick of the enemy. God has someone better for you."

My divorce was a nightmare, just like that of anyone who has had to go through it. (*Insert your own horror story here.*) But what made my story different was that I was listening to what someone else said God said.

A televangelist was on. I despised televangelists. They reminded me of my past. He was flashy in his expensive tailor-made suit, gold watch, gold pinkie ring, and matching cuff-links. He had perfectly coiffed, blondish-white hair, and he was white. I reached for the remote control.

"You!" he said. "God spoke to me and told me to assure you that he has heard your cry."

"Yeah, right!" I said as I took a big swig from the bottle. I picked up the remote to turn the channel.

"I want you to turn with me to John the eleventh chapter," he said.

I took another swig, settled down on my couch, and waited.

Then he told the story about Lazarus being raised from the dead, which I had heard so many times before. But he told it in a way I had never heard it before—from Lazarus' perspective.

It went something like this: Lazarus and his sisters had sent for Jesus because Lazarus, someone whom Jesus claimed to love, was sick and dying. Lazarus knew it should have taken Jesus about an hour at the most to get there, but instead, it took Jesus about four days.

Yet Lazarus told his sisters, "Don't give up. Jesus is on the way."

By the time Jesus got there, Lazarus' friends and family had buried him. They had covered his eyes so that he could not see, bound his hands so that he could not feel, and tied his feet so that he could not walk. Then they had wrapped him in death clothes and stuck him in a shroud. Finally, they had laid him in a cold, damp cave and blocked it with a large stone so that he could not get out.

Lazarus' friends and family did this to him according to the Jewish laws and customs. They thought they were doing what they were supposed to do.

"Some of you are bound and gagged in the cave," he continued. "You have been placed there by family, friends, husbands, and people at work. But don't give up. God is on the way."

That was exactly how I felt—like I was inside a cold, dark cave. In fact, I felt I had lived my entire life that way: bound, gagged, blinded, and put in a cave by those who said they loved me and thought they were doing the will of God.

"I want out of the cave, God!" I cried. "I want out of the cave of guilt, shame, condemnation, fear, and panic attacks. I'd rather be dead than continue to live like this. Either fix me or take me home. God, I want to believe in you. But I don't. I can't. And I don't want to go on any more."

And God spoke to me.

"Write!" he said. "Write your way out of your cave. Chronicle your deliverance. Write about what you have seen and heard, witnessed and experienced. Just write. In so doing, write yourself out of the cave. And don't be afraid to read and expand your knowledge of me. I am not that delicate.

"Read *Conversations with God*. Learn to meditate. Be ye transformed by the renewing of your mind. If all of the things you have seen, heard, felt, and experienced did not shake your faith in me, then neither will expanding your knowledge of me and of what others are saying about me. I speak to you in many forms and through many people."

And so that evening, my spiritual journey began.

When I told Linda that I was taking a meditation class at the Buddhist Center, she became concerned.

"Oooooh! No. Remember what happened to Tina Turner?"

"No. What happened to her?"

"Remember, she started chanting and got caught up in that Buddhist stuff."

"Yeah, but chanting helped her get out of an abusive relationship with Ike Turner, and she is the happiest she has ever been."

Pentecostals are afraid of everything. We seem to believe our faith is so fragile that anything unknown will cost us our faith and anger God. But it doesn't.

I went to meditation classes. My teacher was a Buddhist, but she taught me how to relax my mind. The Bible says to be transformed by the renewing of your mind. My mind had been in some serious trouble. It had needed a whole lot of renewing, not to mention reprogramming. My meditation teacher also spoke about the importance of having love for everyone and love for our planet.

Some time before this, my friend from Jamaica had sent me a book called *Conversations with God*, but I had been too afraid to read it for fear it would offend God. It didn't. It was the first book to describe God's unconditional love for me. Some say God did not tell Neale Walsh to write his book and dismiss him as a heretic. But through his book, my knowledge of God expanded. His book was just the beginning.

I began to see God as loving, kind, and forgiving parents, who only wanted the best for me. I saw God/Goddess love in everyone, in everything and in all that he had created. He certainly wasn't lurking around, waiting for me or anyone else to mess up so he could punish us and banish all of us to a lake of fire because we did not believe as others believed.

I went to back to counseling, too. I took the medication as prescribed and faced the music with my therapist.

Through it all—counseling, prayer, the Bible, other books about God, meditation and exercise, I began to see how I had been controlled my whole life by a religion fueled by fear, anxiety, control and anxiety. How I had lived with a voice that constantly reminded me that I wasn't smart enough, pretty enough, worthy enough, deserving enough of anybody's love, but especially God's.

Through it all, I learned I had to love myself before I could expect anyone else to love me. How could I expect the men I married when I didn't even love myself.

Not only did I find God, but I found my Mother both of whom created me in their likeness and image. So what's not to Love. If God/ Goddess be for me who can be against me. Now, when I drove back and forth across the Coronado Bridge and the fear comes, I simply embraced it as a part of me, lavishing the fear with love. The Bible says that perfect love casts out all fear.

God's perfect love for me gave me the courage to continue and to go on to be the best I can be. If I messed up—and I would— and I did -- who cares. My real parents will never leave me nor forsake me. No matter what. I no longer need to be controlled by fear. I can breathe easy now. That's not to say that on some days, I choose to go the long way around to get to Coronado, and on some days, I just wouldn't go. But that is okay. I AM okay. At least now, when I cross the bridge, I don't feel like jumping.

Finding I AM

Newark, New Jersey
Summer 2005

Jesus said unto them, Verily, verily, I say unto you,
Before Abraham was, I AM. John 8:58

I climbed out of the driver's side of a rented red Mustang convertible and peered over the top of my designer sunglasses. Glancing over the luscious landscape and green terrain, I listened to nature's voices. The sun shone brightly and I turned my head upward to soak in its warm rays.

Ebony, my adult daughter, opened the passenger-side door and stepped gingerly out of the car.

"Don't forget the flowers, Mom," she whispered to me.

Reaching into the backseat, I grabbed the colorful boutique of assorted flowers, dominated by yellow roses.

Hand and hand, Ebony, Shayna, and I tiptoed softly over the grass, careful not to get the heels of our shoes stuck in the dirt. And then we stopped.

"There it is," Shayna, my eleven-year old daughter, whispered. "Why do people whisper in cemeteries?" I asked.

"I don't know," Ebony responded. "I guess it is a sign of respect."

The three of us, my two daughters and I, stood holding hands and looking at the grave marker.

It was beautiful. Jensen Monument had done a great job. Between two praying hands it read, "Bless the Lord, O, My Soul."

My eyes dropped down to the family name: Quick. There was Percy Sr., Eva Torrence, Percy Jr., and finally

BISHOP FRANKIE BELLE ROBERTS

I stood admiring the craftsmanship.

For three years after her death, Mother's ashes sat in my wet bar, snuggled between the Jack Daniels and the tequila. I didn't know where her parents were buried.

During that time I came to terms with my past. God wasn't going to answer any of my prayers until I changed. The Bible says as a man thinketh, so is he. Even though I appeared to succeed in life-- the poor little colored girl who was on her way to the Lake of Fire because her name was not written in the Book of Life self-image --remained subconsciously embedded in my mind. The low self esteem seed was planted in my subconscious mind during early childhood and cemented by religious dogma, education, society, and social media. Fueled by fear, this seed grew and grew into a ugly failure monster. The medication numbed the fear but didn't do anything to disentangle the "I" I believed myself to be. The I AM, I thought myself to be, had to undergo radical change. I had been sinning my whole life. Webster's Dictionary defines "sin" as: missing the mark. I wasn't even aiming for the mark.

Mom had a plot, but I didn't know where. Gloria knew but she was withdrawn from the world. We couldn't talk to her about anything. It was by accident I found it. After mom's death, Linda and I sorted through her belongings. I took Mother's hymnal. Three years later, I opened it while trying to find a song to play on my piano and the death certificates of her parents floated out from between its pages. It was a miracle.

So I brushed the cobwebs off of the United States Postal Service package in which Mom's ashes had arrived and began to make the necessary phone calls.

Ebony and Shayna nudged me.

"You all right?" they asked, in some form or another.

"I'm fine," I said, wiping tears from my eyes.

Now, as I stood over the grave of my ancestors, I wondered if they knew I was here.

"This is Debra, Grandfather. Grandmother Eva, I wished I could have met you. Mother always said I looked like you."

Grandmother Eva died in 1941, and yet her grave had gone unmarked all these years, as had my grandfather's and my Uncle Percy's. So I had asked the monument company to erect something in their honor.

Did they know I had done that for them? I felt their presence and felt them cheering me on.

"You go, girl," Mom was saying. "I knew you had it in you. I am very proud of you." followed by "Oh, De-brat-lee, you did not have to make such a fuss over me," even though she was tickled pink and would boast to her dad, mother, and brother about me. I knew Mom was proud.

Then I introduced them to my daughters Ebony and Shayna, the next generation. And I vowed to find out about the rest of our ancestors.

But for now, I needed closure. Standing at their grave, Ebony, Shayna, and I wished them well and asked them to look over us and protect us and to heal the preacher's daughters by allowing us to make peace with our past.

We climbed back into the Mustang and drove five miles down the cemetery road. I stopped the car and we got out a second time. We walked to a grave marker that read

REVEREND JOHN H. ROBERTS

Shayna placed a large bouquet of colorful flowers on her grandfather's grave, whom both she and Ebony had gotten the pleasure to meet. I opened the container in my hand and sprinkled some of Mother's ashes over Daddy's burial site.

Then I removed a small, heart-shaped necklace from my purse, which also carried some of Mom's ashes. The heart read, "Frankie and Johnnie 4 ever." I knelt down with my daughters and dug a hole in the ground using my bare hands. I placed the heart in the hole and covered it, burying with it my past and all of its religious dogma. Then I said good-bye to my parents.

Hand in hand, my daughters and I turned, and as we walked away, I made a vow to the Lord to never turn back.

Printed in the United States
by Baker & Taylor Publisher Services